Christian Socialism as Political Ideology

Christian Socialism as Political Ideology

The Formation of the British Christian Left, 1877–1945

Anthony A.J. Williams

BLOOMSBURY ACADEMIC
LONDON • NEW YORK • OXFORD • NEW DELHI • SYDNEY

BLOOMSBURY ACADEMIC
Bloomsbury Publishing Plc
50 Bedford Square, London, WC1B 3DP, UK
1385 Broadway, New York, NY 10018, USA
29 Earlsfort Terrace, Dublin 2, Ireland

BLOOMSBURY, BLOOMSBURY ACADEMIC and the Diana logo
are trademarks of Bloomsbury Publishing Plc

First published in Great Britain 2021
This paperback edition published in 2022

Copyright © Anthony A.J. Williams, 2021

Anthony A.J. Williams has asserted his right under the Copyright,
Designs and Patents Act, 1988, to be identified as Author of this work.

For legal purposes the Acknowledgements on p. viii constitute an extension
of this copyright page.

Series design by Adriana Brioso
Cover image: James Keir Hardie at a Peace Demonstration against the 1914 war, London.
(© Hulton-Deutsch Collection/Corbis via Getty Images)

All rights reserved. No part of this publication may be reproduced or transmitted
in any form or by any means, electronic or mechanical, including photocopying,
recording, or any information storage or retrieval system, without prior permission
in writing from the publishers.

Bloomsbury Publishing Plc does not have any control over, or responsibility for, any
third-party websites referred to or in this book. All internet addresses given in this
book were correct at the time of going to press. The author and publisher regret any
inconvenience caused if addresses have changed or sites have ceased to exist, but
can accept no responsibility for any such changes.

A catalogue record for this book is available from the British Library.

A catalog record for this book is available from the Library of Congress.

ISBN: HB: 978-1-8386-0772-2
PB: 978-0-7556-3499-6
ePDF: 978-1-8386-0773-9
eBook: 978-1-8386-0774-6

Typeset by Deanta Global Publishing Services, Chennai, India

To find out more about our authors and books visit www.bloomsbury.com
and sign up for our newsletters

For Hannah
'The heart of her husband doth safely trust in her' – Prov. 31.11

Contents

Acknowledgements	viii
Note on text	ix
Introduction	1

Part One The basis of Christian Socialism

1	The biblical basis	11
2	The church basis	33
3	Other influences	51

Part Two The route to Christian Socialism

4	A democratic-revolutionary synthesis	77
5	The revolution in practice	85
6	Confusion and contradiction	104

Part Three A Christian Socialist society

7	Collectivism and the role of the state	115
8	Democracy, equality and conservatism	133
9	Pacifism and utopianism	153
Conclusion		166

Notes	185
Bibliography	230
Index	237

Acknowledgements

I would like to record my thanks to Dr Kevin Hickson, who both suggested that I undertake my doctoral research into Christian Socialism and then supervised the project to completion. His guidance has been invaluable in writing this book and in setting out on an academic career. Thanks are also due to colleagues including Professor Jonathan Tonge, my internal examiner Dr Stuart Wilks-Heeg, external Dr Matt Beech, and fellow doctoral students, especially Dr Jasper Miles and Dr Keith Roberts, for their help and support.

I would also like to thank the staff and customers of the Augustus John pub for their – at times, rather more questionable – support, as well as my brothers and sisters in Christ at Belvidere Road Church, Calvary Baptist Church and Grace Church Halewood.

I am indebted to the University of Liverpool Arts and Humanities Scholarship fund for providing the financial assistance necessary to undertake this work. I am also grateful for the assistance of staff at the University of Liverpool Sydney Jones Library, the archives of the London School of Economics and Political Science, Gladstone's Library in Hawarden, the Labour History Archive & Study Centre in Manchester, the University of Manchester Methodist Archives and Research Centre, the University of Leeds Brotherton Library, and Liverpool Hope University's Sheppard-Worlock Library, as well as Thomasz Hoskins and Nayiri Kendir at I. B. Tauris for helping transform the thesis into a publishable form.

None of this would be possible without the support of family and friends, especially mum and dad who encouraged a passion for learning, and my sister Margaret with her unfailing enthusiasm about my work. My wife Hannah has spent innumerable hours over the last few years out at work or caring for our children while I tried to make a career out of reading things and writing about them. This book is dedicated to you and to our shared faith in One who 'shall supply all your need according to his riches in glory by Christ Jesus. Now unto God and our Father be glory for ever and ever. Amen' (Phil. 4.19-20).

Note on text

Scripture quotations unless otherwise stated are taken from the Holy Bible: Authorized King James Version. Scripture quotations marked 'ESV' are taken from the Holy Bible: English Standard Version.

Introduction

The past few years have provided ample evidence that any link between politics and religion in Britain is viewed as something suspicious. David Cameron, the Democratic Unionist Party and Jacob Rees-Mogg have all raised the ire of politicians, commentators and the general public for bringing their religious views into the political arena. 'Politicians such as Rees-Mogg are clearly entitled to their religious beliefs', declared sociologist Pam Lowe, 'but this should be kept separate from their public roles.'[1] Suspicion rises still further when the religious individuals or groups in question are not advocating a conservative perspective, as Tim Farron argues: 'When Jacob Rees-Mogg declares his views on the application of faith, he gets mocked, but no one is surprised or confused – he is a traditional conservative, of course he believes those things. When a liberal turns out to be an evangelical Christian, people are surprised and confused.'[2]

This issue has been highlighted by Andy Walton, Andrea Hatcher and Nick Spencer, writing for Theos, who were spurred to carry out their research investigating the 'increasing number of claims that a US-style Religious Right either exists or is rapidly emerging in Britain'.[3] The researchers cite, for example, a 2011 *New Statesman* article by Andrew Zak Williams, which argued 'that the Christian movements both here and in the USA clearly feel most at home on the right. [. . .] [T]he agendas of the Christian church and the political right-wing make comfortable bed-fellows. You know the kind of thing: anti-abortion, anti-unions, opposed to same-sex marriage and tough on crime.'[4]

Such a viewpoint has possibly gained traction due to the close relationship in the United States between the Republican Party and the (white) evangelical church. Since 1980, such Christians have been 'united in supporting Republican presidential candidates; no Democrat since has won a majority of white evangelicals'.[5] This, however, would not be an accurate assessment of the situation in Britain. 'The strength of the Christian involvement in British politics is its multi-party spread', argue Walter, Hatcher and Spencer. 'For every Christian giant of the Conservative Party such as William Wilberforce, there is an equivalent in the Labour Party, such as Keir Hardie; for every Shaftesbury, there is a Lansbury'.[6]

It is those representatives of the Christian left and others like them which are the focus of this study. Such a focus is valuable because the prevailing belief that Christian engagement in politics is necessarily linked with the conservative right can serve to obscure the significance of a Christian Socialist tradition which goes back to the meeting of F. D. Maurice, Charles Kingsley and John Ludlow in 1848.[7] This book focuses on a later period, however, from the late nineteenth to mid-twentieth century: a period in which the more paternalistic ideas of Maurice and the others gave way to a genuinely socialist creed, a creed which would result in the formation of the Christian Socialist Movement – now Christians on the Left – in 1960. The periodization referred to in the title – 1877–1945 – reflects this development. The significance of 1877 is derived from the founding of Stewart Headlam's Guild of St Matthew, an Anglo-Catholic society which is thought to be the first socialist organization in Britain.[8] Christian Socialists since 1877 were largely – though not exclusively – devoted to the labour movement, and therefore the first majority Labour government of 1945 with all its achievements provides a suitable end point. We could point to James Keir Hardie, George Lansbury and R. H. Tawney as just a few of the Christian Socialist contributors to this; it is exemplified by Ellen Wilkinson's role as co-author of the 1945 manifesto *Let Us Face the Future*.[9]

More than being a history of the movement, however, Christian Socialism is here approached from a political theoretical perspective, with the aim of setting out in a systematic way the beliefs, ideas and concepts which make up Christian Socialism as political ideology. To this end, answers were sought to the following questions:

(1) What does Christian Socialist ideology consist of? What principles and concepts are common to Christian Socialists?
(2) To what extent does Christian Socialism draw its ideas from theology or religious teaching, and to what extent from other sources?
(3) What kind of society – if any – do Christian Socialists seek to create? How do they seek to create it – by revolutionary or democratic means?
(4) Is Christian Socialism necessarily distinctive from other kinds of socialism?

The title of this book is *Christian Socialism as Political Ideology*, and therefore it is necessary to provide working definitions of those terms. For our purposes Christianity is identified with mainstream, orthodox, Trinitarian Christianity.

This would include the Church of England, the Roman Catholic Church, and Nonconformist denominations such as Presbyterians, Methodists and Baptists, among others; it would exclude groups such as Unitarians, Mormons and Jehovah's Witnesses who, for example, may have their own scriptures or reject the deity of Christ.

Socialism may be defined as that which is opposed to capitalism and the free market, desiring instead some form of collective, cooperative or planned economy and a society in which people are both formally and materially equal to one another.[10] Again, for our purposes, socialism is that which seeks to replace capitalism with such a cooperative system, rather than simply making reforms to the existing system in order to alleviate the harm it is perceived to cause.

A political ideology is, in effect, a belief system consisting of political ideas which provide for its adherents a guide to political action. 'An ideology', explains Robert Leach, 'involves firstly an interconnected set of ideas which form a perspective on the world. [. . .] Secondly, ideologies have implications for political behaviour – they are "action-oriented".'[11] This twofold definition underpins our approach to understanding Christian Socialism in terms of both belief and practice. We will also draw on Michael Freeden's view of ideologies as 'configurations of political concepts', and his description of the purpose of studying an ideology being 'identifying, describing, and analysing the building blocks that constitute it and the relationships among them' in seeking to draw conclusions about the conceptual structure of Christian Socialism.[12]

A hermeneutic, textual analysis method was followed, focusing on the writings of ten key individuals – some well-known figures, others rather less so – from the Christian Socialist Movement in this period. These were as follows:

- *Margaret Bondfield (1873–1953)* – trade union activist and Labour Party MP; she was the first female cabinet minister.
- *John Clifford (1836–1923)* – Pastor of Westbourne Park Chapel in London; he was the president of the Baptist Union and the Christian Socialist League.
- *James Keir Hardie (1856–1915)* – Labour politician, often considered the founder of the Labour Party; he was the party's first leader and first MP.
- *Stewart Headlam (1847–1924)* – Anglican minister, founded the Guild of St Matthew, one of Britain's earliest socialist groups.
- *Henry Scott Holland (1847–1918)* – Anglican minister, founded the Christian Social Union, a Fabian-type organization for members of the Church of England.

- *Samuel Keeble (1853–1946)* – Wesleyan Methodist minister, founded the Wesleyan Methodist Union for Social Service along similar lines to the Christian Social Union.
- *George Lansbury (1859–1940)* – Labour politician and party leader 1932–5; he is probably best known as a pacifist and a leader of the Poplar Rates Rebellion in 1921.
- *Richard H. Tawney (1880–1962)* – Labour political activist, well known for his writings on politics and economics, including *The Acquisitive Society*.
- *William Temple (1881–1944)* – Anglican minister, successively Bishop of Manchester, Archbishop of York and Archbishop of Canterbury.
- *Wilfred Wellock (1879–1972)* – Independent Labour Party MP, Independent Methodist lay preacher and author of *Christian Communism: What It Is and Why It Is Necessary*.
- *John Wheatley (1869–1930)* – Labour politician, he was one of the 'Red Clydesiders' and the founder of the Catholic Socialist Society.
- *Ellen Wilkinson (1891–1947)* – Labour MP who helped organize the Jarrow March of 1936 and served in the 1945–51 Labour government.

These individuals were chosen, in the main, because they had written books, pamphlets and articles about Christian Socialism and their own political views which provide a basis for our exposition and systematization of Christian Socialist ideology, while other figures – though no less important – had not contributed such texts for analysis. Several also founded their own Christian Socialist organizations, adding another aspect to the study. They were chosen to be as representative as possible: for example, of the twelve, seven are politicians or primarily political thinkers, while five are ministers of religion. There is a reasonable mix of religious denominations, with five Anglicans (Headlam, Holland, Lansbury, Tawney and Temple), six Nonconformists (Bondfield, Clifford, Hardie, Keeble, Wellock and Wilkinson), and a Roman Catholic (Wheatley), as well as of social backgrounds, with some – such as Headlam, Scott Holland and Tawney – coming from quite privileged backgrounds, and others – such as Clifford, Hardie and Wilkinson – coming from poorer, working-class backgrounds.

The individuals chosen for this study had to be those who were self-identified as Christian Socialists, or those who have been consistently recognized as such in previous works. They had to be those who were, in keeping with the definitions, genuinely socialists rather than merely social reformers, and practising Christians rather than merely those who acknowledged in some vague way the morality of Christianity. On the first point, great Christian reformers such as Lord Shaftesbury and William Wilberforce would not be included. On the second, Tony Benn, as an example, would not be included, for though he cited the ethical influence of Christianity, he did not regard himself fully as a Christian. In *God's Politicians* Graham Dale includes a section on Benn, quoting him: 'Anyone who really thinks that Clause 4 and common ownership was invented by Karl Marx [. . .] might go back to the Acts of the Apostles for the idea of all things in common.' Dale, however, also has to quote Benn's answer to the question of whether he believed that Jesus Christ is Lord: 'Since I don't believe in lords in any shape, it is a bit difficult to acknowledge Jesus as one.'[13] Chris Bryant calls Benn an 'agnostic'.[14] Benn's writing of a 'political commitment [which] owes more to the teachings of Jesus – without the mysteries within which they are presented – than to the writings of Marx' has echoes of Clement Attlee: 'Believe in the ethics of Christianity. Can't believe in the mumbo-jumbo.'[15]

This latter issue also caused the abandonment of an investigation into John Trevor, the Unitarian minister who founded the Labour Church Movement. It soon became apparent that Trevor and the Labour Churches could not be regarded as practising Christianity. Peter d'A Jones, for example, argues that Trevor's views 'were closer to the Ethical Culture movement than to Christianity', and states outright that the Labour Churches 'were not essentially Christian'.[16] John Callaghan, in his *Socialism in Britain*, suggests that 'the Labour Churches dispensed with Christianity virtually altogether'.[17] According to Trevor himself: 'The attempt to bring the thought of Jesus into the life of today as a guide and standard is an anachronism. [. . .] [T]he Labour Church is not a Christian Socialist Church, but is based simply on the conception of the Labour Movement as being itself a religious movement.'[18] Here we have moved beyond religious socialism to the idea of socialism as a religion. This is the difference between, for example, Stewart Headlam basing his socialist beliefs on the Christian sacraments of baptism and Eucharist, and J. Bruce Glasier's view that socialism itself was a sacrament.[19] Trevor and the Labour Church Movement were therefore omitted.

In practice, of course, this process proved to be far from an exact science. For example, near the beginning of his *Industrial Day-Dreams*, Samuel Keeble disavows the expression 'Christian Socialism', preferring instead 'social Christianity'.[20] Wilkinson suggests that R. H. Tawney was 'not happy about the idea of "Christian Socialism". [. . .] To blend Christianity and socialism might (he considered) imperil the distinctiveness of each.'[21] Henry Scott Holland, on further reading, might be excluded for being a reformer rather than a socialist, while Keir Hardie might be excluded given that, at least according to Glasier, he had eventually 'given up all belief in the Christian Church as an exclusive means of salvation. [...] [H]e probably accepted the Bahai teaching which would include Buddha and other "Redeemers of Men" in a common brotherhood'.[22] We could, if we were so minded, find grounds to exclude every person in this study, and be left with no study at all. This, however, does not cast doubt over the legitimacy of the study. Instead, it tells us something about the nature of Christian Socialism and hints at its inconsistencies, internal confusions and even contradictions, to which we shall return.

It may also be argued that the study is flawed insofar as figures which fulfil the criteria to the same extent as those included have been excluded. Such argument may be made on behalf of a large group of individuals, such as Richard Acland, Charles Gore, Arthur Henderson, Conrad Noel, Margaret McMillan or Phillip Snowden. A particular example might be made of Gore, a key thinker who argued for the existence of 'what can rightly be called a Christian socialism, by the very fact that the law of brotherhood is the law of Christ' and called for a revolution through 'gradual and peaceful means'.[23] Such objections to the validity of this research are, however, groundless; this study makes no claim to being exhaustive, but rather to being representative. In the particular case of Gore, his close relationship with Scott Holland within the Christian Social Union (CSU) made the inclusion of both men unnecessary. Holland was preferred on the grounds that he appeared to be identified as the more influential figure; Bryant views him as the founder of the CSU, while Wilkinson chose to subtitle his work *Scott Holland to Tony Blair*.[24] The exclusion here of some individuals is therefore no commentary on the worth of their contribution to Christian Socialist thought or their importance within the Christian Socialist tradition.

The book is split into three parts, each consisting of three chapters. Part One considers 'The basis of Christian Socialism', with chapters describing the application of scripture, the use of church teaching and the sacraments, and, finally, other influences on the Christian Socialists. The conclusion that Christian Socialists were influenced by and argued from the Bible and the teaching and example of the church is hardly groundbreaking; however, the extent of the reliance on these sources, over and above other influences such as Karl Marx or Henry George, is well worth noting, for it comes as a corrective to any notion that even these religious men had a pretty much secular outlook and approached politics in a secular way. It was no exaggeration for Keir Hardie to write that 'the impetus which drove me first of all into the Labour movement, and the inspiration which has carried me on in it, has been derived more from the teachings of Jesus of Nazareth, than from all other sources combined'.[25]

Part Two examines 'A route to Christian Socialism' – how Christian Socialists sought to bring about a socialist society. Here will be a systematization of the writings on this topic found in various places and the exposition of a three-stage approach: first, successful persuasion of the deficiencies of capitalism and the need for a socialist alternative; secondly, the election of Labour to a position of power, or the 'conversion' of those already in power to socialist principles, meaning that, in either cases convinced socialists would now be in power; thirdly, the reorganization of society by a socialist state, aided by a supportive and cooperative population. We will be able to conclude that Christian Socialism in this period, by seeking revolutionary change via democratic means, offers a synthesis between revolutionary and democratic socialism; or, as Wilfred Wellock puts it, 'Parliamentarianism [...] combined with a revolutionary spirit and method.'[26] These conclusions, however, will be tempered by a consideration of some of the confusion and inconsistency evident on this point, especially in the writing of Wellock.

Part Three considers 'The Christian Socialist society', describing the kind of society aimed at by the Christian Socialists. This will prove to be a difficult task, first, because of the – sometimes intentional – vagueness on this topic, and secondly, because it is at times unclear if a policy or proposal is being made or supported as part of short-term reforms to the existing system or whether it would be part of a new socialist society. Nevertheless, we will be able to draw some conclusions about the nature of the collectivism and cooperation aimed at by Christian Socialists, as well as other principles which would colour the makeup of any Christian Socialist society. We will conclude that Christian Socialists in general held a utopian vision of the future, in which the establishment of socialism is equivalent to the setting up of the Kingdom of Heaven on Earth, leading to the abolition of war, poverty, overwork and even sickness and premature death.

We will conclude finally that the key concept of Christian Socialism is brotherhood, as derived from the idea of the universal Fatherhood of God, and that other concepts – cooperation, equality and democracy – are drawn from this. Christian Socialism is not distinct from other socialisms in espousing cooperation, equality and democracy, but it is distinct in drawing these from ideas from Christian theology. Christian Socialism has more often been studied and written about in terms of its history as a movement or biography of its individual protagonists, and it is therefore to be hoped that this book offers a fresh perspective in examining in greater detail the ideological content of Christian Socialism. The subfield of religion and politics in Britain is itself one which is still developing, and it is to be additionally hoped that this book will serve to enlarge our understanding of religious political thought and practice in general.

Part One

The basis of Christian Socialism

1

The biblical basis

Christian Socialists are marked out by their use of the Christian religion as a basis for socialism, rather than economic or sociological analysis in the manner of Marxism or Fabianism. In that sense, Christian Socialism is 'rightly bracketed with other "ethical" socialisms. But although it has fed from them and into them, it rests on unique foundations.'[1] These foundations include the Bible, as well as the teaching and sacraments of the church. James Keir Hardie, for example, 'would as easily apply the Old Testament as the New, and also argued from the practice of the early Church and the teaching of the Church fathers. [. . .] [T]he overriding force is of a simple appeal to the ethical wisdom of the Bible.'[2] The same is true of Stewart Headlam, whose political views were 'firmly based on the Bible and the creeds', and George Lansbury, who was 'a Socialist because the Christian religion teaches us that love, co-operation, brotherhood are the way of life which will give us peace and security'.[3] Wilfred Wellock saw that '[m]ost socialists rested their case solely on the economic argument, whereas I saw the basic error of capitalism in certain spiritual deficiencies'.[4]

Politics then was viewed in moral terms by Christian Socialists, with capitalism viewed as immoral. Wellock writes of 'the inhumanity, the moral bankruptcy of capitalism [. . .]. It is obviously immoral, and a colossal social crime that almost all the economic benefits of mass-production should be reaped by a minority.'[5] R. H. Tawney, similarly, views the 'industrial problem is a moral problem'.[6] Tawney believed then in the application of morals to industrial questions. While, on the face of it, these morals may have been sourced from any religious or ethical system, or simply those arrived at by Tawney himself, in practice his morals – like those of all Christian Socialists – were drawn from Christianity.[7] Tawney sums this up: 'The essence of all morality is this: to believe that every human being is of infinite importance, and that no consideration of expediency can justify the oppression of one by another. But to believe this it is necessary to believe in God.'[8]

Christian ministers who espoused socialism pointed to this disconnect between the capitalist system and Christian morality. John Clifford, the Baptist pastor, wrote in a tract for the Fabian Society, that free-market capitalism was 'more in keeping with the gladiatorial than the Christian theory of existence. It provides for ruthless self-assertion rather than self-restraint. It does not inspire brotherly helpfulness, but the crushing of competitors and thrusting aside of rivals.'[9] Samuel Keeble, a Methodist minister, agrees:

> No system of industry which proceeds upon the principle of unscrupulous competition, of treating human labour as a mere commodity, and human beings as mere 'pawns' in the game of making money, as mere means to a selfish end; of taking advantage of one man's poverty and necessity, and of another man's ignorance; which sanctions the law of might, and not of right, and the principle of survival of the fittest for success in the scramble for material wealth – no such system [. . .] can by any stretch of generosity be called Christian.[10]

The same stance was taken by career politicians, a class of people who today might be expected to avoid such statements of religion or morality. George Lansbury wrote that '[m]y reading and my prayers and all united to confirm my faith that Socialism, which means love, co-operation and brotherhood in every department of human affairs, is the only outward expression of a Christian faith'.[11] Hardie, in similar vein, remarked that '[t]he only way you can serve God is by serving mankind. There is no other way. It is taught in the Old Testament; it is taught in the New Testament.'[12] Margaret Bondfield's 'socialist belief followed naturally from the biblical texts and congregational preaching she absorbed in her youth'.[13]

Lansbury refers to his reading, Hardie to the teaching of the whole Bible and Bondfield's biographer to 'biblical texts' and Bible-based preaching. The Bible was one of the key sources – if not the key source – from which Christian Socialists gained the basis for their socialism. 'The Bible', argues Catterall, 'was not just the source of political language which gained power through the beauty and familiarity of the King James Version, but it was also a series of statements of what should be and of how men should order their society under God.'[14] Theologically different Christian Socialists had different views of the Bible: Keir Hardie refers to it being 'inspired' (or, at least, that Christians are 'taught to look upon [it] as inspired'), while Stewart Headlam refers to the Bible 'not as the infallible Word of God, but as the most inspiring literature of a nation whose best men were convinced that there was one righteous God, and that personal and social righteousness was the main thing'.[15] Nevertheless, each one appears to have found in the scriptures arguments, justifications and a basis for socialism. In this chapter we will consider the basis for socialism as drawn from the Bible.

The Fatherhood of God and the brotherhood of man

A key theme in Christian Socialist writing is that all men are brothers, and that all humanity – far from being a disparate collection of individuals – comprises one big family. This idea was also based on, to take one key example, the words of Christ recorded in Gospel of Matthew: 'But be not ye called Rabbi: for one is your Master, even Christ; and all ye are brethren. And call no man your father upon the earth: for one is your Father, which is in heaven.'[16] Stewart Headlam, to give another example, points to the words of Paul in his letter to the Ephesians: 'For this cause I bow my knees unto the Father of our Lord Jesus Christ, of whom the whole family in heaven and earth is named.'[17] '[H]ere is St. Paul', writes Headlam, 'dwelling on the universal Fatherhood of God.'[18] A theological emphasis on this theme had become more pronounced in British Christianity – Nonconformity in particular – in the mid-nineteenth century, perhaps reflecting the work of German theologian Adolf Harnack, itself influenced by Kantian philosophy.[19] This idea of, as Lansbury phrased it, God's 'Fatherhood and the consequent Brotherhood of man', or in the words of Hardie, 'that Gospel [. . .] proclaiming all men sons of God and brethren one with another', was for Christian Socialists an argument against capitalism and in favour of socialism.[20]

Samuel Keeble identified 'the great Christian principles of the Fatherhood of God and the Brotherhood of Man' as in tension with the selfishness and individualism of capitalism. Competition, according to Keeble, 'is contrary [. . .] to the teaching of the Christian religion, which [. . .] condemns selfishness, and demands that men love their neighbour as themselves. It is contrary, because Christianity proclaims the brotherhood of men.'[21] Lansbury agrees with Keeble's analysis, writing that despite this 'brotherhood' and the fact that 'men and women are equal in the sight of God' it remains the case 'that under our present social conditions this equality is not realized.'[22] The problems of capitalist society exist, according to Lansbury, because 'we have refused to believe that it is possible to live as brothers and sisters should live'. 'I believe', he adds, 'in the Fatherhood of God, in the Brotherhood of Man, and in the fact that men and women can co-operate, if they will.'[23] John Wheatley took up a similar theme in a letter to the *Glasgow Observer*, 'A Catholic Defence of Socialism', asking: '[I]n a society which is one of the swindler versus the swindled, how can there be brotherly love?'[24] For Ellen Wilkinson, Christians were called to combat 'injustice' wherever it afflicted 'human beings, the children of God'.[25] It is clear then that to Christian Socialists this idea of God's Fatherhood and the familial relationship between all the people He has created meant that Christianity and capitalism were completely at odds with one another; capitalism stood condemned because it ignored and made impossible to practice the brotherly relations that should be exercised by God's children.

If capitalism denies this idea of universal brotherhood, Christian Socialists believed that socialism was the economic and social system which enshrined it. This was proclaimed in the declaration of John Clifford's Free Church Socialist League:

> Believing that the principle of Brotherhood as taught by Jesus Christ cannot adequately be wrought out under existing industrial and commercial conditions, and that the faithful and commonplace application of this principle must result in the Socialization of all natural resources, as well as the instruments of production, distribution and exchange, the League exists to assist in the work of eliminating the former by building the latter Social Order.[26]

In the words of Keeble, '[t]he other great cry of Socialism is for *brotherhood* – the most Christian of cries'. 'The Socialist', writes Keeble, 'who demands brotherhood in industry is far nearer the mind of Christ than the economist who clamours for "free" competition.'[27]

This is also the view of Henry Scott Holland, who writes that it is socialism which 'tells of the Fatherhood of God, bringing Peace and Goodwill: of the universal brotherhood of men'.[28] Wheatley agrees, writing that it is socialism 'which emanates from that spirit of brotherhood which is ever present in the heart of man but is so often suppressed by the struggle for existence'.[29] The idea also seems to have found acceptance in the writing of Tawney, who calls for 'a society which [. . .] holds that the most important aspect of human beings is not the external differences of income and circumstance that divide them, but the common humanity that unites them, and which strives, therefore, to reduce such differences to the position of insignificance that rightly belongs to them'.[30] 'Surely there is a better way', declared Wellock, 'a nobler motive in industry than greed, a right above that of the few to amass huge fortunes whilst others starve! Is it beyond our dreams that society can function as a great brotherhood, can co-operate as fellow citizens instead of exploiters and exploited? What say you who profess Christianity?'[31]

It is clear then that for the Christian Socialist, socialism is simply a natural consequence or outworking of Christianity; the Bible teaches that God is the Father, and socialism is the system whereby the people of the world or of a particular society can live as brothers and sisters. The practice of Christianity should, therefore, necessarily lead to the practice of socialism, as George Lansbury proclaimed: 'If anywhere in the world there is true Christianity it will be found ranged on the side of International Socialism, proclaiming in clear language the Fatherhood of God and the Brotherhood of Man.'[32] For Lansbury, therefore, a Christianity that did not accept and support socialism was not worthy of the name, not a 'true Christianity'.

While Lansbury offers the opinion that a Christianity which rejects socialism is false, William Temple makes the related point that a socialism which rejects Christianity is completely without foundation:

> Apart from faith in God there is really nothing to be said for the notion of human equality. Men do not seem to be equal in any respect, if we judge by the available evidence. But if all are children of one Father, then all are equal heirs of a status in comparison with which the apparent differences of quality and capacity are unimportant; in the deepest and most important of all – their relationship with God – all are equal.[33]

Here, Temple observes not only that this Christian doctrine is a basis for socialism, or that Christianity should lead to socialism, but also that there is no other reason to accept or implement socialism. For Temple, faith in God as the Father is the only reason to accept equality, because without this fundamental belief human beings are clearly unequal, and an unequal capitalist society is merely a reflection of that natural inequality. Keeble expresses a similar view: 'In so far as Socialists wish for brotherhood, Christians are with them, but the "brotherhood" of secularist Socialists is indeed a sentimental thing. There is no brotherhood where there is no Fatherhood.'[34]

The example of Christ

Christian Socialism has been described as 'a "Christ-centred faith" in that it focused on the life and message of Christ'.[35] This, it has been argued, was particularly the case for Nonconformists who did not place as great an emphasis on sacramental theology and were consequently less likely to use sacramental arguments.³⁶ As an example Keeble, a Wesleyan Methodist made the following argument:

> It is high time, then, that Christian teachers proclaimed that Christian business men, at least, are expected to respect the dignity of human nature in the humblest of their servants, to remember that Christ died for the day-labourer as well as for his master, and that if they be Christians, even rough, unskilled labourers are temples of the Holy Ghost and kings and queens unto God, most precious in His sight.³⁷

Keeble adds that 'a system which unblushingly proceeds upon the principle of selfishness must be contrary, as a system, to the teaching of Christ'.³⁸ Keeble's fellow Wesleyan Ellen Wilkinson wanted to see society brought back to the principles taught by Christ.³⁹ Clifford, a Baptist pastor, declares that 'no other name than that of Christ is given whereby we can have social salvation', and that if individualistic capitalism 'is in the least bit in accordance with the mind of Christ, then I must confess that I have failed to read aright its wonderful contents'.⁴⁰

Hardie, a member of the Evangelical Union, explained that 'the impetus which drove me first of all into the Labour movement, and the inspiration which has carried me on in it, has been derived more from the teachings of Jesus of Nazareth, than from all other sources combined'.⁴¹ Hardie here expresses the extent to which Christ is the basis of his socialism and his commitment to the labour movement – 'more than all other sources combined' – more than the rest of the Bible; more than church teaching or the sacraments; and more than the economics, sociology and philosophy that provided the basis for other types of socialism such as Marxism or socialist societies such as the Social Democratic Federation or the Fabian Society. On a speaking tour of France and Belgium Hardie declared: 'It was reading the Gospels and studying the life of Jesus Christ and his spirit and teaching that brought me into the labour movement [. . .] without the spirit and teaching of Jesus Christ you will fail to realise your ideal of the reconstruction of society on a juster [sic] and more human basis.'⁴² We can see, therefore, the importance of Christ's work and teaching to Nonconformist Socialists as a basis to their ideology.

Yet the writings of Christian Socialists from other denominational backgrounds suggest that Jesus Christ was no less significant for them. Stewart Headlam, an Anglo-Catholic, also saw Christ as the basis for socialism: 'All those ideas which we now express vaguely under the terms solidarity, brotherhood, co-operation, socialism, seem to have been vividly present in Jesus Christ's teaching.'[43] For Headlam, Christ was 'a radical reformer', 'a Socialistic carpenter' and a 'revolutionary Socialist from Galilee'.[44] John Wheatley, a Roman Catholic, similarly argued that the 'Divine Founder' of the church 'on every occasion condemned the accumulation of wealth'.[45] This view is expounded by Wheatley in *How the Miners are Robbed*, in which he imagines a trial of capitalists and those who have supported them. One of the witnesses called to give evidence before the magistrate on behalf of the capitalist accused is a clergyman:

> Mag. My dear sir, you are injuring Christianity by trying to explain away that on which it was founded. Did not its Divine Founder say – 'Woe to the rich, for you have your consolation.'?
>
> Wit. Yes, your honour; but I think He meant they should use their wealth properly.
>
> Mag. Why close your eyes to the fact that it is not the mismanagement of wealth, but the possession of it that is here condemned?[46]

George Lansbury, another Anglican, also declares the significance of Christ: 'I am a socialist pure and simple. I have come to believe that the power which should and which will, if men allow it, work our social salvation, is the power which comes from a belief in Christ and his message to man.'[47] Lansbury went so far as to describe Christ as 'the greatest revolutionary force of His times', adding in a reference to the Christian doctrine of the Resurrection that 'I believe, too, that He lives now to give men and women the revolutionary spirit'.[48] For Lansbury, Jesus was 'the lonely Galilean – Communist, agitator, martyr – crucified as one who stirred up the people and set class against class'.[49] This is an example of the tendency not just to follow the teaching of Christ, but to also identify Him as a practising socialist and member of the working class.

Wheatley did similarly to Lansbury, arguing that Christianity was founded by a member of the working class – Christ.[50] Here Wheatley can claim that Christianity in general or Roman Catholicism in particular is the basis for socialism and supportive of the rights of the workers because it is the creation of a working-class man. Henry Scott Holland, an Anglican priest, argued that the solution to social problems could only be found in 'the person and life of Christ', and – refuting the notion that followers of Christ should focus merely on spiritual matters, or life after death – that 'the more you believe in the Incarnation the more you care about drains'. 'If we believe in the Incarnation', wrote Holland, 'then we certainly believe in the entry of God into the very thick of human affairs.'[51] A similar argument was advanced by a Nonconformist, Keeble: 'The Immanence of God in the world [. . .] calls for Christian effort to make society sensitive and responsive to the divine presence and power.'[52] On this reading, Christ appears to have a clear significance for Christian Socialists of all denominational types.

Christ's Sermon on the Mount was a particular influence on Christian Socialists.[53] This was especially the case for Keir Hardie, who refers to the Sermon frequently. 'Socialism', wrote Hardie, 'is the application to industry of the teachings contained in the Sermon on the Mount', which is 'a consistent and powerful argument against property'. The Sermon, 'whilst it perhaps lends but small countenance to State Socialism, is full of the spirit of pure Communism', and it would be 'an easy task to show that Communism, the final goal of Socialism, is a form of Social Economy very closely akin to the principles set forth in the Sermon on the Mount'.[54]

Verses such as 'Blessed are the poor in spirit: for theirs is the kingdom of heaven' and 'Blessed are the meek: for they shall inherit the earth' were given socialist interpretations:[55] the Kingdom of Heaven belonged to the poor rather than the rich; the Earth would be inherited by the meek rather than being controlled by the capitalist and landlord class. In *Christian Communism*, Wilfred Wellock implies that these Beatitudes are ignored and even reversed by capitalism: 'To oppress and disinherit the meek and increase the power of the mighty; to denounce and imprison the peacemakers and extol the preachers and doers of violence; to scoff at the advocates of justice, honesty and mercy; and persistently crush the economically weak.'[56] Lansbury agrees, arguing that 'we are in that condition because we have not taken the Sermon on the Mount as the guiding star of our lives'.[57]

Another key section of the Sermon comes where Christ explains: 'No man can serve two masters: for either he will hate the one, and love the other; or else he will hold to the one, and despise the other. Ye cannot serve God and Mammon.'[58] The word 'Mammon' traditionally refers to material wealth, as is reflected in more recent translations of the Bible: 'You cannot serve God and money.'[59] Christian Socialists pointed to this verse to show that capitalism was immoral because it involved the worship of money and profit rather than the Christian God. For example, Lansbury wrote that '[w]e have succeeded in setting up a god whose name is Mammon, and in creating poverty in the midst of plenty'.[60] Lansbury condemned a society which was built not on obedience to Christ but on the worship of material wealth.[61] Hardie argued that society should be 'cleansing our moral sewers of the poisons with which selfishness and Mammon-worship have tainted them', and that the work of the Independent Labour Party (and the labour movement generally) was to rescue '[h]umanity from the brutalizing power of Mammon'.[62] Wellock pointed to the condition of the European continent in the aftermath of the First World War, writing that 'Europe lies in ruins, a deliberate, daring sacrifice to the god Mammon'.[63]

Christian Socialists made reference to other of what Hardie called 'Christ's denunciations of wealth' in the Gospels.[64] There are, for example, Christ's instruction to the rich young man, 'sell all that thou hast, and distribute unto the poor, and thou shalt have treasure in heaven', and the account of the rich man and Lazarus, in which the rich man is condemned to hell while Lazarus – a beggar – is welcomed into the presence of God.[65] In a sermon Stewart Headlam argued that this parable was a warning to those 'who are in positions of power or influence, but are not socialists in their use of their various powers', while in his tract for the Fabian Society Headlam explained that 'the rich man was in Hell simply because he allowed the contrast between rich and poor to go on as a matter of course, day after day, without taking any pains to put a stop to it'.[66] Hardie went even further: 'Dives was sent to Hades for apparently no other reason than that he was rich, Lazarus went straight to Abraham's bosom because of his earthly poverty'.[67]

In the same way Keeble pointed to the warning against seeking material again: 'And he said unto them, Take heed, and beware of covetousness: for a man's life consisteth not in the abundance of the things which he possesseth.'[68] Scott Holland concludes that Christ 'denounced vehemently the sins to which the rich were so inevitably prone, and enthusiastically praised the virtues that sprang inherently out of simplicity of life, and are found so characteristically of the poor'.[69] These denunciations were a powerful argument for Christian Socialists against capitalism, which appeared to rely upon the pursuit of wealth and profit, even at the expense of others. According to George Lansbury, the 'gospel tells us that we have got to go out into the world and preach the gospel; not get on and get rich! We have got to preach the gospel that you and I are part of one another; my life is no good unless yours is good; yours is not good unless my life is good.'[70]

Christian Socialists used the other parables and teachings of Christ as arguments in favour of socialism, or even in favour of specific policies. Margaret Bondfield noted the injunction of Christ, 'Thou shalt love thy neighbour as thyself', arguing: 'It is in the degree [the nation] brings politics in line with the Golden rule that we shall be judged by the generation to come.'[71] Ellen Wilkinson pointed to the parable of the sheep and the goats, in which Christ judges the world in righteousness, commending those who provided for the poor and needy and condemning those who failed to do so.[72] Headlam also referred to this passage, arguing: 'It is this parable which seems to compel every Christian to be a socialist.'[73] Headlam went further than this in his Fabian tract, arguing that

> even in the case of those who said they did not know God, who would call themselves or be called by others Atheists, Jesus Christ said that if they were taking pains to see that the people were properly clothed, fed and housed, however much they might say that they did not know God, God knew them and claimed them as His.[74]

For Headlam, therefore, socialism was such an outworking of Christianity that even those who outwardly denied this were doing God's work. Hardie agrees with this assessment, writing that 'the Socialist who denounces rent and interest as robbery, and who seeks the abolition of the system which legalises such, is in the true line of apostolic succession with the pre-Christian era prophets [and] the Divine Founder of Christianity'.[75] Samuel Keeble similarly invoked the parable of the Good Samaritan to argue that when the churches (represented by the two religious Jews who refused to help the injured man) ignore the needs of labour or the working class, God will send to society a 'Good Samaritan' in the form of socialism from outside the church.[76]

Keeble also uses the phrase from the Lord's Prayer 'Give us this day our daily bread' as an argument in favour of a living wage.[77] He backs up this argument with a reference to the Parable of the Vineyard, in which a man hires workers for his vineyard, paying each one a denarius though some have worked all day, others only half the day, and some just an hour or two.[78] Keeble argued that, a denarius per day being a reasonable amount on which to live, each of the workers in the parable received a living wage, even those who had not been hired for a full day. Keeble elaborates:

> Our Lord makes the man in the parable fix his wages not by the laws of any political economy, but by the law of justice, in its widest sense. 'Whatsoever is *right* I will give thee.' [. . .] The whole parable of the labourers in the vineyard turns, so far as its business aspect is concerned, on the employer refusing to pay less than the wage determined.[79]

Scott Holland also references this parable:

> Remember that text which is so direly misquoted: 'May I not do that what I will with mine own?' The words are flung at us, as if they would justify the most harsh and arbitrary exercise of the rights of property. In reality, they are used in

the parable to justify action of exactly the opposite character. The Master of the Vineyard [...] is arguing for that liberty to be humane and equitable, and kindly, which every man claims in cases where he is own master.[80]

The teaching and example of Christ, therefore, proves to be vital in providing a basis or underpinning to Christian Socialism. The Christian Socialists showed the immorality of the capitalist system from the Gospels and pointed out that Christ taught and practised socialism – or, at least, principles of brotherhood, cooperation, care for the poor and condemnation of the rich which were embodied in the modern world by socialism. As Keir Hardie summed up: 'Christianity on its social side can never be realised – if it is to be interpreted in the light of Christ's teaching – until there is full, free Communism.'[81]

New Testament

The life and teaching of Christ were not the full extent of Christian Socialist argument from the Bible; many other passages from both Old and New Testaments served as part of their basis for socialism.

Christian Socialists, for example, found as persuasive argument for socialism from other New Testament denunciations of wealth and warnings to the rich as those of Christ. Headlam cited the condemnation of those who become rich at the expense of their workers in the Epistle of James: 'Go to now, ye rich men, weep and howl for your miseries that shall come upon you. [...] Behold, the hire of the labourers who have reaped down your fields, which is of you kept back by fraud, crieth: and the cries of them which have reaped are entered into the ears of the Lord of sabaoth.'[82] 'The cry of the reapers', wrote Headlam, 'who have been defrauded of their wages enters into the ears of the God who fights.'[83]

Hardie referenced the earlier passage, pointing out that 'James the Epistolian called upon the rich to weep and howl for the miseries awaiting them in the world to come', and that 'St. James in his Epistle rivals the old prophets in his treatment of those who grow rich at the expense of the poor'.[84] The tract issued by Lansbury and the other Poplar 'rebels' in answer to accusations made against them also included a quote from the Epistle of James: 'Pure religion and undefiled before God and the Father is this, To visit the fatherless and widows in their affliction.'[85]

Headlam also goes back to the opening chapter of Gospel of Luke, before the birth of Christ, to the words of Mary (sometimes referred to as the Magnificat) upon hearing the news of her virgin conception. Mary sings: 'My soul doth magnify the Lord, and my spirit hath rejoiced in God my Saviour. For he hath regarded the low estate of his handmaiden [. . .]. He hath put down the mighty from their seats, and exalted them of low degree. He hath filled the hungry with good things; and the rich he hath sent empty away.'[86] Headlam writes: '[L]et Socialists turn to Our Lady's song, the Magnificat – "the hymn of the universal revolution" – "the Marseillaise of humanity," which tells of the disposition of the mighty, the scattering of the proud, the emptying of the pockets of the rich.'[87] Keeble also held that the Magnificat indicates the damage to character rendered by the possession of riches.[88]

One passage cited by a number of Christian Socialists is Paul's commandment to the Thessalonians 'that if any would not work, neither should he eat'.[89] While this verse could be used as a defence of the capitalist system which compels men to work for a living, for Christian Socialists it was a condemnation of a ruling class who gained their living from the work of others. Hardie interpreted the verse in this way, as did Headlam, whose Guild of St Matthew declared: '"If a man will not work", the apostle had written, "neither let him eat". Christians were thus enjoined, like socialists, to condemn an economic system that allowed the idle few to extort rent and interest from the labouring many.'[90] This is also the interpretation arrived at by John Wheatley, who in his fictional court case has the magistrate confront the pro-capitalist clergyman:

> Mag. You must have learned that St. Paul said – 'If any man will not work neither shall he eat'.
> Wit. I explain that away, your honour.
> Mag. My dear sir, you are injuring Christianity by trying to explain away that on which it was founded.

Tawney may also have had this verse in mind when he argued that landowners who currently perform no function ought to produce something in return for the income they receive: 'The surest way to encourage production is to make it clear that those who do not produce will not consume.'[91]

Keeble's view was that these 'stern words were never meant to apply to the sick and the feeble, the aged and unfortunate', but rather to the 'luxurious unemployed' and the 'rich unemployed', for 'every man should earn his daily bread, and not live idly on the compulsory labours of others'.[92] In even harsher words, Keeble argued that

> it is distinctly laid down in the New Testament that if, in a Christian society, a man will not work, neither shall he eat. Therefore a system which produces

a class of idlers, of consumers who are not all producers or necessary to production, who do nothing for their living, is a system self-condemned, however it may legalize the status of such social parasites. Such men have no moral right to eat.[93]

Keeble also reverses the commandment, arguing that – logically – if those who refuse to work should not eat, then those who do work should expect to eat. In a capitalist society, argues Keeble, this is not the case, as many of those who work the hardest are paid much less than is necessary for them to provide enough food for themselves and for their families.[94]

Paul's description of the body of Christ in 1 Corinthians was also 'important to Christian Socialists with its image of the body where every part has a function and where the body prospers by mutual inter-dependence and fellowship'.[95]

> But now are they many members, yet but one body. And the eye cannot say unto the hand, I have no need of thee: nor again the head to the feet, I have no need of you [. . .] that there should be no schism in the body; but that the members should have the same care one for another. And whether one member suffer, all the members suffer with it; or one member be honoured, all the members rejoice with it.[96]

Wilkinson suggests that 1 Corinthians is particularly evident in R. H. Tawney's writings, for example, when Tawney writes: 'A well-conducted family does not, when in low water, encourage some of its members to grab all they can, while leaving others to go short. On the contrary, it endeavours to ensure that its diminished resources shall be used to the best advantage in the interests of all.'[97] William Temple similarly 'compared Labour's ideal of brotherhood with the Pauline image of believers as the body of Christ'.[98] Keeble declared that this image to be 'the pattern to society. This is how men are meant to dwell together on all the face of the earth.'[99]

Christian Socialists also argued for a collectivist order of society from Acts of the Apostles, in which Luke records that 'all that believed were together, and had all things common; and sold their possessions and goods, and parted them to all men, as every man had need'.[100] These verses seemed obviously to commend common ownership, as explained by Keir Hardie:

> Here we have it clearly brought out that the direct outcome of the teachings of Jesus upon those who lived nearest to His time, and who became His followers, was to make them Communists. These early Christians found it impossible to retain property after they became Christians, since it raised artificial class distinctions in their midst and prevented the free play of that

spirit of fraternal brotherhood which Jesus taught as one of the characteristics of the Kingdom of God.¹⁰¹

It is interesting to note that Hardie reads into the passage that the motivation for collectivism was equality: in this case the abolition of 'class distinctions'. We also see that Hardie links back to the key concepts of brotherhood and the teaching of Christ. Similarly to Hardie, Headlam comments that that 'the first result of God's good spirit working on men after the day of Pentecost was, that they had all things in common'. 'The first Christians were, as you well know, in the simplest sense of the word communists – they put all their goods into a common fund and distribution was made to very man according to his need'.¹⁰² William Temple also describes this practice of the early church as 'voluntary communism', albeit drawing a distinction between this and '[m]odern communism'.¹⁰³

Other New Testament verses were cited by Christian Socialists in their arguments for socialism. Scott Holland, for example, made reference to another section of 1 Corinthians, Paul's words about love: 'So now faith, hope, and love abide, these three; but the greatest of these is love.'¹⁰⁴ Holland mockingly remarked '[i]magine putting up a stained-glass window to Faith, Hope and Political Economy'.¹⁰⁵ John Clifford provides another example, invoking the words of Paul in 2 Corinthians: '[F]or the weapons of our warfare are not carnal, but mighty through God to the pulling down of strong holds; casting down imaginations, and every high thing that exalteth itself against the knowledge of God, and bringing into captivity every thought to the obedience of Christ.'¹⁰⁶ Clifford viewed socialism as the means by which this was to be accomplished, writing that socialism 'is an ethical and religious effort, proceeding from within the soul of the human race, for pulling down principalities and powers, and spiritual wickedness in high places, and bringing every thought of men into the obedience of the teaching and spirit of Jesus Christ, the Saviour and Leader of men'.¹⁰⁷

George Lansbury and Keir Hardie both turn to Paul's sermon at the Areopagus in Athens, as recorded in Acts of the Apostles. Paul declares that God 'hath made of one blood all nations of men for to dwell on all the face of the earth'.¹⁰⁸ Lansbury writes of having 'learned the truth "God has made of one blood all the nations of the earth". Because this is so we sing of the Red Flag and look forward to the day when the nations of the world will gather under this Red Flag and fling down their arms, destroy their custom houses, break down all barriers.'¹⁰⁹ Hardie argued that 'Socialism would give reality to the claim often insisted upon from the Christian pulpit, and yet so universally belied by our every day deeds, that God hath made of one blood all nations of the earth to dwell together in unity'.¹¹⁰ Although this is a New Testament reference it speaks of an Old Testament doctrine, that of creation, and Christian Socialists were just as capable of making arguments from socialism from the Old Testament scriptures.

Old Testament

Samuel Keeble described how it is that '[t]he principles of a Christian social order are gathered, of course, from the teaching of Christ in the Gospels, and the teaching of the other writers of the New Testament; but they arise out of the social principles of the Hebrews, those of the Old Testament, given in the Law and the Prophets'.¹¹¹ The Old Testament doctrine of creation, drawn primarily from the book of Genesis, was key to the thinking of Christian Socialists; we have already seen that in Lansbury and Hardie quoting from Paul's declaration in Athens. The concept of God's Fatherhood is also linked to creation, as is the brotherhood that exists between those He has created. Part of the importance of this doctrine was that human beings were created in God's image, as described in the opening chapter of Genesis.¹¹² Wilfred Wellock, for example, argued that the issue of whether a society should be socialist or capitalist 'depends upon whether we are going to regard man as a beast or a soul, a collection of physical appetites or a spiritual being made in the image of God'.¹¹³ Tawney, for another, viewed the consequences of capitalism as 'an odious outrage on the image of God'.¹¹⁴ Hardie agreed, asking 'how long do you intend to submit to a system which is defacing God's image upon you [. . .] which is blurring and marring God's handiwork, which is destroying the lives of men, women and children?'¹¹⁵

Temple also drew on the doctrine of creation and the consequent fellowship that should exist between people:

> Man is created for fellowship in the family of God: fellowship first with God, and through that with all God's other children. And that is the primary test that must be applied to every system that is constructed and every change in the system that is proposed. Does it help us nearer towards the fullness and richness of personal fellowship?¹¹⁶

From this Temple argued that democracy was the best system, for by including everybody in the political process it led to the greater expression of fellowship.

Another important implication is that the land being created by God, there was no right for it to be controlled exclusively by a land-owning class. In a speech, Lansbury told his audience: 'What we Socialists want is, you should claim that land was not made by man but by God, and belongs to the whole people, for the use of mankind and not for the profit of the idle few.'[117] The inference of Christian Socialism then is that land created by God should be owned universally by all of His children. This theme was taken up by John Wheatley, responding to a group from his local church who, incited by the parish priest, had protested outside his house:

> Don't you know that God who gave you life has created for you green fields and sunny skies, that he has given you the material and the power to have in abundance beautiful homes, healthy food, education, leisure, travel and all that aids in the development of cultured men and women. These gifts of God have been stolen from you.[118]

For Wheatley, as God's creation was intended for all people, the ownership of the land by a specific land-owning class was nothing more than theft. Stewart Headlam also took up this theme, paraphrasing from the Psalms – 'The earth is the Lord's, and the fulness thereof; the world, and they that dwell therein' – arguing: 'The earth is the Lord's, and therefore not the landlord's; the earth is the Lord's, and He hath given it unto the children of men.'[119] The same verse is cited by Wellock, who viewed it as another statement into which 'society [should] be brought into absolute conformity'.[120] Ellen Wilkinson imagines a deputation to God receiving this response:

> Have you not the land? Have I failed in the yearly harvest and seedtime? Does not the earth bring forth her fruit? Does not the rain come and the showers? Has the sun failed to shed forth its beneficent beams? Have you not more goods than you can use? My child, the fault is not with Me but with yourselves. Learn to use your brains. Learn to care for one another, and to observe the Golden Rule. It is a problem of distribution. There is plenty for all if it is equally shared.[121]

Headlam also points to the account of the Exodus, in which the Jewish nation escaped from the rule of Egypt; he argues that the Passover meal 'commemorated, what we should nowadays call the great strike or revolution, which Moses headed against the Egyptian tyranny'.[122] Samuel Keeble also refers to the Exodus account of Pharaoh denying the Israelite slaves the proper materials in order to make the bricks with which they were required to build.[123] 'Capitalists must not', writes Keeble, 'try to make God's children provide bricks without straw, for if they do there is for them a fearful looking for of fiery indignation and wrath. God is not dead, and He will hear the cry of the oppressed.'[124] Keeble here takes up Headlam's theme of 'the God who fights', pointing to the eventual judgement carried out against Pharaoh and Egypt as a warning to the capitalist class.

Headlam is quoted arguing: 'The earth is the Lord's, and therefore not the landlord's.' Keeble makes just the same argument: 'The Hebrew regulations concerning the Sabbatic year, land-debts, rural housing, the pledge, and the year of Jubilee, all declare that 'the earth is the Lord's', and not the landlord's, and they all aim at preserving the economic freedom of the worker and his family. There is no absolute property in land in the Bible.' For Keeble, this 'Hebrew code is based on freedom, equality, justice, and aims at securing them, especially for the week and defenceless'.[125] According to Headlam, 'a study of Hebrew polity shows that careful arrangements were made, by the Jubilee laws especially, to deal righteously with the land, to see that the whole community enjoyed its value'.[126] Likewise, Hardie writes that 'land could neither be sold outright nor held for more than a limited period as security for debt; even the debtor was freed from all obligations when the year of Jubilee came round'.[127]

Temple agrees with this, writing: 'There were thus to be rights to property, but they were to be rights shared by all, and were subject to the overruling consideration that God alone had ultimate ownership of the land, the families to whom it was allotted being His stewards.'[128] Temple also values the Jubilee laws, mentioned by Headlam and Hardie, and referred to by Keeble as 'the Sabbatic year'. This law stated that every fiftieth year land that had been bought and sold was to return to those to whom it had originally been allotted – 'And you shall consecrate the fiftieth year, and proclaim liberty throughout the land to all its inhabitants. It shall be a jubilee for you, when each of you shall return to his property and each of you shall return to his clan' – and Temple argued that this law should be reinstated in order to prevent monopoly of land.[129]

In a similar way to these references to Old Testament land law, Christian Socialists could refer to the Ten Commandments to argue in favour of socialist principles. 'In every church throughout the world', wrote George Lansbury, 'the words "Remember the Sabbath day to keep it holy" are said by the minister, and yet all these ministers know that hundreds of thousands of men and women, boys and girls, are not allowed to rest from their labours.'[130] Elsewhere Lansbury declared that '[t]he grievous spectacle of seven days' work per week in a country which professes to honour the Sabbath has to be abolished'.[131] Keir Hardie attacked the factory owner Lord Overtoun along these lines, accusing him of the gross hypocrisy of being a member of a society for preservation of the

Sabbath while forcing his employees to work seven days a week, denying them any opportunity for rest or church attendance on the Lord's Day.[132] Bondfield takes up a similar theme, criticizing the hypocrisy of shop owners who professed to honour the sanctity of the Sabbath by allowing their employees to finish work at 11.55 pm on Saturday.[133]

Headlam refers to the command 'Thou shalt not steal', applying it to wealthy in capitalist society:

> [I]t is just as possible, indeed much more probable, that the rich will rob from the poor, as that the poor will rob from the rich. 'Thou shalt not steal' is just the commandment we want to get kept; we want to put a stop to the robbery of the poor by the rich, which has been going on for so long.[134]

Tawney shows the influence of the second commandment which forbade idolatry – 'Thou shalt not make unto thee any graven image [. . .] Thou shalt not bow down thyself to them, nor serve them' – in viewing the status of money in capitalist society as idolatrous: 'To kick over an idol, you must first get off your knees. [. . .] Either the Labour party means to end the tyranny of money, or it does not. If it does, it must not fawn on the owners and symbols of money.'[135]

'Social equality and fierce denunciations of the rich form the staple of the writings we are now taught to look upon as inspired', wrote Keir Hardie. 'What is now known as Socialism is woven from the same loom as was the vision of Isaiah', and 'the prophets of Israel are fiery publicists of the description we should now call Socialists or Anarchists.'[136] 'As a matter of fact', concludes Keeble, 'the literature and law-books of the world, ancient and modern, cannot equal the social teaching of the Law, the Prophets, and the Psalms, and that teaching is the Christian's by inheritance. It is really his prerogative and function to do with it what the Hebrew could not – make it operative.'[137]

Arguing from scripture

We saw earlier that opponents of socialism offered an interpretation of Paul's statement that 'if any would not work, neither should he eat', and how this was refuted by the Christian Socialists. Supporters of capitalism and opponents of socialism were just as capable of using the Bible in order to make their case, and Christian Socialists were forced to make counterarguments in order to uphold their beliefs. For example, in his Fabian tract John Clifford complained that the opponents of socialism 'denounce ministers who hold and teach that the laws of God run everywhere, even into wages and prices, into houses of toil and the sanitary conditions of factories and drapery establishments'.[138] Such were those who held that Christianity was a personal, individual matter and could not be applied to industry or to the economy. Samuel Keeble, who in his writings makes a point of countering the arguments made against Christian Socialism, dismissed this argument:

> Against Christian Individualism, which demands 'the simple gospel', Christian Socialism maintains that the Christian Gospel is twofold – individual and social – that the former never has been, and never can be, neglected, but that the latter both has been and is grossly neglected. The social gospel is as sacred and as indispensable as the individual gospel – the two are complementary, and the neglect of either always brings its penalties.[139]

Opponents would use specific verses and passages in order to disprove the claims of Christian Socialists; for example, the words of Paul in his first letter to Timothy – 'if we have food and clothing, with these we will be content' – were used as an argument against stirring up discontent among the working class.[140] This was a serious argument against Christian Socialism which sought, in the words of Headlam, 'to stir up a divine discontent in the hearts and minds of the people with the evils which surround them'.[141] Keeble, however, completely turned the argument on its head: many working-class people did not have food and clothing, and were therefore logically 'not to be content'. 'There is nothing', continued Keeble, 'to make either Christian individuals, Christian churches, or Christian communities contented when workers have not the necessities of existence, but, on the contrary, discontented.'[142] Keeble made the same point more fully elsewhere:

> A Christian, honest and industrious, conscientious and careful, who finds himself lacking [food and clothing], is not here to be exhorted to be contented. Both the circumstances themselves and the teaching of this very passage warrant the most energetic and definite discontent. If the wages and profits of labour and toil do not suffice to bring in this necessary minimum of food, clothing, fire, and house-room, Christians are justified both in being discontented themselves and in making other social victims discontented also. They suffer social injustice. In the Acts of the Apostles, we read that there was discontent in the Apostolic Church because the 'widows were neglected', they did not receive their 'daily bread'. The result of this discontent was not Apostolic rebuke but social reconstruction, the appointment of Stephen and others to the diaconate.[143]

In a similar way, the instruction of John the Baptist in the Gospel of Luke to 'be content with your wages' was also used as an argument against socialism.[144] Keeble, however, refuted this argument, pointing out that 'these words were spoken to Roman soldiers, who were guaranteed by the State a good "living wage", food, fire, clothing, and shelter, with perquisites and pickings, employment, and pension till death. Such, indeed, should be content with their wages – they had no grievance – a very different position from that of the average workman in Christian Europe and Christian England'.[145] For Keeble, the command to 'be content' came to those who enjoyed the benefits of a living wage; that was not true for the working class in capitalist society, and therefore discontent was perfectly justified.

Another argument put forward from opponents of socialism is that Christ both blessed the poor in the Beatitudes and stated that 'ye have the poor with you always'; therefore, attempts to eradicate poverty were both undesirable and unworkable.[146] Headlam opposed this notion in his Fabian tract, writing, first, that Christ meant 'that these poor men, notwithstanding their poverty, were better and happier men than their opponents', but that this in no way suggested 'that poverty – especially the grinding poverty which is found in our modern centres of civilisation – is the normal condition of things'.[147] Secondly, Headlam argued that Christ, in saying 'ye have the poor with you always', was simply noting the persistence of poverty in society, going on to add that even 'under the best Socialist *regime* imaginable, if a man is a loafer [and] refuse[s] to work when he has every facility and opportunity for working, he will fall into poverty'.[148] Scott Holland also detailed a counterargument on this point, arguing that the poverty that Christ blessed was a simple, non-materialist way of living, which nonetheless provided for basic needs, as opposed to the desperate poverty of capitalist society. '[D]o we suppose', asked Holland, 'that Jesus Christ has laid his Blessing on this unholy Poverty? Do we really imagine that this is what He had in His eyes as He pronounced the benediction?'[149]

> After all, Jesus did not intend to perpetuate even the Poverty that He blessed. He did not say 'Blessed are the Poor! – therefore keep them poor.' [. . .] The best of Poverties, the blessed Poverty, is to find its blessing in the riches of the Kingdom of Heaven. How much more, then, is that evil Poverty, that wicked Poverty, that fatal Poverty, which withholds from the Kingdom – to cease and disappear? Herein lies our task, the special task of Social Reform.[150]

'Poverty', wrote Keeble, 'miserable tragic poverty, is no "divine institution". Nine-tenths of it is of human origin, due to unbrotherliness, injustice and greed. It is "always with us" because individuals and society will not take the necessary steps, log ago indicated by Christ, to remove it.'[151]

The idea of 'divine institution' could be used against socialism, in the argument that the world was as ordained by God and ought not to be changed. This was refuted by Lansbury: 'Poverty, unemployment, casual labour, slums and all the social and economic evils from which we suffer, are not sent by God or Nature. They all arise out of conditions created by man, and by man can be removed.'[152] Lansbury declared: 'We talk about God's poor and God's rich, but you can search the Book right through and you won't find a word in the Master's philosophy that has anything to do with the creating of rich and poor.'[153] Wilkinson credits the influence of Scott Holland's CSU with the fact the verse

> The rich man in his castle
> The poor man at his gate,
> God made them, high or lowly
> And ordered their estate

was removed from the hymn 'All things bright and beautiful' in the 1906 version of *The English Hymnal*, for the idea had spread that poverty was not ordained by God.[154]

On a similar note, Keeble takes issue with the teaching of Thomas Malthus, the Anglican minister and economist: 'Malthus declared that "The Great Author of Nature, with that wisdom which is apparent in all His works, has made the passion of self-love beyond comparison stronger than the passion of benevolence". Hence, Malthus makes the Second Commandment false, which at least puts regard for others on a level with regard for ourselves.'[155] Keeble refutes the notion that the selfishness exhibited in capitalist society has been ordained by God. In an article for the *Baptist Times* George Lansbury offered this challenge:

> If we who based our Socialism on Christian ethics are wrong, you who think the present system right must find a way out of the morass which compels millions of our brothers and sisters to live a miserable existence on public and private charity. [...] If we believe Him and His teaching, then we dare not accept as final the economic situation which faces us.'[156]

Conclusion

It is at once apparent that Christian Socialism a Bible-based ideological position. The examples discussed in this chapter serve to demonstrate that references to scripture were not merely allusions or rhetorical flourishes in order to make socialism appear attractive in an age more characterized by religiosity that our own. Rather, Christian Socialists of different theological positions delved deep into the Bible in order to demonstrate the rightness of socialism. The key idea – one which is at the conceptual centre of Christian Socialism – is the Fatherhood of God and consequent brotherhood of all people. The life, teaching and example of Christ, allied to passages which demonstrate the need for equality, cooperation and collectivism and denounce the worship – even the possession – of wealth are woven into a scriptural foundation for socialism.

2

The church basis

We have seen that the basis of socialism for Christian Socialists is ethical, and that these ethics are drawn from Christianity. Chapter 1 dealt with arguments for socialism from the Bible; this chapter considers the basis for socialism found in the church. Throughout the writings of the Christian Socialists there are references to ways in which the church has provided for them a basis for socialism. Peter d'A Jones identifies an argument from patristics, being 'that many of the church fathers were socialists and communists', and from the sacraments of the church such as communion and baptism, being 'that the modern church in its worship, symbol and ritual exhibits a socialist faith'. To this latter phenomenon Jones gives the name 'sacramental socialism'.[1] We could add to the influence of the 'church fathers' – men such as Augustine of Hippo Regius – the modern-day teaching of the church, including Catholic social teaching, the foundation of which was laid in 1891 with Pope Leo XIII's encyclical *Rerum novarum* (otherwise known as *The Condition of Labour*) which 'confirmed the need for the state to intervene to protect workers and poor people'.[2]

Which church?

Christian Socialists and those who have written about Christian Socialism have sometimes taken it as evident that Catholicism – whether in the form of Roman Catholicism or Anglo-Catholicism – is more suited to socialism than Protestantism. In the period we are considering, 'the distinction between Protestant individualism and Catholic cooperation was becoming an intellectual commonplace'.[3] One writer points to 'the mythology of the age, which lays it down that Protestantism, especially in such advanced forms as English Dissent, is necessarily individualistic, without social content, and inevitably and inseparably associated with Capitalism'.[4] Stewart Headlam's view was that, by contrast, 'the Catholic Faith is essentially at one with the Socialist ideal', and

John Wheatley argued that '[t]he Catholic church has always leaned more to socialism or collectivism and equality, than to individualism and inequality. It has always been the church of the poor and all historical attacks on it have emanated from the rich.'[5]

One reason for this, as suggested earlier, is that the universal claims of Catholicism stand in contrast to the individualistic nature of much Protestantism, especially Nonconformity. One Roman Catholic writer describes how, in this view, the Nonconformist or evangelical view of the church is quite different from the Catholic view:

> The sect type, as a small radical group, regards the world as evil and thus removes itself from the world so that the Christian community can live and follow the biblical demands of Jesus without being forced to compromise or be contaminated by the evil world. The church type, on the other hand, comprises saints and sinners, lives in the world, and attempts to have a direct influence on what transpires in all aspects of worldly existence. [. . .] [B]ecause the Roman Catholic Church is the best illustration of the church type, it will be concerned about what happens in the world. The history of the Catholic Church testifies to its involvement in working for a better society.[6]

Another reason is that, as explained more fully later, arguments for Christian Socialism have often been made from the sacraments of the church, particularly baptism and communion. Anglo-Catholics raised these to the position of utmost importance in worship, while Nonconformists tended to focus more on the ministry of the Word than the ritual of the sacrament. This difference is emphasized by the interior design of church buildings, as Headlam explains, declaring in a sermon that the Catholic tradition, as followed in the Anglican Church, makes 'the worship of Jesus Christ the central act of our service: go into almost any Church you like and it is the altar, not the pulpit, which is the most prominent and exalted place'.[7] 'The Bible, and the Bible only, may be the religion of Protestants', wrote Headlam, 'but the Catholic Faith, with its one unique Christian service bearing witness to the Eternal Presence of Jesus Christ, is not founded on a book but on a Person.'[8] It is the sacramentalism of Anglo-Catholicism allied to the strong association between sacramentalism and Christian Socialism which leads to the linkage of socialism with Catholicism.

These two reasons – the claims to universality and the focus on sacraments – are also drawn together, in that an understanding of the latter in light of the former is conducive to socialism. Take, for example, baptism. Headlam, again, writes that 'we claim every little baby born into the world as being equal with every other little baby, no matter whether it be the child of a costermonger or the child of a prince', before adding, in an aside to Protestants, especially those who practice believer's baptism, 'not waiting for conversion or illumination, or election or proof of goodness, but simply because it is a human being, we claim it as of right a member of Christ, the child of God and an inheritor – not merely a future heir but a present inheritor – of the Kingdom of Heaven'.[9] For Headlam, socialist equality made perfect sense under a system in which all children in a country were christened, but not under a system in which either the children of believers only were christened or the mature believers themselves baptized. 'Infant baptism', writes one of Headlam's biographers, 'was the surest safeguard against exclusiveness and the sectarian mentality which Headlam saw to be subversive of both Catholicism and Socialism.'[10]

This view has sometimes led to criticism of Protestantism by Christian Socialists, such as those essayists from the Church Socialist League who in *Return to Christendom* attacked Protestantism for its individualism and ignoring of social problems, and argued that the Reformation had undone the Christian values which had underpinned medieval society.[11] R. H. Tawney, in the words of a biographer, argued that 'Protestantism, and Calvinism in particular, replaced social solidarity with individualism, and encouraged the separation of economic and ethical interests'.[12] John Wheatley, similarly, contrasted the collectivist spirit of the Church of Rome with the individualism of Protestantism, following on from the Reformation.[13]

These views, however, are countered by some writers on this subject and by the Nonconformist Christian Socialists themselves. Interestingly, it is a biographer of John Wheatley who notes that the 'Labour movement in Britain would never have come into existence without the belief, particularly strong among Nonconformist Christians, that this could, and must, be done', adding that Wheatley's 'task was perhaps a harder one, coming as he did from a church with a tradition of formidable sanctions against intellectual dissent among its own ranks'.[14] Another writer argues that 'the kind of Christianity which counted for most in the history of the Labour movement was that kind which found its formal expression in the several denominations of Nonconformity'.[15]

Nonconformist Christian Socialists were just as capable of finding from within their own tradition a basis for socialism. Samuel Keeble, a Wesleyan Methodist minister, saw socialism displayed in England's Protestant tradition: 'In the past the Church has been very prominent in all the social revolutions of England – the Lollard movement owed much to Wyclif and his poor priests, and the Stuart tyranny was struck down by the Puritans.'[16] Keeble elsewhere cites the Puritans of England and Covenanters of Scotland as part of this socialistic tradition.[17] Wilfred Wellock, an Independent Methodist lay preacher, noted in similar vein that the socialist movement followed 'in the spirit of men like Wyclif, Luther, Knox'.[18] Keir Hardie, a Congregationalist, also points to this tradition, writing of John Ball, the 'Communistic teachings of Wycliffe', 'John Huss the Communist', Thomas Muntzer, the Anabaptists and the Levellers.[19]

Keeble admitted that '[t]he Roman Catholics, making much more of the Church, the Christian body politic, and less of the individual than Protestants, naturally were earlier in the field of the social question', adding that 'Protestantism has grievously suffered from the individualism grafted upon it – bad stock on a good stem'.[20] Keeble then accepts part of the case against Protestantism, but argues that a disinterest in the welfare of society is not natural to Protestantism but an unfortunate mistake, due to the Reformers' 'zeal for the emancipation of the individual from superstition and spiritual tyranny'; they nevertheless 'did not wholly lose sight of [the] social environment'.[21] The Baptist minister John Clifford goes on the offensive against Catholicism, referring to Ernest Renan's writing about the Church of Rome: 'Renan has described the steps by which the "Church became all in Christianity"; and so displaced much of Christianity; and then he speaks of the one step more by which "a bishop becomes all in the Church", and thus gets rid of much of the Christianity that remained.' Clifford concludes: 'We do not recognise that bishop. We are not of that Church, and refuse to take our social and economic ideals from either him or it.'[22]

Church teaching as a basis for socialism

The writings of Christian Socialists nevertheless indicate that, whatever church background they were from, they in part derived their socialist beliefs from the teaching of the church. John Wheatley's political beliefs, for example, have been described as 'socialism illuminated by these insights into its relationship with church teaching and moral law'.[23] In his *Catholic Working Man* Wheatley's arguments were 'reinforced with wide-ranging quotations from the church fathers, Cardinal Manning and, perhaps most effectively in its immediate local context, Archbishop Maguire himself', Maguire being the Archbishop of Glasgow who had criticized Wheatley for his socialist views.[24] We see here that Wheatley employs a mix of church teaching both historical and contemporary, including reference to 'the church fathers', the patristic argument identified by Jones. The same line is taken by Hardie, who argues that the 'early Church Fathers' were those who 'spoke out fearlessly [. . .] on the side of Communism', adding 'that for nearly seventeen centuries the common people and their leaders believed Communism and Christianity to be synonymous terms'.[25] '[I]f men accepted the teaching of the Christian Church', wrote R. H. Tawney, 'they would have a body of principles not only resting on authority [. . .] but setting out the main lines of a moral scheme of the universe and deducing man's duties and rights, freedom, responsibility, justice, etc.'[26]

It is Samuel Keeble who gives the most extensive treatment of the teaching and example of the church throughout history, giving in his *Christian Responsibility for the Social Order* – after a similarly extensive discussion of scriptural reasons for socialism – just over forty pages to a chronological account of socialism throughout the history of the church. We shall therefore follow his chronology. Keeble begins by noting the contribution of the earliest Christians to social reform, adding that the earliest Christians 'protected the poor, the widow, and the orphan', and 'dignified labour by engaging in it'.[27] Temple also appeals to the behaviour and example of the early church as a whole rather than just those regarded as fathers of the church: 'The primitive Church expressed its intimacy of inner fellowship by a spontaneous community of goods. It was a small fellowship of persons filled with the spirit of Christ and therefore with love for one another. This expressed itself in a voluntary communism.'[28] Hardie does likewise, explaining that 'it is now known that Communism in goods was practiced by Christians for at least three hundred years after the death of Christ'.[29]

Keeble then references some of the apocryphal gospels and epistles from the early church, quoting first the *Epistle to Diognetus*: 'It is not by exercising lordship over his neighbours, or by desiring to be greater than those that are weaker, or by being rich and oppressing those who are poor, that happiness comes, nor can anyone by these things become and imitator of God, but whoso bears his neighbour's burden.' Keeble then points to the 'Way of Darkness' described by the writer of the *Epistle of Barnabus* – 'not to administer righteous judgement to the widow and orphan and to have no compassion on the poor, nor to take any pains for such as are heavy-laden and oppressed; it is to be advocates of the rich, but unjust judges of the poor' – and contrasts it with the writer's 'Way of Light' – 'thou shalt communicate to thy neighbour all thou hast; thou shalt not call anything thine own'. It is particularly this latter command that points to communal ownership rather than merely care for the poor. Finally, Keeble quotes from the *Shepherd of Hermas*: 'Justify the widow, judge the cause of the fatherless, and spend your riches and your wealth in such works as these.'[30]

Keeble then moves on to the writings of those regarded as the church fathers, first pointing to the words of Tertullian: 'We who mingle in mind and soul have no hesitation as to fellowship in property.' Cyprian is then quoted, commanding that Christians should 'imitate the equality of God in the common gifts of nature, which the whole human race should equally enjoy'. 'The unequal division of wealth', writes Ambrose of Milan, 'is the result of egoism and violence'.[31] Again, these quotes appear to compel both equality and common ownership.

Keeble also writes of Augustine of Hippo Regius, who is elsewhere quoted: 'Let us, therefore, my brethren, abstain from the possession of private property, or from the love of it if we cannot abstain from the possession of it.'[32] William Temple also points to Augustine in his discussion of private property. According to Temple, 'St. Augustine taught explicitly that private property is the creation of the State and exists only in virtue of the State's protection. But the state, according to him, has its origin in the sinfulness of men, which must be kept within bounds. So the state has a divine authority, yet was instituted only because of men's sin.' The point of this in Temple's view is that property rights 'are always an accommodation to human sin, are subordinate to the general interest, and are a form of stewardship rather than of ultimate ownership'.[33] Temple's view would agree with that of Tawney – that property rights are not absolute but rather 'subordinate to the general interest' – but the significance here is his appeal to a church authority, Augustine, to make his point.

Keeble then looks to a later period of church history, arguing from the teaching of John Wyclif – 'the ideal remains that no man should hold separate property, and that all should be had in common' – and his contemporary, John Ball – 'things would never go right in England as long as goods were not in common, and so long as there were villeins and gentlemen'. Keeble offers some praise for Martin Luther but criticizes Luther for his opposition to the peasants, which 'accounts for the atheistic and material form which German socialism has generally assumed. [. . .] It was pitiful that "the monk that shook the world" for religious freedom, who, like a lion, confronted Pope and Emperor, should quail before property.' Instead Keeble quotes Thomas Muntzer: '[O]ur sovereigns and rulers are at the bottom of all usury, thievery, and robbery; they take all created things into possession.' Keeble turns to other figures from this period, such as Jean Calvin, Hugh Latimer and Thomas More.[34] We have already noted instances of Wilfred Wellock and Keir Hardie citing individuals and movements from the Reformation era as examples for socialism.

Christian Socialists not only looked back to the church of the past for inspiration but also found elements of socialism in the modern-day church.

Stewart Headlam, according to one biographer, 'used the Book of Common prayer as a textbook in socialism'.³⁵ Headlam also gave a socialist interpretation to passages from the Anglican Catechism. The Catechism, for example, reads: 'My duty toward my neighbour is to love him as myself, and to do to all men as I would they should do to me.' According to Headlam, this is a condemnation of 'those who say that it is my duty [...] to get all I can out of my neighbour, to take advantage of him, to catch him when he is weak and alone, when he has a large family, and make him work for me at just as low wages as I can get him to take'.³⁶ Headlam quoted the Catechism instruction to 'hurt nobody by word or deed', arguing that 'we can't quite, according to the Catechism, leave these matters to supply and demand'.³⁷

Headlam also cited the Catechism on entering into a debate about the role of such teaching in an industrial dispute. 'It was, for instance, claimed during the lock-out of the agricultural labourers that the low condition of the workers was in part due to the teaching of the Catechism about submissiveness. Headlam soon stressed that the Catechism spoke of "that state of life into which it *shall* please God to call him", not "*has* pleased", thus encouraging, as he said, a "divine discontent"'.³⁸ For Headlam, the Catechism spoke of socialism because it did not call men to submit to any other conditions but the condition of life which God shall eventually call them, that being a socialist way of life; therefore they should be discontent with anything less than that. It may be that George Lansbury also held to this interpretation of the Catechism, as evidenced in the statement he made of himself: 'He did not believe that God was pleased to call people to live in slums or workhouses, prisons and such-like places, brought there by man-made conditions.'³⁹

Tawney references the Book of Common Prayer in arguing that a prosperous society 'depends upon co-operative effort, and co-operation upon moral principles. And moral principles are what the prophets of this dispensation despise. So the world "continues in scarcity," because it is too grasping and too short-sighted to see that "which maketh men to be of one mind in a house"'.⁴⁰ The phrasing here shows that it is God that makes men of one mind, able to co-operate in the way Tawney views as necessary in order for society to prosper.

Catholic social teaching

That which came to be known as Catholic social teaching has been identified as important in the political thought of John Wheatley.⁴¹ 'Catholic social teaching unequivocally maintains that the purpose of the state is to promote the common good, both for individuals and in terms of conditions appropriate for all.'[42] The only major document to have been written during Wheatley's lifetime was Pope Leo XIII's *Rerum novarum* or *On the Condition of Labour* in 1891, an encyclical written in response to the problems caused by the Industrial Revolution. '*Rerum novarum* – in opposition to laissez-faire liberalism and individualism – called for government intervention to protect workers. The state should intervene not only for the good of all but for the good of a particular class.'[43]

It is not difficult to see why such a document could be used by socialists such as Wheatley to argue for socialism, or as a basis for their personal socialist beliefs. For instance, Leo writes: 'But all agree, and there can be no question whatever, that some remedy must be found, and quickly found, for the misery and wretchedness which press so heavily at this moment on the large majority of the very poor.'[44] Again, Leo refers to 'the cruelty of grasping speculators who use human beings as mere instruments for making money' and calls for rulers to ensure that the poor are 'housed, clothed and enabled to support life'.[45] Here Pope Leo seems to be supportive of socialist ideas.

However, *Rerum novarum* 'had, in fact, rejected socialism as an answer to social problems'.[46] Pope Leo opposed socialism for its rejection of private property – 'the main tenet of socialism, the community of goods, must be utterly rejected' – and for giving too much power to the state, despite his not fully rejecting state intervention. He also believed that equality in society was unobtainable: 'in capability, in diligence, in health, and in strength; an unequal fortune is a necessary result of inequality in condition'.[47] This rejection of socialism was the Vatican's consistent position: Pope Pius IX had rejected socialism and communism in his *Syllabus Errorum* (the *Syllabus of Errors*) in 1864, as did Pius XI in *Quadragessimo anno*, (*In the Fortieth Year*, so called because the encyclical was written in 1931, forty years after the publication of *Rerum novarum*). Indeed, Pius XI was specific in his condemnation:

> Whether socialism be considered as a doctrine, or as a historical fact, or as a 'movement', if it really remains socialism, it cannot be brought into harmony with the dogmas of the Catholic Church. [. . .] 'Religious socialism', 'Christian socialism' are expressions implying a contradiction in terms. No one can be at the same time a sincere Catholic and a true socialist.[48]

According to the Church of Rome, then, socialism is a worse evil than capitalism; 'socialism', explains one writer, 'is intrinsically evil because it contravenes basic Christian teachings on private property and class relations, whereas capitalism is not intrinsically evil but often leads to abuses. Thus, the condemnations are not symmetrical. Socialism alone is intrinsically evil.'[49]

Given then that *Rerum novarum* specifically rejected socialism, how could an argument for socialism be framed from Catholic social teaching? It was perhaps 'by virtue of its consistent endorsement of the legitimate claims of the working class', and that the encyclical 'had endorsed many aspects of the labour movement's social and political programme, particularly affirming some of the political devices by which socialism was to be approached (a living wage, rights of association)'.[50] These things being so clearly stated, socialists could argue that *Rerum novarum* in practice did support their cause. This was the case for Samuel Keeble, who cited Pope Leo, 'though he condemned Socialism'.[51]

Wheatley additionally argued that the socialism rejected by the Vatican was different to the socialism espoused by the British labour movement. Early in his political life, Wheatley wrote to the *Glasgow Observer* in reply to an antisocialist lecture given by the Catholic Truth Society in which he distinguished between moderate socialism that did not threaten the church and more radical socialism which was anti-Christian.[52] In response to Pope Leo's specific point about property rights, Wheatley wrote in his *Catholic Working Man* that 'Socialism is defined as the public ownership of land and capital. This does not mean the abolition of all private property'.[53] One Roman Catholic writer describes how, according to Catholic social teaching,

> Socialism violates the right to private property which allows persons to sustain their lives and the social good by the free and intelligent use of their possessions. Likewise it intrudes on family, not only by denying private property, but also by its conception of an all-encompassing state (since the state is suppose[d] to represent the will of a classless society). State socialism undermines the relationship between parents and children.[54]

Wheatley, as it were, refutes this, arguing: 'Our Socialism is not confiscation nor robbery nor the destruction of family life, nor anything like what you have heard our opponents describe it. It is simply a scheme to abolish poverty.'[55] Wheatley's socialism then, on paper at least, is perfectly compatible with the teaching of the Vatican. In this way Wheatley became 'an effective and eloquent protagonist of a non-Marxist socialism which Catholics could in good faith espouse'.[56]

Wheatley, however, did sometimes fail to reconcile his political and religious beliefs. When a letter from a priest, Leo Pusissant, used quotes from *Rerum novarum* to attack Wheatley's socialism, this 'led Wheatley to call in question the claims of that encyclical to *ex-cathedra* status'.[57] In effect, Wheatley was reduced to denying that *Rerum novarum* embodied the infallible teaching of the Pope, implying therefore that the document was not binding on Roman Catholics. Beatrice Webb recalls a meeting with Wheatley shortly before his death, in which, losing faith with a parliamentary route to socialism, he told her that '[h]e would be a Communist if he were not a pious Catholic'.[58] However, despite these difficulties, we can see how Wheatley found some basis for his socialism in Roman Catholic social teaching, and how other Christian Socialists found arguments for their socialism in the teaching of the church both past and present.

Sacramental socialism

Peter d'A Jones identifies the sacraments as an important aspect of Christian Socialist belief. To this Jones gives the name 'sacramental socialism', explaining this as 'a phrase which stands for the belief that the best proof and witness of the socialism of Christ is in the Holy Sacraments of the Church – especially Baptism and the Mass (or, as some Anglicans preferred to call it, the Lord's Supper)'.[59] We have seen earlier that the sacraments as a basis for socialism carried more weight with those from a Catholic tradition, particularly Anglo-Catholics, and it is Stewart Headlam who focuses more than any other on the connection between the sacraments and socialism. Headlam writes, 'Baptism, the Sacrament of Equality, and Holy Communion, the Sacrament of Brotherhood: these two are fundamental, the one abolishing all class distinctions, and admitting all into the Christian Church, simply on the ground of humanity; the other pledging and enabling all to live the life of brotherhood'.[60]

Headlam saw that his followers in the Guild of St Matthew were also given to the same understanding of the sacraments as representing socialism, writing that '[w]e have from the beginning in this Guild, and rightly, connected the restoration of the Mass to its proper place with our secular and political work; our sacramentalism with our Socialism [. . .] we are Socialists because we are Sacramentarians'.[61] James Adderly, a Guild member, said that baptism is 'the entrance of every human being into the greatest democratic society in the world', while the Mass is 'the weekly meeting of a society of rebels against a Mammon-worshipping world order'.[62]

Headlam viewed the Mass or Lord's Supper as important, partly because of its origins in the Old Testament Passover meal; the Passover, he wrote, 'commemorated, what we should nowadays call the great strike or revolution, which Moses headed against the Egyptian tyranny'.[63] Its greatest significance, however, was as a symbol of brotherhood and equality. This view was shared by Henry Scott Holland, who linked the 'social solidarity of man' with 'the essential solidarity of Church fellowship' as expressed in the Eucharist.[64] William Temple, similarly, viewed the Eucharist as 'the perfect picture of the Christian society'.[65] Holland's CSU passed a resolution that its members should be those who had a 'bond of union in the Sacrament of Christ's body', on the grounds that this allowed the CSU to 'demand from Communicants that social service to which their Communion pledges them'.[66] Headlam reportedly declared that 'those who come to Holy Communion must be holy communists'.[67] Both the CSU and the Guild of St Matthew asked that members pray for their societies at communion services.[68]

As well as representing brotherhood and equality, the communion service helped those who were present to live a life committed to those socialist values; as Headlam says, 'pledging and *enabling* all to live the life of brotherhood'.[69] Holland believed that 'this supreme effort to create a new social conscience in Church workers, must of sheer necessity involve corporate Acts of worship, Communion with one another, in the intimacies of the innermost shrine, gatherings around the one Altar, to partake of the one Bread, and to drink of the one Cup'.[70] George Lansbury also speaks of the meaning of this sacrament, writing that 'the Communion service to me is not only the sacrifice again of Christ but a reminder of all the good men and women who have made their sacrifices in order to make the world better'.[71] For Lansbury then, the significance is a reminder of sacrifices made for socialism.

Headlam linked the Mass with baptism as we have seen earlier, writing that 'baptism demonstrates the equality of all children, regardless of the economic or social class into which they are born'. Headlam viewed the two sacraments as complementary:

> And so, just as the most old-fashioned clergyman, whatever may have been his politics, or views on social questions, was by the mere fact of his baptising the labourer's little baby bearing witness to the truths of equality in a more far-reaching way than any French Revolution ever did: so the quietest and the most retiring of you when you kneel on Easter morning to receive Jesus Christ for your strength and refreshment, are also bearing witness to truths which, when realised, will regenerate the world: which will put down the mighty, scatter the proud, empty the pockets of the rich.[72]

Headlam also makes brief mention of other sacraments.[73] 'Confirmation', writes Headlam, is that 'by which the child, beginning the critical period of adolescence, is strengthened by his conscious membership of the Socialist Society'. Marriage, according to Headlam, serves as a reminder of duties towards that society, while penance promotes progress by encouraging the acknowledgement of mistakes.[74] We can therefore see that for Stewart Headlam, as well as for other Christian Socialists, the sacraments of the church provided a basis for their socialist beliefs.

Church opposition to socialism

Despite the enthusiasm of Christian Socialists for the socialism, which they saw preached in and through the church's teachings and sacraments, there was a problem with this perspective – namely that the church was often opposed to socialism. We have already encountered the view that the Reformation and Protestantism had ushered individualism into the life of the church and prevented it from being that which held society together as an ethical community; we have also seen that, despite the influence of Roman Catholic social teaching, successive popes have rejected socialism as unworkable and, in any case, wicked. Establishment, in the view of Christian Socialists from various traditions, was also a major factor in compromising the church's socialist message. Keir Hardie alleges that '[t]he Church only began to reject Communism after it became part of the state'.[75] John Clifford similarly argues that establishment 'tends to make the Church self-seeking instead of self-sacrificing, unprogressive and reactionary instead of leading the highest and best movements of mankind'.[76] George Lansbury criticizes 'official Christianity' for giving its support to war, 'as it always has done on behalf of all war since that fateful day in the history of Christianity when Constantine established the Christian religion as part of the State machinery of Government'.[77]

For this reason some Christian Socialists were opposed to the church being part of the state. Clifford sees a remedy in the church being 'free in all its activities from the control of Princes and Parliaments, and from the interference of civic and political organisations of every kind'.[78] Headlam agreed with his fellow Fabian Clifford on this point, writing in his Fabian tract on *Christian Socialism*: 'A complete Christian Socialism cannot be brought about until the Church is free to use influence and discipline for the establishment of the Kingdom of

Heaven upon earth.'[79] This theme was taken up again by Headlam a few years later, when he argued that Anglicans should 'want to help set the Church free to manage her own affairs, to elect her own clergy, to be a real power to help bring about those secular reforms which are necessary in order to make this diocese of ours into a part, a beautiful part, of the Kingdom of Heaven upon earth'.[80] Clifford and Headlam both mention that the church must be 'free' from the state in order to function properly and truly espouse socialism. Tawney also views freedom of the church as a priority; the church, he writes, 'must be free to be a servant', adding his support for disestablishment by arguing that '[t]he ancient question of whether church is to be above state or state is to be above church, finds its solution in a free church refusing the temporalities for the sake of the spiritualities'.[81]

Because of these issues – individualism, establishment, opposition to socialism – Christian Socialists were often found criticizing the church. This is a theme that Keir Hardie repeatedly returns to in his tract *Can a Man be a Christian on a Pound a Week?* 'In what follows', Hardie begins, 'I do not seek to assail Christianity or impugn its teachings. But I cannot accept current theology as being other than a travesty of what Christ taught.' Hardie goes on to criticize those who profess Christianity and yet live 'an idle luxurious life at the expense of the poor toil-worn workman with his pound a week', while the workman himself is excluded from the fellowship of the church for being unable to 'wear good clothes, pay seat rents, and subscribe to the minister's salary'. Hardie concludes that 'modern Churchianity is not only un-Christian, but anti-Christian. I can find no points of correspondence between the teachings of Jesus, as contained in the New Testament, and the teachings of the modern pulpit.'[82]

A particular example is found in Hardie's anger about the relationship between the church and Lord Overtoun, a Scottish factory owner known to be a particularly harsh employer. For example, as already noted, Hardie accused Overtoun of the hypocrisy of being a member of a society for preservation of the Sabbath while forcing his employees to work seven days a week, denying them the opportunity to attend church on Sunday. Hardie writes,

> I mean to try whether the Christian Church cannot be so stirred up on this matter as to insist on men who make so much profession of Christianity as Lord Overtoun makes first of all giving some evidence of the faith that is in them by their treatment of the workpeople. If they will not treat these humanely, then the Church should not accept for its altar the blood-stained gifts which have been procured by the destruction of men, body and soul.[83]

Whether that could be the case is in Hardie's view doubtful; as he notes elsewhere 'the political economist wields more influence in church councils than does the Religious Teacher, and that Adam Smith and "The Wealth of Nations", is a more potent factor than the Sermon on the Mount, and the Apostle'.[84]

Hardie could be virulent in his denunciation of what he saw as hypocrisy within the church and among Christians: 'If the spiritually proud and pride-blinded professors of Christianity could only be made to feel and see that Christ is here ever present with us, and that they are laying on stripes and binding the brow afresh with thorns, and making shed tears of blood in a million homes.'[85] John Clifford recalled that Hardie 'was pained by the excessive care which the Churches showed for the "respectable", and what seemed to him their cruel indifference to the oppressed and the poor'.[86]

Yet Hardie's was not the only voice criticizing the church in this way. Clifford himself, in milder language, writes that the church has shown 'little courage in championing the cause of justice and social betterment'.[87] Stewart Headlam agrees, asking 'is it not true that the Church has, for the most part, either ignored or opposed those in our own times who have done most to this end?'[88] 'Church people', in the view of Henry Scott Holland,

> were hopelessly behind in all the movements for Social Reform. They did not count, practically, in the Cause. They held coldly aloof from the struggle. They bore no part of the burden. They, more than any, refused to bring their Faith to bear upon the actual facts of Commerce and Industry. They shut it up within the closed doors of sacred Churches, and left the outer world of temporal affairs to go its own bad way, as if it could never be expected to conform to Christian Ethical standards, or to glorify God in Jesus Christ our Lord. They continually formed a block of solid and stolid obstruction to every movement of the Spirit as it strove to transfigure Society into something that would reflect the City of God. The main mass of the Church's folk had betrayed the Creed that they professed to hold.[89]

R. H. Tawney argued that compromise should be 'as impossible between the Church of Christ and the idolatry of wealth, which is the practical religion of capitalist societies, as it was between the Church and the state idolatry of the Roman Empire', and that a 'Christianity which resigns the economic world to the devil appears to me, in short, not Christianity at all'.[90] George Lansbury agreed, writing: 'If Christian ministers decide that the principles of our religion cannot be practiced, we ought to close up our churches and cease praying in our Parliaments.'[91]

John Wheatley offered specific criticism of his own parish priest, Andrew O'Brien: 'One of his favourites poses is as the friend of God's poor. While God's poor are prepared to act like slaves and sycophants they are flattered, but independence is treated as a deadly sin.'[92] Wheatley indicates in his fictional trial of capitalists and their allies that the church is often on the side of the capitalists, having the workman 'Old Dick' include the 'clergymen' in the list of those who had told him 'not to listen' to the socialist, and having the two capitalists call upon a clergyman in their defence.[93]

Wilfred Wellock points to the hypocrisy of society as a whole: 'We call ourselves a Christian people and the most civilised nation on the face of the earth, and yet our civilisation is characterised by methods of refined barbarism.'[94] Tawney, again, takes up a similar theme:

> To suggest that an individual is not a Christian may be libellous. To preach in public that Christianity is absurd is legally blasphemy. To state that the social ethics of the New Testament are obligatory upon men in the business affairs which occupy nine-tenths of their thought, or on the industrial organization which gives our society its character, is to preach revolution.[95]

'The church', complains Ellen Wilkinson, 'suffers a great deal from some of the petty little people who take its name as their badge.'[96] It is for these reasons that Samuel Keeble urges patience with socialists' opposition to Christianity, writing that the 'Christian Socialist has to bear all this meekly, knowing that the Christian Church has given only too much ground for this hostility and suspicion.'[97]

How then could Christian Socialists take the church as a basis for their socialism? The reason is that, in the view of Christian Socialists, in opposing socialism the church was opposing its own teaching. Therefore, Lansbury observes that the 'Churches are bankrupt because they are not true to their creed', and Tawney similarly argues that the churches failed to repel individualism because 'they did not possess [. . .] faith in their own creed'.[98] 'Tawney's charge', suggests one biographer, 'was that the Christian churches combined a doctrine about the importance of treating people as ends with an acquiescence in a social and economic system which treated them unequally and instrumentally as means.'[99]

In this conception then, the Christian Socialists found their basis for socialism in the creeds of the church – creeds which the church itself often failed to live up to. Stewart Headlam explains, for example, that '[i]n order to understand the connection between the Church and Socialism, we must blot out from our memory the Bishops' votes in the House of Lords: the action and talk of the highly-placed laymen and lay-women [. . .] and go straight to the basis and Sacrament of the Church'.[100] This is reflected in the criticisms of Keir Hardie. He writes that the 'rich and comfortable classes have annexed Jesus and perverted His Gospel', and that the 'modern Christian Church is a reflection of the modern business world'.[101] 'The Christian world', writes Hardie, 'has gone sadly astray. They do not know that they have forgotten the centre cross and are worshipping at the cross of the thief'.[102] The criticism here is of the 'modern church' – the one that has 'gone sadly astray', having allowed its creed to be 'annexed' by the capitalist class. 'Christianity is no longer a reality', Hardie concludes. 'The religious form may still exist, but once again the spirit has passed away and has found embodiment elsewhere.'[103]

There was, therefore, an ideal church, which existed in the past – hence references to the church fathers or the early church – which was still reflected in some of the modern church's teaching, liturgy and sacraments. Christian Socialists felt themselves to be representing this ideal church having understood properly the true meaning of both the church's teaching and the Bible; by contrast, many within the church – including its modern-day leaders – failed to understand, having been corrupted by individualism and capitalist economics.

Hardie's writings reflect a pessimism about the state of the church, writing, as we saw earlier, 'Christianity is no longer a reality [. . .] the spirit has passed away and has found embodiment elsewhere'. One of Hardie's biographers argues that he 'never claimed that socialism replaced Christianity or the church', yet Hardie's suggestion that 'Christianity is no longer a reality' and that 'the spirit' of Christianity 'has found embodiment elsewhere' suggests that this indeed was his view.[104] In a speech Hardie is reported to have said: 'Christianity today lay buried, bound up in the cements of a dead and lifeless theology. It awaited decent burial, and they in the Labour movement had come to resuscitate the Christianity of Christ.'[105] We may then conclude that Hardie did believe that the spirit of Christianity had passed away from the church and was now embodied in the socialist or labour movement.

This, however, was not the view of other Christian Socialists. R. H. Tawney, in the final chapter of *The Acquisitive Society*, sees the church has having a vital role, supplying the moral and ethical basis for his functional society. The church

> will define [. . .] the lines of conduct and organization which approach most nearly to being the practical application of Christian ethics in the various

branches of economic life, and having defined them, will censure those of its members who depart from them without good reason. It will rebuke the open and notorious sin of the man who oppresses his fellows for the sake of gain as freely as that of the drunkard or adulterer. It will voice frankly the judgement of the Christian conscience on the acts of the State, even when to do so is an offence to nine-tenths of its fellow-citizens. Like Missionary Churches in Africa to-day, it will have as its aim, not merely to convert the individual, but to make a new kind, and a Christian kind of civilization.[106]

For Tawney, the church's involvement in and support for a new society is not just desirable, but necessary. William Temple argues that the church 'has a concern for the basic needs of citizens, and must point out conditions which flout Christian conscience'.[107] John Clifford suggests a similar role, writing that the 'churches can and ought to keep the minds of men alert to note every existing wrong in the framework of society'.[108] Clifford believed that the Holy Spirit would 'convince the churches of their sin in not undertaking with more definite purpose and sustained enthusiasm the greater and inclusive task of social salvation'.[109] Wilfred Wellock argues that 'instead of the churches "standing off" where politics are concerned [. . .] they must go right into politics, taking the Gospels with them', while Samuel Keeble sees a role for the church in 'declaring social duties, and pointing out social perils and evils'.[110] Here the Christian Socialists see the church living up to its creed and playing its part in bringing about socialism. For Stewart Headlam, 'the Christian Church [. . .] might be, and ought to be, *the* great agency for human progress in religion, politics, society, customs, and institutions'.[111]

Conclusion

In a similar way to the Bible, church teaching and practice formed for Christian Socialists a foundation underpinning their ideological commitment to socialism. The church fathers, the saints of early Christianity, the Protestant Reformers and theologians of all ages – the teachings and examples of all seemed to compel Christians to be socialists. The sacraments were also clear demonstrations of socialism, especially for Anglo-Catholics such as Headlam, signifying equality, cooperation, human dignity and the presence of Christ in the created, material world. The relationship of Christian Socialists to the church though was not always an easy one. Wheatley could point to the denunciations of free-market capitalism in *Rerum novarum*, but struggled with the Roman Catholic official line on socialism. Hardie, among others, saw the modern church as hopelessly hypocritical. Yet this was not because the teaching of the church was wrong; rather the church as an institution had failed in large part to live up to its own teaching.

3

Other influences

In the two previous chapters we have seen how the Christian Socialists, as we might expect, derived their political views from the teaching and tradition of Christianity. This includes the Bible itself – most notably the idea of the Fatherhood of God and the life and teaching of Christ, though there are examples of Christian Socialists making arguments for socialism from all sections of scripture – the teaching of the church – including reference to the church fathers, the teaching and example of prominent Christians from all ages and the sacraments administered by the church. In this chapter we will examine other key influences on Christian Socialism.

There are many sources of influence that appear in the writings of these Christian Socialists or have been identified in their thinking by others. For example, we have seen in the previous chapters that Samuel Keeble based his argument against interest or usury on the Bible, as well as on the early church and theologians both of the Church of Rome and of Protestantism; however, he also chooses to cite Aristotle as an authority in his argument.[1] R. H. Tawney quotes Matthew Arnold against inequality.[2] Wilfred Wellock follows the example of Gandhi (Wellock published *Gandhi as a Social Revolutionary* in 1950), as does George Lansbury in *My Quest for Peace* in 1938.[3] One writer points out that 'Henry Scott Holland and the young William Temple both drew on Bosanquet's idea that the individual only found full development in the state'.[4] Another sees that John Wheatley was influenced by the Roman Catholic economist Francesco Nitti, who 'argued that Christians should hold everything in common, and, if need be, this could be done through the moral agency of a collectivist state'.[5] Thomas Wodehouse's *A Grammar of Socialism* has been identified as an influence on Stewart Headlam; similarly, we may cite the influence of Robert Blatchford's *Britain for the British* and *Merrie England* on Ellen Wilkinson.[6]

It is not possible to include every single reference or quote used by these Christian Socialists to someone or something which has influenced them and their beliefs. In this chapter we will consider persons or ideas which are mentioned or alluded to frequently, and therefore constitute a key influence or contribute to a pattern of political thinking. These include Christian Socialists of previous generations (the likes of Frederick Maurice and John Ruskin, as well as T. H. Green), as well as other socialist thinkers and traditions (particularly Karl Marx and Henry George, and also including Fabianism, guild socialism and Chartism). We will conclude that Christian Socialists drew their beliefs and ideas from wide variety of sources, although the weight of evidence suggests that it is the Bible and the teaching and history of the church which dominate Christian Socialist thought.

Other Christian Socialists

Christian Socialists in this period were inspired and influenced by those previously identified as Christian Socialists and sometimes considered to be the founders of the movement, including F. D. Maurice and Charles Kingsley. A 1908 report by the Pan-Anglican Conference described 'the Guild of St Matthew, the Christian Social Union [and] the Church Socialist League' as the 'children of Kingsley and Maurice'.[7] One writer points to William Temple and his career within the church as being 'the logical conclusion of the Christian Socialist Movement begun by Maurice'.[8]

Stewart Headlam, in a lecture entitled *Maurice and Kingsley: Theologians and Socialists* credits those men with 'revealing the theological basis of Socialism, by showing how essentially Christian it was', adding that '[t]hey brought into the world of thought all the suggestion which is contained in that most pregnant phrase, "Christian Socialism"'.[9] Headlam's view of his own Guild of St Matthew in this lecture is that it has 'to some degree carried on the tradition' established by these early Christian Socialists, especially Maurice.[10] In *Priestcraft and Progress* Headlam speaks of his 'great obligations to Mr Maurice' and thinks of his own work as 'an earnest attempt to apply his principles and teaching to the needs of our time'.[11] One of Headlam's biographers points to the influence of Maurice on Headlam, explaining that 'Maurice's insistence on the Fatherhood of God and the Brotherhood of Humanity through the Eternal Sonship of Christ came as an immense liberating experience to Headlam'.[12]

In the same way the Christian Socialism of Samuel Keeble is said to have drawn 'its inspiration from the earlier work of F.D. Maurice and his stress on the Fatherhood of God and the ethical imperatives of Christ's teaching as the Incarnate God at work in humanity'.[13] In *Christian Responsibility for the Social Order* Keeble, as part of his detailed historical account of the spirit of

Christian Socialism, expresses his admiration for Maurice and his companions, writing that they 'rendered most valuable service on sanitation, sweating and co-operation, and still more valuable in their very able and informed application of Christian principles'.[14] Keeble's biographer points to Maurice as one architect of the 'Social Gospel' that Keeble espoused.[15] George Lansbury praises Charles Kingsley, among others, for 'a great effort to stir the conscience of the church', while James Keir Hardie lists him and Maurice as examples of establishment figures who came to believe in and campaign for socialism.[16] William Temple and Henry Scott Holland both demonstrate the influence of Maurice in their formulation of socialism as an ethical rather than purely materialistic creed.[17]

Jones, however, has argued that although Christian Socialists 'owed a debt to F.D. Maurice', this was 'perhaps not as heavy a debt as one might have supposed'.[18] References to Maurice and his colleagues do not appear regularly, or even at all, in most of the Christian Socialist writings being considered here. Although, as Jones points out, Maurice clearly had some influence, the scarcity of references to him and his work from the likes of Hardie, Lansbury, Tawney and Wheatley suggest that his influence is limited, particularly, for those Christian Socialists who operated primarily as politicians rather than churchmen.

Even Headlam, while perhaps unusual in his devotion to Maurice, differed from him and the early Christian Socialists in key respects. This 'second generation of Christian Socialists' was 'still imbued with Maurice's religious humanism' but wished to 'associate more immediately with progressive developments in secular politics'. This included Stewart Headlam.[19] Indeed, one of Headlam's biographers suggests that 'Maurice would have disapproved of Headlam's full-blooded radicalism'. As well as this, Maurice's belief was that the Kingdom of Heaven had already been established on Earth, while Headlam – and the majority of others in this study – held that it had yet to be established. Nevertheless, this biographer concludes that Maurice's 'ideas are the foundation upon which Headlam built his faith and politics'.[20]

Part of the reason for the limitation of Maurice's influence may be that he was not as fully committed to socialism as those of the later generation, as Jeremy Morris argues that 'he remained a sort of cautious Gladstonian Liberal at best', and Chris Bryant states that 'much of the first Christian Socialist writings seem to be no more than pious, paternalist but benevolent Toryism'.[21] If we accept that Maurice would have disapproved of Headlam's radicalism, we are left in no doubt as to how he would have viewed the Labour politics of Hardie or Lansbury. It should, however, be noted that John Ruskin has also been described as a 'Tory paternalist', yet he is still quoted and referenced by the Christian Socialists of this period.²² According to Bryant, 'Ruskin was by no means a conventional Christian Socialist', but he was to prove 'a significant link' between Maurice, Kingsley and Ludlow, 'and their successors in the Guild of St Matthew and the Christian Social Union'.²³ Ruskin, says another writer, 'was not a Christian Socialist, though in more recent terminology he might be called a fellow-traveller'.²⁴ Headlam's Guild of St Matthew is described as 'Ruskinite'.²⁵

The Radical Tradition, a collection of essays and articles by Tawney, includes a section on Ruskin in which Tawney praises his contribution and credits him with articulating the following idea:

> The purpose of industry is service [. . .] industry should be subordinated to the community in such a way as to offer the best service technically possible; that those who offer faithful service should be honourably paid, and that those who offer no service should not be paid at all, because industry is a social function, and it is the essence of a function that it should find the meaning in the satisfaction not of itself, but of the end which it serves.²⁶

Tawney quotes Ruskin arguing that men should only be paid for their service, and that landlords should only be paid insofar as they work, not merely because they possess land.²⁷ These are the same ideas and principles that Tawney would later expound in *The Acquisitive Society*. According to Wilkinson, Tawney drew 'upon John Ruskin's teaching that the function of the manufacturer is no more to work for profit than a priest's function is to earn his stipend'.²⁸ This is also evident in the work of Samuel Keeble, who quotes Ruskin in full: '[T]he merchant's function is to provide for the nation. It is no more his function to get a profit for himself out of the provision that it is the clergyman's function to get his stipend.'²⁹

Keeble quotes Ruskin often throughout the essays published as *The Ideal of the Material Life*, for example: 'True justice consists mainly in the granting to every human being due aid in the development of such faculties as it possesses for action and enjoyment.' 'The characteristic of man', writes Keeble, 'is that he is a moral being, and therefore moral considerations, in his world, must take the first place. No one puts this better than Ruskin, who says that things can never be right, until the question with us every morning is, not how to do the gainful thing, but how to do the just thing.' Keeble also expressed his admiration for Ruskin as a person:

> Few greater and nobler sacrifices of property for the good of society have been made than that of John Ruskin, who sacrificed the whole of the fortune bequeathed him by his father – £127,000 – in social experiments and services

for his country's good. In addition to this, he gave his country his brain – his brilliant brain – imagination, insight, prophetic, literary and artistic gifts.[30]

In *Christian Responsibility for the Social Order*, Keeble praises Ruskin, writing of his 'masterly Christian and economic criticisms of industrialism and commercialism', and numerous other references to Ruskin are found in Keeble's work – for example, in *Industrial Day-Dreams* and *Christianity and Socialism*.[31]

Keeble makes particular mention of *Unto This Last*, in which Ruskin argues against free-market economics and in favour of what today might be termed a planned economy and a welfare state.[32] George Lansbury, according to his son Edgar, was also greatly influenced by Ruskin, and especially by his book *Unto This Last*. Edgar writes,

> I can imagine only one condition upon which he [George Lansbury] would willingly attend say the Lord Mayor's Banquet; it would be that he might read to the assembled notabilities a page or two from Ruskin's *Unto This Last*. He quotes it often, in and out of the House of Commons, because he thinks it contains the key to the so-called problem of poverty.[33]

An example is found in Lansbury's *Your Part in Poverty* in which he urges the better off to consider the plight of the poor: 'As Ruskin has well said, the cruellest man living cannot sit at his feast unless blind to the misery and evil which accompanies his wealth.'[34]

It is worth noting Alan Wilkinson's view that 'Ruskin did not belong to the Christian Socialists and thought little of Maurice', but even if he was not part of Maurice's circle he appears to have espoused a form of Christian Socialism – he is included in the works of both Wilkinson and Bryant – and in any case he seems to have been at least as influential on the next generation of Christian Socialists as Maurice himself.[35] As an example, in 1893 all forty-four members of a branch of Henry Scott Holland's Christian Social Union had read *Unto This Last*.[36]

While Jones points out that the debt to Maurice is perhaps not as great as might be imagined, he points to the influence of the 'philosophical idealism' of T. H. Green.[37] Green, according to Wilkinson, 'produced a philosophical foundation for the New Liberalism and for Anglican socialism. [...] He believed that the state ought to promote the common good [and] taught that only in community could the individual find true significance and that the church and its gospel must advance social welfare and political justice.'[38] Green's 'Constructive Liberalism', according to one writer, was 'in essence the same' as the 'ethical socialism' advocated by R. H. Tawney.[39]

'The influence of T.H. Green was strongly felt' in the work of Tawney, 'with its Idealist analysis of the derivation of rights from functions and its consequences for a "politics of conscience"'.[40] Tawney followed Green in his 'belief in an immanent God, in the moral personality of individuals, a commitment to a notion of common good and a Functional Society, and an ethical rather than economic approach to social reform', as well as his belief that 'every individual should possess equality of moral value' while still accepting 'differences in material equality'.[41] 'Green argued that the essential part of being a moral person is that we should always be treated as an end and never as a means'; he 'went beyond' the idea of equality of opportunity 'and argued for a stronger form of equality'; he 'was critical of landlords who have been allowed to misuse their land and pursue ends that conflict with the social good'.[42] All these things are also true of Tawney. Tawney also shared Green's positive conception of liberty, as demonstrated in this passage:

> [I]f the rights are to be an effective guarantee of freedom, they must not be merely formal, like the right of all who can afford it to dine at the Ritz. They must be such that, whenever the occasion arises to exercise them, they can in fact be exercised. The rights to vote and to combine, if not wholly valueless, are obviously attenuated, when use of the former means eviction and of the latter the sack; the right to the free choice of occupation, if expenses of entering a profession are prohibitive; the right to justice, if not poor man can pay for it; the right to 'life, liberty, and the pursuit of happiness', if the environment is such that a considerable proportion of those born will die within twelve months, and that the happiness-investments of the remainder are a gambling stock.[43]

Edward Caird's writing on Green could equally be applied to Tawney: '[He held] an intensely democratic or Christian tone of feeling that could not tolerate the thought of privilege, and constantly desired for every class and individual a full share in the great heritage of society.'[44]

Green was 'the chief intellectual influence on Henry Scott Holland Holland', who 'belonged to Green's inner circle of students' at Oxford.[45] Holland wrote that he had 'taught us the reality of the co-operate life and the inspiration of the community. He gave us back the language of self-sacrifice, and taught us how we belonged to one another in the one life of organic humanity'.[46] Holland points, as an example, to 'T.H. Green's pamphlet on Liberty of Contract', which 'taught us how positive and constructive a policy is needed in order to ensure the conditions which would enable men to be free to make a contract. Competition was, then, to be no blind mechanical force. We were deliberately to provide adequate equipment for the competitors'.[47] Holland here also follows Green's positive conception of liberty. Holland and his CSU colleague Charles Gore are even described as 'Greenians'.[48] Green is also among those referenced by Keeble in *Christian Responsibility* and is recognized by Bryant as an influence on William Temple.[49]

While considering the contribution of Christian Socialists from a previous generation, we should not discount the influence that the Christian Socialists in this study had on each other. There are many examples in the writings of Samuel Keeble; for example, in *Christianity and Socialism* he regards John Clifford and Henry Scott Holland as influences on his political thought.[50] In *Christian Responsibility for the Social Order* he cites Stewart Headlam alongside Holland. Holland's CSU in particular was the impetus for Keeble's own Wesleyan Methodist Union for Social Service.

Keeble attended William Temple's Conference on Christian Politics, Economics and Citizenship (COPEC), writing a report in which he praised Temple and the conference, approvingly quoting Temple's description of 'a great movement within the Church for the Kingdom of God on earth'.[51] Keeble also quotes the work of Tawney a number of times; taking Tawney's idea of an 'acquisitive society', he writes that '[t]here is no moral and spiritual health in such a society. It is sick unto death.'[52] Keeble also refers to Tawney's work for the Sankey Commission in *The Ethics of Public Ownership*, concluding in like manner to Tawney that '[a] system by which 3,000 pits are owned and worked by 1,500 companies or individuals, with discontented workmen, is now finally condemned as wasteful and inefficient'.[53] Hardie prefigures the work of Tawney by declaring in 1907 that '[t]he landlord, *qua* landlord, performs no function in the economy of industry or of food production. He is a rent receiver and nothing more'; so does Wheatley in 1908, who imagines his 'Socialist' character being asked by the 'Magistrate': 'Are those shareholders unnecessary?', and replying 'Absolutely unnecessary, your honour; they are not managers, neither are they workmen'.[54]

The close working and personal relationship between Temple and Tawney is well known; Tawney was also involved in COPEC, while sections of Temple's *Christianity and the Social Order* were influenced by the work as well as by the criticism and suggestions of Tawney, especially the appendix which suggested a programme of action in keeping with the principles expounded in the rest of the book.[55] Tawney was also 'attracted by Henry Scott Holland's mixture of socialism and Christianity', and for this reason he joined the CSU.[56] Tawney's *Religion and the Rise of Capitalism* was the inaugural set of Henry Scott Holland Memorial lectures before it was published as a monograph.⁵⁷ We may also note that George Lansbury was a regular columnist in the CSU's *Commonwealth* magazine.⁵⁸

Lansbury and his colleagues on Poplar Council enjoyed a measure of support from John Wheatley as the minister responsible for local government, and Wheatley praised the council for its work of 'social emancipation'. It was, according to Wheatley, 'only as the policy of Poplar permeated the country that they would march towards a different order of society'.⁵⁹ Wilfred Wellock, too, points to the example of Poplar Council in raising awareness of an ongoing injustice.⁶⁰ Lansbury, in turn, praises Stewart Headlam, writing of his 'magnificent work' in raising awareness of poverty within the church.⁶¹ Wellock also calls for society to accept the teaching of and be re-made in the spirit of Keir Hardie.⁶² Hardie, as we have seen, was also praised by John Clifford, who wrote that he 'read human life through Christ's teaching – felt the compassion of Christ for those who were in any way wronged by others. [. . .] He was pained by the excessive care which the Churches showed for the "respectable", and what seemed to him their cruel indifference to the oppressed and the poor.'⁶³ Clifford was also a supporter of Margaret Bondfield's campaign against the living-in system for shop workers.⁶⁴

This is not to suggest that there was always harmony and agreement among this generation of Christian Socialists. We will note Headlam's opposition to the creation of a Labour Party and could also mention the personal dislike that existed between Headlam and Keir Hardie.⁶⁵ John Clifford, as a Baptist minister, attacked the Church of England, offending both Headlam and Scott Holland.⁶⁶ As cabinet ministers in the 1929–31, Margaret Bondfield supported the cautious economic policies of Chancellor Phillip Snowden while Lansbury was opposed – though Bondfield had been a critic of Snowden during the 1924 and subsequently following the formation of the National Government.⁶⁷ Even Temple and Tawney did not always agree: Tawney was critical of Temple's decision to leave the Labour Party upon being created Bishop of Manchester, but Temple felt a bishop should not be a member of a political party.⁶⁸ Temple criticized *The Acquisitive Society* for failing to consider the usefulness to society of the profit motive and the desire for individual betterment.⁶⁹

Tawney was also criticized by Lansbury, who opposed setting up a branch of Tawney's Workers' Educational Association in Poplar, fearing that it may distract workers from playing a part in the labour movement. Tawney had reportedly argued 'that the Labour Party ought to get and train its young men', to which Lansbury responded: 'I don't altogether agree: I'm very much afraid of taking them away from their work. They tend to become superior and "intellectual" [. . .] I think the only "intellectual" in our party has not been good for it.' In turn, 'Tawney was equally critical of Lansbury's anti-intellectualism'.[70] Lansbury, however, was not always so critical of Tawney. 'Having served on the Archbishop's Committee on the Church and the Labour movement [Lansbury] criticized the other members, except Tawney, for rejecting Socialism, and considered himself a voice in the wilderness on this committee, again except for Tawney.'[71]

There were also differences between Headlam and Holland, and their respective organizations. It has been suggested that the CSU was founded in order 'to create a group which could be "Christian Socialist" in a broad way without having to live with Stewart Headlam'.[72] 'The founders of the CSU were troubled by Headlam's revolutionary rhetoric and contempt for ecclesiastical authority. Headlam's heart was in the right place, they agreed; the same could not be said for his head.'[73] Despite all this though, it seems clear that the Christian Socialists of this period were just as influenced by each other as by their predecessors Maurice, Ruskin and Green.

Marxism

Christian Socialism was also influenced by other socialist traditions, including Marxism. Tawney, for example, refers to 'the genius of Marx' in foretelling the effects of inequality in society: 'They divide what might have been a community into contending classes, of which one is engaged in a struggle to share in advantages which it does not yet enjoy and to limit the exercise of economic authority, while the other is occupied in a nervous effort to defend its position against encroachments.'[74] Headlam similarly suggested that Marx had 'formulated the scientific basis which underlies the ethical teachings of the New Testament.'[75] Keeble was also influenced by Marx and 'is reputed to be the first Methodist to have read *Das Kapital*'.[76] Keeble takes a very even-handed approach, writing of *Das Kapital* that '[i]t is a wonderful book, full of genuine learning, passion, and love for the people', and yet 'much marred by materialistic philosophy, Hegelian jargon, and economic errors'. Again Keeble writes that '[i]n reading *Capital*, while annoyed by the Hegelian jargon and by the profanity which frequently mars it, as well as at Marx's false logic and crude theorizing, the reader cannot fail to be impressed by the new spirit which he introduces into political economy'.[77]

Keeble accepted the idea of surplus value as used by Marx and Engels: 'Beyond question, Marx shows that in modern industrialism capital gets more than its share. His main indictment of capitalism is true and awful. He makes an effective point when he shows that capitalist production rests on the appropriation of surplus value derived from the labour of the workers and benefitting from a surplus army of labour.'[78] Keeble, however, did not believe that the labour theory of value employed by Marx and Engels was accurate, and he praised the Fabian Society for their rejection of it.[79] Tawney also criticizes Marx's economics, writing that he 'took an unduly mechanical view of the operation of economic factors and greatly underestimated the importance of factors which are not economic'. Despite Marx's emphasis, 'economic forces act, not directly but through human minds and wills'.[80] Despite this though, Keeble argues that '[n]o weakness in Marx's theory of value can impair the truth and importance of his revelation – for revelation it was – of the innate tendencies of the capitalistic system of industry to exploit the labourer'.[81]

Keir Hardie perhaps makes the most overt references to Marx in his work, especially in *My Confession of Faith in the Labour Alliance* and *Karl Marx: The Man and His Message*. In the latter, Hardie refers to the *Communist Manifesto* as 'the birth certificate of the modern Socialist movement'.[82] In the former Hardie concludes: 'The policy of the I.L.P. is in line with that preached and practiced by Karl Marx [and] Friedrich Engels. [. . .] That policy is also mine, and I want the party to grasp it more fully.' He then closes with these words, derived from the *Communist Manifesto*: 'WORKERS OF THE WORLD UNITE; YOU HAVE ALL TO GAIN, AND NOTHING TO LOSE BUT YOUR CHAINS.'[83] A similar declaration is made in *From Serfdom to Socialism*: 'Workers of the world unite, wrote Karl Marx; you have a world to win, and nothing to lose but your chains.' Here Hardie demonstrates the influence of Marxist ideas, such as the theory of alienation: the result of factory working conditions, he wrote, 'is to produce demoralisation of the most fatal kind. There is no sense of unity between the man and his work. He can have no pride in it since there is nothing personal to him which will attack to it after it is finished.'[84] Hardie also demonstrates influence by the Marxist view of there being several stages of history:

> Socialism we believe to be the next step in the evolution of that form of State which will give the individual the fullest and freest room for expansion and development. State Socialism, with all its drawbacks, and these I frankly admit, will prepare the way for free Communism in which the rule, not merely the law of the State, but the rule of life will be – From each according to his ability, to each according to his needs.[85]

The same influence is shown elsewhere by Hardie, writing: 'Communism, the final goal of Socialism, is a form of Social Economy very close to the principles set forth in the Sermon on the Mount.'[86] Here Hardie, like Marx, explicitly names communism as the stage which will follow socialism. Unlike Marx, he equates it with the realization of the teaching of Jesus Christ.

This being the case, it is hard to sustain Bob Holman's view that Marx's influence on Hardie was minimal, although there may be some truth in Holman's assertion that 'Hardie read some Marx and selected bits which fitted with his own views of an ethical and peaceful socialism', such as 'Marx's later claim that in some countries socialism could be achieved by a peaceful process'.[87] Nevertheless James Maxton was able to recall that Keir Hardie 'was probably more Marxist in practice than those who paid greater deference to Marxist theories'.[88]

Maxton perhaps has in mind H. M. Hyndman's Social Democratic Federation (SDF), of which Keeble joked that they 'swear by Karl Marx, and almost believe in the verbal inspiration of his *Capital*'.[89] Hardie disagreed with the SDF refusal to support the Labour Party, writing that they 'are not only not representing the Marxist tradition; they are outraging every principle of Marxian Socialist tactics', as Hardie believed that the 'Labour party is the only expression of orthodox Marxian Socialism in Great Britain'.[90] This assertion is based on his understanding, expressed in *Marx: The Man and His Message*, that Marx's 'abiding thought was that freedom could only come by the gradual evolution of a properly-equipped working-class party, taught class consciousness by actual experience gained in the struggle with Capitalism', and that 'Marx only knew of one way; the organisation of a working-class movement, which would in process of time evolve the Socialist state'.[91] For Hardie this 'working-class movement' was the labour movement and the 'working-class party', the Labour Party; in refusing to support Labour the SDF was refusing to support a working-class party and thereby rejecting the teaching of Marx. Indeed, Hardie quotes Engels:

> The Social Democratic Federation here shares with your German-American Socialists the distinction of being the only parties to accomplish the bringing down of the Marxian theory of development to a rigid orthodoxy. According to them the working man is not to attain to this complete development ('class consciousness') through an evolution set in operation by his class feeling; but he has to swallow it down immediately as an article of faith and without development. Therefore, both remain only sects, and come, as Hegel says, from nothing, through nothing, to nothing.[92]

Hardie views these words of Engels as 'a biting criticism of the S.D.F. attitude in standing outside the Labour Party'.[93]

Keeble is also critical of Hyndman and the SDF for their unquestioning acceptance of the labour theory of value, while Tawney makes a similar criticism, writing in his diary that 'Marxian socialists are not revolutionary enough. They say that capitalist society is condemned because the worker does not get the equivalent of what he produces. He does not. But why should he? The real condemnation of the capitalist spirit is contained in the suggestion that men should get only what they produced.'[94] In 'The Choice before the Labour Party' Tawney writes: 'The British Labour movement was offered in its youth a foreign, and peculiarly arid, version of Marxian socialism. It very sensibly rejected it – very sensibly, not because the doctrine was Marxian, but because, in its pedantry and lack of historical realism, it was anything but Marxian.'[95] Therefore we can see, as Wright concludes, that Tawney was influenced by and praised Marx, but did not believe that those who labelled themselves Marxist were necessarily following Marx.[96] We see the same pattern in the work of Hardie and Keeble.

Ellen Wilkinson was committed to Marxist thought for much of her career, as demonstrated by the Marxist analysis of war *Why War? A Handbook for Those Who Will Take Part in the Second World War*, published in 1934 and co-authored with the Marxist scholar Edward Conze. Here Wilkinson and Conze argued that war was a symptom of capitalism. 'As experience shows, modern capitalism is constantly faced by the danger of 'over-production, which does not mean that more goods are produced than needed, but that more goods are produced that can be sold as a profit.'[97] This situation was endemic to capitalism: 'Marxists at least can find no comfort in opiate myths. Capitalist imperialism produces war as inevitably as an explosion of oxygen and hydrogen produces water.'[98] The only way in which war can be prevented is to 'abolish imperialism itself, and with it the capitalist system of which is the root of imperialism and hence of war.'[99]

Wilkinson was a co-founder of the British Communist Party, arguing that 'there is but one aim for us – the overthrow of world capitalism. To secure this there can only be one army, the International of the World Proletariat' and the communists must 'prepare workers for the social revolution and the dictatorship of the proletariat'.[100] Wilkinson resigned from the Communist Party in 1924, arguing that she disagreed with the party's attacks on the Labour Party and its authoritarian nature, though perhaps also because her association with the party preventing her from being selected as a Labour candidate.[101] Despite this though 'she joined communist-led organisations and agreed with much Communist Party propaganda', declaring in 1930: 'Yes, I am a Communist.'[102]

Often the Christian Socialists do not mention Marx or Engels by name, but still make points that seem to be derived from Marxist thought. George Lansbury – who had been a member of the SDF early in his political career, and according to a biographer, had studied Marxism and accepted some of its teachings – provides a number of examples.[103] For example, in a 1913 article on 'Socialists and Socialism' from the *Daily Herald*, Lansbury declares that 'everything of worth is produced by labour, and that those of us who obtain things without labour obtain them from those who do'.[104] In a 1912 *Labour Leader* article titled 'How I Became a Socialist', Lansbury makes the same point: 'The poor are robbed daily. Members of Parliament, Cabinet Ministers, and all the classes who are not engaged in manual labour, live on the backs of those who toil.'[105] The same ideas are drawn upon in Lansbury's condemnation of childhood poverty: 'These children are in these conditions because somebody is getting the result of the labour of their parents or of working-class parents generally.'[106]

John Wheatley also appears to have been influenced by these ideas, attacking those who made money from housing without contributing any labour:

> [I]f all those who, by hand or brain, give service to the production of the house, take 3s. 3d., that section of the community who lend, not their labour but their credit, their surplus wealth – usually, not their savings but their leavings – take twice as much out of the rent of the house as all the useful contributions to the erection of the house.[107]

The same thinking is indicated in some of the exchanges Wheatley describes in his imaginary trial of capitalism, first between the judge and 'The Duke of Hamilton', a landowner ('Pris.'), and secondly between the judge and 'Old Dick', a miner:

> *Pris.* I don't require to work.
>
> *Mag.* No successful robber does. Why don't you require to work?
>
> *Pris.* I'm a wealthy man, sir.
>
> *Mag.* How did you come to be wealthy seeing you don't work, and wealth is the product of labour?
>
> [...]
>
> *Mag.* Then I suppose you were not aware that the market price of the coal you have produced would be £15,000?
>
> *Dick* I was not aware of that, your honour.
>
> *Mag.* What wages have you received?
>
> *Dick* On average 25s a week.
>
> *Mag.* Great Heavens! That means you have been swindled out at nearly £12,500![108]

Headlam makes the same argument in his Fabian tract: '[T]he reason why so many have to work under such evil conditions for so long a time is because they have to produce not only sufficient for themselves and their families, but also sufficient for a large number of others who are themselves producing nothing, or nothing adequate, in return for what they consume.'[109] Perhaps for this reason Headlam's Guild of St Matthew pointed to 'the present contrast between the great body of the workers who produce much and consume little, and of those classes which produce little and consume much' as being 'contrary to the Christian doctrines of brotherhood and justice', and point (b) of the Guild's platform was 'to bring about a better distribution of the wealth created by labour'.[110]

Henry Scott Holland's view, similarly, was that 'the work of the master-capitalist consists more and more in sheer manipulation of the resources and opportunities supplied to him by the organised labour of others', and William Temple asserts: 'All wealth is a product of human labour expended upon God's gifts.'[111] Hardie, who we have already seen was an admirer of Marx, demonstrates his influence in *Can a Man Be a Christian on a Pound a Week?*: '[T]he total income of the nation is £1,750,000,000 a year, of which the usefully employed wage-earners receive less than £600,000,000 [. . .] he is paid one-third the value of his labour.'[112] Margaret Bondfield argues: 'Under capitalism the function of the distributive trade is to make profits for employers and shareholders. To make these profits large, labour and the shopping public are being exploited.'[113]

Bondfield grew frustrated at the refusal of female shop workers to organize into a trade union. This was due, despite their impoverished circumstances, to a view of themselves as middle-class workers – a view that Bondfield's biographer describes as 'an artificial distraction from the reality of their economic and social conditions. [. . .] To Bondfield the message was clear: to stop dreaming or indulging in a false consciousness about their situation, accept their true social and economic status, and claim a fair share of the profits to which they contributed so much.'[114] Here Bondfield sees the workers as blinded to their material reality and instead in the thrall of the false ideological superstructure. Bondfield however did not agree with the Marxist conception of class warfare, for this reason preferring to join the Independent Labour Party (ILP) rather than the SDF.[115]

Bondfield believed that the rise of socialism was inevitable, and there is also evidence that along with certain elements of Marxist economics some of the Christian Socialists accepted what is described, in reference to Lansbury's beliefs, as 'the stages theory of history [. . .]. Just as the "break up of feudalism" had constituted a revolutionary transformation, so the capitalist system that has replaced it would inevitably be swept away by a higher stage.'[116] We have already noted the influence of this idea on Hardie, and it is also evident in John Clifford's

Fabian tract *Socialism and the Churches*. Clifford reflects the sense of inevitability in writing that socialism is 'a movement, a tendency, a pushing forward of the inner soul of humanity towards its predestined goal'.[117] For Clifford, capitalism is the present stage of human history, while socialism is the next stage which will inevitably take its place. Clifford goes on:

> I do not say that this movement is the *final* form of human society. [. . .] But Socialism is the next, the necessary, the vital, the saving movement. Yet, just as the wage-earning period with its colossal capitalists; its giant plunderers, usurers, and sweaters; its princes of philanthropies; and its myriads of miseries and cruelties, was confessedly an advance in the conditions of slavery; so Socialism may only be a stage in the wonderful evolution of the manifold life of the children of God.[118]

Clifford here does not mention Marx by name, and therefore his ideas could be derived from another source: perhaps a purely Fabian idea of society's progress; possibly Clifford's reference to a 'predestined goal' indicates influence by the Calvinist idea of predestination; or a view of progress as the working of God in history.[119] However, the above-mentioned quote shows that Clifford saw stages of human history, each an improvement on the last: first slavery, then a 'wage-earning' capitalist period, then socialism and then perhaps a further stage of improvement which would be brought about by the socialist stage; this leaves open the possibility of the communist stage which Marx believed would follow the socialist stage which would constitute the final stage of human existence. This then indicates Clifford's influence by, if not slavish adherence to, the teaching of Marx, albeit with religious sentiments added.

The Christian Socialists also showed some support for the Russian Revolution. A few of them were members of the 'Hands Off Russia' campaign against British military intervention, including Wilfred Wellock, John Wheatley and George Lansbury. Lansbury was 'a passionate supporter of the early gains of the Russian Revolution'.[120] At an event to celebrate the revolution, Lansbury declared to the crowd: 'You are celebrating tonight a tremendous thing, the Russian Revolution. It is a fine thing to cheer these people, fine to feel you can sing about them, talk about them; a finer thing still is to emulate them and follow their example.'[121] Elsewhere Lansbury declared: 'You have been told that Russia is in the grip of a gang of despots. The fact is that Lenin and his supporters have no individual power other than that delegated to them by the Soviets.'[122]

Lansbury travelled to Russia in 1920, publishing his findings and his experience that same year as *What I Saw in Russia*, in which he is fulsome in his praise of the revolutionaries and the new society which they are building against the odds: 'In my judgement, no set of men or women responsible for a revolution of the magnitude of the Russian Revolution ever made fewer mistakes or carried their revolution through with less interference of the rights of individuals, or with less terrorism and destruction, than the men in control in Russia.' Lansbury was able to meet with Lenin, afterward describing him as a 'champion in the cause of economic and social freedom'.[123] This assessment may, of course, be challenged, but our purpose is simply to show Lansbury's influence by the revolution. Lenin explained to Lansbury that he was a convinced atheist, but Lansbury replied that 'to me your idea of life is the only Christian way of living'. Lansbury goes so far as to write that 'if it is true that we "worship God by doing good, that deeds not words are understood", then these Bolsheviks, feared and hated because they are feared, are the true Christians of today'.[124]

Ellen Wilkinson was also a keen supporter of the Revolution, praising post-revolutionary Russia for establishing sexual equality and arguing: 'In Russia they estimate the needs of the people and they set out to produce what the people need without considering the profit of private speculators.'[125] She worked closely with Zinoviev and lobbied for the UK government to allow Trotsky to settle in the country after his expulsion from Russia.[126] According to one biographer she was 'in denial about repression in the Soviet Union', though an earlier biographer has suggested that 'her enthusiasm for the Russian Revolution was later modified'.[127] Certainly, she withdrew from all communist organizations and ceased her unofficial support for the British Communist Party after the signing of the Nazi–Soviet pact.[128]

Others were more reserved in their praise for Soviet Russia. Wellock, who visited Russia in 1927, was later critical of the loss of workers' freedom and self-management under the rule of Stalin, writing: 'Whatever soul Russian communism ever had – and I had felt its impact in 1927 – Stalin's purges seemed to have obliterated. He inherited from Lenin a considerable spiritual legacy, and left behind a spiritual wilderness.'[129] Tawney's view in 1949 was that '[o]nly ignorance or prejudice would deny the technical and economic achievements of the Soviet Union; but dams, bridges, power-plants and steel-works, however admirable, are not a substitute for human rights; and the contrast between Russian Police Collectivism and the socialism of Western Europe is too obvious to need emphasis'.[130] Bondfield was initially sympathetic towards the Russian Revolution and visited Soviet Union in 1920. Even at this early stage though she noted the threat of authoritarianism and was uneasy about the move away from voluntary agricultural co-operation to state-managed centralization of farming. Shortly afterwards Bondfield was part of the team negotiating terms of co-operation between the Labour Party and the British Communist Party; she concluded from these talks that the authoritarian nature of the Communist Party rendered the two parties incompatible.[131]

Henry George

Another key influence was the work of Henry George, who in *Progress and Poverty* and other works proposed a tax on land values in order to abolish peacefully private ownership of land.[132] In *Thy Kingdom Come* George calls for 'taxation for the use of all that value which attaches itself to land, not as a result of individual labour upon it, but as a result of the increase in population, and the improvement of society. In that way everybody would be equally interested in the land of his native country'.[133] More than anyone else Stewart Headlam advocated the proposals of George; in the words of Jones 'it remained his main economic goal at all times'.[134] Headlam's thinking was 'dominated' by George's ideas; 'he remained all his life more of a Georgeite than a Socialist'.[135] These ideas were reflected in the published aims of Headlam's Guild of St Matthew, of which the first was 'to restore to the people the value which they give to the land'.[136] Headlam, in his Fabian tract, calls the redistribution of land values 'the main plank in the platform of the Christian Socialist, the chief political reform at which he aims'.[137] Headlam continues his argument:

> Why, you find land in the City of London worth more than £30 per superficial foot, land in Belgravia worth more than land in Bethnal Green; land in Bethnal Green worth more than land in Epping Forest. Now what is it that makes the land more and more valuable? Simply the people living or working in any neighborhood, or wanting to live and work there. Yet into whose pockets does the whole of this value go? Not into the pockets of the men and women who create it, but into the pockets of those who, often simply because they are the sons of their fathers, are the owners of the ground rents and values. Robbery is the only accurate word which a Christian Socialist can use to describe this state of things.[138]

Headlam goes on to argue that not just the land itself but the minerals produced beneath it, as well as the produce of the seas and rivers are claimed by 'robber landlords', 'so that, as Henry George has well said, every salmon which comes up from the sea might just as well have a label on it, "Lord or Lady So-and-So, with God Almighty's compliments"'.[139] These sentiments match those of George where he writes of his disgust that 'our laws say that this God's earth is not here for the use of all His children, but only for the privileged few'.[140]

George Lansbury was also a supporter of Henry George's scheme, writing that 'I see no means for dealing effectually with the land question as a whole except by making all those who would wish to use land pay, not to private individuals, but to the State, for the use of such land', and calling for 'taxation of land values'.[141] In Lansbury's view 'Henry George, when he had called attention to the land question thirty years ago, was on perfectly sound ground. We cannot hope for a reformed society if land remains private property and all the value which the pressure of population gives it goes into the pockets of private people.'[142]

Keir Hardie was a member of George's 'Land for the People' campaign.[143] Henry Scott Holland writes of

> the flaming portent of Henry George [. . .]. He paraded the irony of the rich growing ever richer by the very same law by which the poor became ever poorer. No one who had once read *Progress and Poverty* could remain the same man that he had been. It changed the atmosphere. It left a mark that could not be effaced.[144]

Further, while it is not evident that Tawney was a supporter of George's scheme, he does share George's aim of 'mak[ing] the holding of land unprofitable to the mere owner, and profitable only to the user'.[145] This same theme is evident in Tawney's *Acquisitive Society*; Tawney criticizes 'the practice of payment in virtue of property rights, without even the pretence of any service being rendered', arguing 'that industry should be subordinated to the community in such a way as to render the best service technically possible, that those who render that service faithfully should be honourably paid, and that those who render no service should not be paid at all'.[146] 'Tawney is looking for a society where the exercise of economic power is contingent on social obligation. In such a society, individual rights and property could not be seen as absolute, but conditional only on the ordering and use against a greater principle or social object.'[147] For both George and Tawney the possession of land was not an evil in of itself, only the wealth gained by land owners who did not work at the expense of those who did. William Temple takes a similar view, writing that a man who owns land must own it 'not as a possessor of so much material resources, but as a steward and trustee for the community. Land not beneficially used should involve liability to fine, or, in extreme cases, to forfeiture'.[148]

Jones, however, points out that not all Christian Socialists were as committed to George's ideas as Headlam, asserting that '[i]t was misleading that Headlam claimed to speak for *all* Christian Socialists, because the majority of them were not in fact satisfied with George's theory', citing 'the Christian Social Union, the Labour Church, and the Christian Socialist Society, none of which accepted the Single Tax'.[149] Indeed, one of Hardie's early biographers records that he came to believe 'that George's panacea, the Single Tax on land, was not enough. Hardie wanted a legal eight hours' day for the miners, and other industrial legislation which George regarded as unwarranted interference with individual liberty'.[150] Similarly, as early as 1895, George Lansbury writes in an election address that 'I should support the taxation of ground values up to 20s in the £', but adds, 'though that is not going to improve the condition of the workers so long as they are compelled to labour for wages for the benefit of the employing classes'.[151] In *Karl Marx: The Man and His Message*, Hardie credits Marx rather than George with advocating public use of land: '[A]bout the time Henry George was due to be born, Karl Marx was recommending that the rent of land should be taken by the State and used for public purposes'.[152] Yet despite the reservations of Hardie and Lansbury, and that, as Jones points out, Holland's Christian Social Union did not accept the Single Tax as an official policy, we can see the influence of Henry George on the Christian Socialists, especially on Stewart Headlam and the Guild of St Matthew.

The Fabians

The Fabian Society was also an influence on the Christian Socialists. Margaret Bondfield, John Clifford, Keir Hardie, Stewart Headlam, George Lansbury, R. H. Tawney, William Temple and Ellen Wilkinson were all members, while Clifford and Headlam both wrote Fabian tracts.[153]. Headlam was part of the committee that drew up the 'basis' of the Fabian Society in 1887, 'and, according to Sidney Webb he was responsible for some of the most extreme items'.[154]

Fabians held a belief in 'the inevitability of progress', which we see reflected in Clifford's 'feeling that tomorrow must grow out of to-day, just as whatever elements we have of order and of progress, of liberty and good legislation, have grown out of yesterday'.[155] While his references to stages of history owe more to Marx, the general idea of progress inevitably taking place equally demonstrates a Fabian pattern of thinking. Scott Holland also demonstrates this, writing of socialism having 'got hold of the real trend of things, under which we are all inevitably and rationally moving'.[156] Holland's CSU followed a Fabian pattern of working:

> We form Reading Circles. We gather round the study of this or that qualified and adequate book. We meet to talk it round, and through, and over. [...] At the end. We, perhaps, can manage to formulate certain conclusions, certain definite issues, which have resulted from the talks. Those can be reduced to print, and circulated. Our experiences are recorded; and we can go on to the next book.[157]

As Jones observes: 'In all this activity the CSU method was very Fabian.'[158]

In this the CSU was followed by Samuel Keeble's Wesleyan Methodist Union of Social Service: 'Its object was defined as "the collection and study of social facts, the pursuit of social service, and the discussion of social problems and theories from the Christian stand-point, with the view to educate the public opinion and secure improvement in the condition of life"'.[159] Keeble praised the Fabians, writing that Fabian socialism 'is a comparatively moderate and practicable thing [...] with its moderation, its spirit of compromise, its practical nature, its freedom from abstractions and logical pedantry, and, above all, its harmony with the methods of Democratic Constitutionalism'.[160]

It should be noted regarding Tawney's membership of the Fabian Society that he has been viewed as simply a passive member, who 'rejected their state-centric view of socialism', and therefore should not be associated too closely with the Fabians. 'Fabianism was about efficiency and mechanism; socialism, to Tawney, was about morality and individual generation.'[161] Tawney had written in his diary that

> the Fabians are inclined to go wrong. They seem to think that you can trick statesmen into a good course of action, without changing their principles, and that by taking sufficient thought society can add several cubits to its stature. It can't as long as it lives on the same spiritual diet. No amount of cleverness will get figs off thistles.[162]

Guild socialism

Guild socialism – the idea of introducing workers' control of industry via guilds for individual trades – also had an impact on the Christian Socialists.[163] According to one writer, guild socialism 'was a principle which had an obvious appeal to a Christian Socialist, in that it was a return to a new form of the original ideals of Ludlow and Maurice'.[164] 'It seemed most natural', writes another, 'for the CSL to support the principles of Guild Socialism, given that the guild idea was developed in the Middle Ages to accompany a Catholic interpretation of life.' A Church Socialist League (CSL) statement argued that guild socialism was 'the best method of giving effect to the essentially Christian principles of liberty, equality and fraternity'.[165]

Tawney was a member of the London CSL, a branch which was 'instrumental' in promoting guild socialist ideas in 1913.[166] 'Tawney, along with the Guild Socialists and thinkers like Harold Laski, did not – first and foremost – advocate extensive public ownership or welfarism, but the extension of democracy into areas of life that had hitherto escaped its influence.'[167] This meant that workers should have control of their own industry, rather than it being directed solely by owners of industry who did not necessarily perform a function or seek what was best for society. This was another key part of Tawney's *Acquisitive Society*. Tawney points to the creation of 'guilds' in the building trade which encouraged 'the discharge of professional duties'.[168] This step was necessary for all industry, 'because the conduct of industry for public advantage is impossible as long as the ultimate authority over its management is vested in those whose only interest in it is the pursuit of gain'.[169] For Tawney the control of industry by guilds would allow industry be conducted in a professional spirit of service to the nation, like the work of teaching or medicine, or the armed forces. Keeble also made an example of the building guilds, arguing that the practice 'seems to help the workers and the community and to hurt no-one'.[170] Hardie pointed to 'the Middle Ages' as 'a time when every private interest was held in subordination to the common weal' and industry was managed by 'the Guilds, the trade unions of the period, in which the craftsmen were banded together for mutual aid and support'.[171] Wellock also supported guild socialism, believing that it would ensure fair distribution of both labour and reward and endorsing it in *Christian Communism*.[172]

Lansbury was another supporter of guild socialism, and was the CSL president at the time it came to recommend the guild system.[173] '[T]he workers must', he wrote, 'if they are to get any kind of control over their lives, join together in great industrial unions or guilds, representative of particular industries, within which guilds a brain-worker and a hand-worker shall organise side by side and, in contract or partnership with the nation, carry on the work of supplying the nation's needs.'[174] Lansbury suggests as further reading on the topic A. R. Orage and S. G. Hobson's *National Guilds: An Inquiry into the Wage System and the Way Out* and G. D. H. Cole's *The World of Labour: A Discussion of the Present and Future of Trade Unionism*, as well as suggesting readers might write to the

National Guilds League. Had he been writing a decade later, Lansbury might well have urged his readers to turn to *The Acquisitive Society*. That being said, it is the view of one biographer that Tawney should best be understood as 'an unorthodox guild socialist'.[175] There were some ideological differences between Tawney and Cole:

> [I]n giving his own understanding of guild socialism as the 'conduct of industry by professional organisations for public service', it was clear why [Tawney] differed from some of its exponents. In particular, he could not share the 'sectionalism' of the functional democracy advocated by Cole, the leading guild theorist, with its erosion of the role of a supreme authority. [. . .] [U]nlike Cole, his emphasis is less upon the assertion of democratic rights and more upon the assumption of professional responsibilities.[176]

Yet, it seems clear that guild socialism was an influence on Tawney's thought – even if there are different emphases in Tawney's work and more orthodox guild socialism – as well as on the thought of Lansbury and Keeble.

Chartists and syndicalists

The Chartists seem also to have had some impact on Christian Socialism, especially the moral-force strand of Chartism which sought the moral and spiritual improvement of those to whom the Chartists wanted to extend democratic rights. John Clifford's family were Chartists in his youth and that formed part of the experience which influenced his political life thereafter.[177] Keeble's view of William Lovett and the moral-force Chartists was that 'they were but applying the Christian truths they had learned of from Wesleyan Methodism and the Christian Scriptures'.[178]

Tawney's *The Radical Tradition* includes a section on Lovett in which he describes Lovett's views as being that 'democracy is less an expedient than an ideal, the vision of liberty, fraternity, and equality. [. . .] It is the only guarantee against mis-government and the one remedy for economic oppression.'[179] Tawney shares with Lovett this view of democracy.[180] Tawney also quotes directly the words of Lovett: 'Whatever is gained in England by force, by force must be sustained; but whatever springs from knowledge and justice will sustain itself.'[181] He also asserts that the Chartist movement is so important because '[i]t was, as Marx pointed out, the entry in politics not merely of a new party, but of a new class'.[182] According to one biographer, Tawney's division between those who work

– manual workers and managers – and those who don't – owners or shareholders which perform no function – 'was the sociology of the Chartists in the 1830s'.[183]

We can also identify in the writings of Keir Hardie, though he does not mention the Chartists by name, the moral-force way of thinking. Hardie, for example, calls for socialists to pledge themselves to abstain from alcohol, arguing: 'The moral force of the Movement would be perceptibly increased if this were done, and it is moral force which carries a movement forward.'[184] More generally Hardie writes that 'with all respect to many a good comrade who I know differs from me strongly on this point, I reaffirm my conviction that only by moral power can the necessary zeal and self-sacrifice be developed to carry this work through'.[185]

We may also note the connection between George Lansbury and the syndicalists. Lansbury joined the Industrial Syndicalist Education League in 1912, 'though', according to one contemporary journalist, 'he does not believe in Syndicalism'.[186] 'I want the Syndicalist and the Socialist to march side by side', wrote Lansbury.[187] One writer describes Lansbury's view as being that there was 'truth in all these various expressions of socialist and anarchist faith, but none have all the truth'.[188] Tom Mann, the syndicalist activist, described Lansbury's visit to Liverpool to support the 1911 strike, and how Lansbury had been influenced by syndicalism, but had not fully accepted it:

> From that time his attitude was changed, and his faith in industrial solidarity grew; but George was, and, I suppose, still is a State-ist; he views the state as Society; he does not take the Syndicalist view that the organised State, with its government and officials and armed forced, was brought into existence by the opponents of the Workers, and functions only in the interests of the enemies of the workers.[189]

While therefore Lansbury was influenced by the syndicalists, he never fully accepted their ideas. The same is true of Hardie, who wrote that '[s]yndicalism is the direct outcome of the apathy and indifference of this house towards working class questions and I rejoice on the growth of syndicalism', but in practice rejected the syndicalist eschewal of parliamentarianism.[190]

Conclusion

Overall then we can trace in Christian Socialism the influence of moral-force Chartism, guild socialism and the Fabian Society, while the ideas of Karl Marx and Henry George seem to have had a major impact on the Christian Socialists. At times the references to these thinkers and organizations are explicit; at others we can perhaps trace the influence hidden from view. While Christian Socialists built their political beliefs on a range of sources – whether declaredly socialist or perhaps more in line with modern liberalism and other progressive movements – the weight of evidence nevertheless suggests that it is the Bible and the teaching and history of the church which dominate Christian Socialist thought.

Part Two

The route to Christian Socialism

4

A democratic-revolutionary synthesis

Having considered the basis of Christian Socialism we must consider the question of how Christian Socialists believed that socialism would be brought about. It is one thing to express a belief in socialism, to argue its Christian basis and its moral and practical superiority to capitalism, but another to answer the question of how a socialist society would actually come into existence. In this chapter the question of whether Christian Socialism was a democratic or revolutionary form of socialism will be examined, with the conclusion that Christian Socialists sought to revolutionize society by peaceful, democratic means, thereby presenting a synthesis of democratic and revolutionary socialisms. In the following chapter the methods by which Christian Socialists sought to carry out this democratic revolution will be sketched out as a three-stage process.

Contradictory language

It should first be noted that the Christian Socialists could express themselves using quite revolutionary language. George Lansbury, for example, wrote in 1929 that when he returned from Australia in the 1880s, he did so as 'a rebel, and I am still a rebel against the present man-made poverty and destitution'.[1] Lansbury had an uncompromising message for the oppressed of the capitalist system: 'You have a right to rebel when you are tricked and deceived, it is the only course open to you. [...] Burn and destroy property or anything you like.'[2] A newspaper account of a speech by Lansbury similarly reports him as saying that '[t]he best message they could send to the poor was the preaching of revolt in order that they might seek to change their present conditions'.[3] James Keir Hardie wrote of his belief in 'the conquest of political power as the method by which the workers would achieve their political emancipation'.[4] Hardie's view was that the workers must 'succeed in capturing and controlling the machinery of the State'.[5] At Christmas,

Hardie offered '[t]he season's greetings to all who are remembering that Christ came "not to send peace but a sword" against wrongdoing in all its forms'.[6]

Stewart Headlam enjoined the working class to 'strike down all evil customs and circumstances', and that 'in the light of the incarnation the social revolution, in the plain meaning of the words, is justified, nay, demanded'. One biographer notes that 'Headlam's revolutionary rhetoric' was troubling to the founders of the Christian Social Union, including Henry Scott Holland.[7] Another affirms that 'Headlam was a revolutionary', adding that '[f]or this reason he was almost as much a misfit in the circles of the Fabians, "the patron saints of reformism", as he was in those of conventional religion'.[8] Similarly, a biographer of John Wheatley notes the 'cutting and militant edge' to his speeches.[9] Wheatley despaired of achieving socialism through Parliament, as did Wilfred Wellock, who called it 'the grave of the people's conscience'.[10] John Clifford, in one place, appears to refute the efficacy of a parliamentary route to change, writing: 'If the progress of England depended to any considerable extent on parliament we might at once prepare for the utter collapse of our nation, and the Gibbon of to-day would find material for the story "Decline and Fall of Great Britain" more abundant in House of Commons than in any other part of England.'[11] Wellock and Samuel Keeble both called for a revolution.[12] R. H. Tawney did likewise, arguing during the First World War that 'it is not true that war cannot be carried on during an internal revolution. It would be truer to say that it is only by means of something like an internal revolution that a war of principles can be carried on.'[13]

Christian Socialists, as already noted, were generally welcoming and supportive of the Russian Revolution of 1917. Hardie, Lansbury, Wellock and Wheatley were among those who were part of the 'Hands off Russia' campaign against British counter-revolutionary action. Lansbury was particularly vocal, declaring at an event celebrating the revolution that '[i]t is a fine thing to cheer these people, fine to feel you can sing about them, talk about them; a finer thing still is to emulate them and follow their example'.[14] Ellen Wilkinson, a keen supporter of the Revolution, argued that revolution was necessary in order to accomplish socialism, mere reform of working conditions and industrial relations being insufficient to banish the exploitation and injustice of capitalism.[15]

In other places, however, the Christian Socialists gave the impression of favouring an evolutionary rather than revolutionary route to socialism. Keeble writes that 'force is anti-social and the programme of Socialism can be realised far more surely by evolution than by revolution'.[16] Elsewhere he makes the same point: 'Rash, violent revolution is no remedy. It retards growth.'[17] Indeed, in Keeble's view Christianity was able to prevent 'revolutionary violence'.[18] Wilfred Wellock, like other pacifists, condemned both 'international war' and 'class war'.[19] Nor is this simply a disagreement between individuals. In spite of his revolutionary comments Lansbury, in a speech opposing militarism, agrees with Wellock, referring to 'murder pure and simple, and as such to be condemned, whether committed in the name of war by Governments, or in that of Revolution by individuals'.[20] On this basis a biographer concludes that Lansbury was 'a pacifist socialist, not a revolutionary socialist'.[21] Keir Hardie, similarly, 'opposed the use of violence as a means to political ends'.[22] Here the pacifism of Christian Socialists overrules, with violent revolution and war between different classes held to be just as immoral as war between nations.

Hardie, like Keeble, saw evolutionary methods as the surest way of bringing about socialism, writing: 'The walls of the industrial system, with its great wealth and resources, will not fall at the blast of any trumpet. The reconstruction of society on a Socialist basis must proceed by the same methods of evolution which have called the existing order into being.' 'With the enfranchisement of the masses', he also wrote, 'it is recognised that the ballot is much more effective than the barricade.'[23] Hardie therefore matched his fierce rhetoric with a parliamentary, constitutional campaign for socialism.

Hardie was instrumental in the creation of the Labour Party, having first been at the forefront of the Scottish Labour Party and the Independent Labour Party. The whole point of the labour movement was to secure working-class representation in Parliament and thereby bring about at least some measure of socialism; Hardie writes in *My Confession of Faith in the Labour Alliance* of his belief that socialism could be brought about through Parliament.[24] Such was his view of electoral politics as the means to bring about socialism that after the defeat of 1895 he complained that there were '[s]ix years of Conservative rule to look forward to before another opportunity comes', adding: 'Fight every bye-election, fight the Municipal Elections as they come around, prepare for the grand struggle at the next election.'[25] For Hardie every election was a fight for socialism. He 'was never in favour of violence. [. . .] Hardie was a constant believer in democracy and in the expectation that eventually an elected Labour government would legislate for much public ownership.'[26]

The same view could be inferred from the career of Wilkinson, who served as a Labour MP, chair of the party and – after 1945 – Secretary of State for

Education. Bartley suggests that Wilkinson, despite having 'worked tirelessly to promote revolution', eventually 'relocated her reforming zeal to Parliament'. She still sought a socialist society, but according to Bartley came to believe in 'a parliamentary road to it rather than a revolutionary one'.[27] A report of a speech in 1934 stated: 'Miss Wilkinson said she wanted Socialism to come in this country as quickly as they could get it, but she believed in the traditions of this country and in Parliamentary Government.'[28] For this reason she was accused of abandoning a commitment to revolution in favour of mere reform.[29]

John Wheatley held a similar commitment to constitutional methods, arguing that 'granted political liberty and constitutional respect, I would regard a resort to violence as a terrible crime'.[30] Tawney was another committed to the democratic process.[31] He argued that socialists should give up any suggestion 'that violence is a card which socialists keep up their sleeves, to be played when they think fit', and that voting rights were 'the only guarantee against mis-government and the one remedy for economic oppression'.[32] Lansbury made a similar argument, voicing his support for female suffrage because 'to obtain possession of the land and to obtain possession of the railways and other means of life, we shall need political power'.[33] Lansbury declared that 'I have never accepted the theory of sudden revolution', and that 'whatever ultimate system is brought about, it will not be done by a sudden change or break'.[34] John Clifford concludes: 'Few now expect a sudden revolution; most work to hasten a natural and orderly evolution of the Socialistic State.'[35]

It could be added that Christian Socialist support for Russia was not absolute. In *What I Saw in Russia*, Lansbury writes of 'how impossible it is for me to discriminate between one form of killing and another'.[36] A large part of the reason he felt able to support the Russian Revolution was set out in the introduction to the book, where he writes of his belief – sincerely held, whether or not we would think it justified – that 'no set of men or women [. . .] ever made fewer mistakes or carried their revolution through with less interference of the rights of individuals, or with less terrorism and destruction, than the men in control in Russia'.[37] Samuel Keeble held a similar position of critical support, showing 'considerable sympathy for the Soviet economic experiment; nevertheless, he thought Stalin was a murderer, and he said so to pro-Soviet friends'.[38] Wellock also describes his disappointment with what he saw as the loss of workers' freedoms under Stalin.[39] Lansbury argued: 'To do as they did in Russia, wipe out a system with blood and fire, is simple; I do not say easy, but we, you, and I, want to transform, without killing anybody, private ownership into public ownership.'[40]

Synthesis

How can we reconcile the revolutionary and evolutionary thought evident in the Christian Socialist writings? A large part of the reason for the apparent contradiction is that Christian Socialists did seek to revolutionize society, but by peaceful means. Wilfred Wellock explains that 'widely different things are meant and conveyed by the word revolution. Communism does not supply the only revolutionary policy conceivable, nor is there any reason why Parliamentarianism should not be combined with a revolutionary spirit and method'; Wellock goes on to illustrate this point by arguing that the 'strength of the Communist Party lies in the fact that it stands for revolution; its weakness lies in the fact that it endorses violence'.[41]

Wellock 'believed in the possibility of a nonviolent, peaceful change of society, a revolution through reconciliation which could avoid the worst manifestations of class conflict'; he sought after 'a *process* of revolutionary change'. 'A "revolution by consent", a revolution by constitutional means, was what Wellock demanded and urged. It was a strange conjunction of the orthodox socialist's analysis of the workings of impersonal economic forces and the moral crusader's faith in the possibility that those vested interests whose existence he condemned might be persuaded to divest themselves of their privilege for their own and the wider community's sake.'[42]

Wellock was not the only one to hold views such as this. We saw Headlam described as 'a revolutionary', yet Headlam eschewed violence as the means by which to bring about the revolution. 'The kingdoms of this world were indeed destined to become the kingdoms of our God and of His Christ: the Church was to conquer the Roman Empire: the revolution was to be accomplished: but the *method* by which this was to be done was to be all important. These good results were not to be snatched at, but to be brought about by moral means, *gradually*.'[43] Headlam wrote of his belief in 'the Social Revolution – which, I take it, will not come suddenly, but like the Kingdom of Heaven, of which it is a part, "without observation"'. This revolution was to be achieved without violence or the shedding of blood. 'What! It is answered, a bloodless revolution – that is impossible! [. . .] but the blood of the Head and Representative of the whole human race was shed on Calvary, that was an all-sufficient blood-shedding, and by the power of that perfect sacrifice, if men choose, their Social redemption may be accomplished.'[44]

A report of a speech by George Lansbury records his view 'that Socialism was simply an organised state of Society, growing out of the present state and gradually coming into being by the consent and assistance of the people'.[45] This was also the view he expressed in conversation with Lenin, arguing 'that we had all the machinery of administration; that we had our great trade union and co-operative movement and friendly societies; that all these organisations, national, municipal and voluntary are training men and women for the work of administration, and that it would be quite easy for us to take over whenever the workers really desire to do so'.[46] 'During the best part of my life I was a revolutionary', declared Lansbury, 'I am still, since I want to help transform society into a co-operative commonwealth. But I always thought violence was wrong – and futile. You cannot coerce people into the Kingdom of Heaven.'[47] Instead, '[t]he revolution we advocate is a revolution of thought expressed in legislation', 'a great revolution in men's thoughts and action'.[48] It is for this reason that an interviewer of Lansbury writes: 'It would be perfectly safe to describe Mr Lansbury as a revolutionist if it were clearly understood that a revolution does not mean a revolt.'[49] It also explains how we are to understand Lansbury's support for the Russian Revolution. Lansbury did want to see the workers 'emulate' the revolutionaries of Russia 'and follow their example', but peacefully.

Keir Hardie, it is argued, also 'believed that workers could achieve a social revolution by democracy'.[50] This view explains how Hardie could hold a belief in parliamentarianism and also 'the conquest of political power', urging workers to aim at 'capturing and controlling the machinery of the State'. Similarly, the *Methodist Times* records that 'Mr. Keeble would appear to approve a socialism whose spirit is Christian and whose method is revolutionary, but not a materialistic socialism based on revolutionary violence', adding that 'if this is so, Keeble certainly does not stand alone'.[51] Keeble himself wrote that '[i]t is true that Christians are not red revolutionaries, but they are revolutionaries. They seek to revolutionize, by peaceful, and if possible, evolutionary, means'.[52] It is for this reason that Tawney could write in 1952 of the growth of the labour movement as representing a 'revolt of ordinary men against capitalism', and yet on the next page describe Labour's method as 'democracy [...] the sole political method discovered by man of effecting bloodless change'.[53] John Clifford similarly wrote of '[t]he quietly operative energy of the popular vote' being 'at its revolutionary work', while John Wheatley believed that a 'Labour government' could 'accomplish peacefully one of the most beneficent revolutions in the world's history'.[54]

This view was explained further by Margaret Bondfield in a 1922 election speech: 'I am opposed to all forms of violence, whether organised by the proletariat or the capitalist government. I believe in a policy of peaceful revolution by mental processes – a revolution of the mind and heart.'55 This was a view reiterated during the Second World War:

> The process of revolutionary change does not require bloody upheavals so much as a greater effort of mind and will to reap an over-ripe harvest. We shall conquer the evils of the capitalist system most quickly by demonstrating our capacity to distinguish the nature of those evils, and by building in constitutional ways the public ownership and control of essential services.[56]

In another wartime pamphlet Wellock sets out a typology of revolutions in order to explain more carefully his view of a 'spiritual revolution, a social transformation arising from a deep realisation of the emptiness and falsity of capitalist values, and of the desirability of bending individual and national effort to the creation of a good society'.[57] There are, according to Wellock, three courses: 'Revolution; Counter-revolution; and Revolution by consent.' A revolution is a struggle for power by the left accompanied by political violence, followed by a period of 'terror' in order to preserve the revolution; a counter-revolution is the gradual gaining of power by the right, resulting in a totalitarian system.[58] Wellock presumably had the Soviet Union and Nazi Germany in mind as the key examples of these phenomena. By contrast,

> A revolution by consent would be democratic in the completest sense, and therefore peaceful. Those elected to carry it through would naturally appeal to the public for support at every stage in their advance. As their aim would be the common good, they would take the public into their confidence, and so win it, and make it a co-partner in the task of constructing a new social edifice and a good society.[59]

Christian Socialists did therefore believe in revolution, but a revolution brought about by peaceful, democratic, parliamentary and constitutional means. This then represents a synthesis of democratic and revolutionary socialist methods.

Conclusion

There is, on first reading, a real lack of clarity in the Christian Socialist approach to bringing about changes to the political and economic system; class for revolution appears alongside a clear commitment to parliamentarism. Figures such as Keir Hardie and Lansbury who called for revolution against the existing order would at the same time assume leadership of the Labour Party in a sincere effort to establish socialism via the existing democratic structures. Some resolution can be found in that Christian Socialists explicitly argued that the revolution for which they advocated was a non-violent, peaceful and spiritual revolution. This was to be a revolution of the system – capitalism was to be abolished and replaced with socialism – as it was to be a revolution in the hearts and minds of people everywhere. But it was nevertheless to be accomplished without taking up arms, shedding blood or violently seizing power.

5

The revolution in practice

Given that Christian Socialists aimed at a revolution, but one which would be undertaken without force of arms or any violence at all, how could such a revolution be carried out? Sometimes this was not clear, and we shall examine some of the contradictions and confusion in the thinking of Christian Socialists on this matter in Chapter 6. It, however, may be possible to discern a process that Christian Socialists expressed as the means by which socialism would be brought about, leaving our consideration of some of the flaws to one side for the time being. The process might be sketched out as follows: first, persuasion of the deficiencies of capitalism and the need for a socialist alternative followed by, secondly, the election of Labour to a position of power, or the 'conversion' of those already in power to socialist principles. In either case convinced socialists would now be in power, and the third stage would be the reorganization of society by a socialist state, aided by a willing and supportive population.

Persuasion

The first step then in the Christian Socialist method of transforming society was the persuasion of the population to reject capitalism and embrace socialism. 'If a Socialist government means business', wrote R. H. Tawney, 'then it must take the initiative, force the pace, and – I won't say compel – but persuade men to be free.'[1] This process, however, had to begin well before a socialist party took office; indeed, it was necessary for that to happen, as Tawney explained: 'Labour will not, however, win power in the first instance, or be in a position to use it, when won, with the vigour required, unless it has behind it, not merely a majority of voters, but a temper in the country which will see the job through'; for this reason, said Tawney, socialism must 'argue and persuade'.[2]

This was also the view of James Keir Hardie, who wrote that 'Socialism cannot be imposed on an unwilling or unready people. The organisation of the masses, their training in politics, and their being made to feel a sense of responsibility for working out their own industrial, political and economic salvation, are all a necessary part in the evolution of the Socialist State.'[3] Margaret Bondfield described a 'political approach to Socialism' which 'has as its subject the conversion of the people to the view that land and industry should be publicly owned, and the utilisation of Parliament and of the local authorities to secure the necessary transfer from private to public hands'.[4]

We observed in earlier chapters that the Christian Socialists derived their socialism in large part from the reading of scripture and from the teaching and practices of their churches. The corollary to this is that Christian Socialists saw the church and its proclamation of Christian teaching as one of the ways in which society could be persuaded to reject capitalism and seek the alternative. In his diary, Tawney argues for the application of 'certain principles of social and economic conduct', adding that '[t]his knowledge is, I would urge, the common property of the Christian nations'.[5] For Tawney then society should be governed by Christian principles, and in the final chapter of *The Acquisitive Society* he argues that the responsibility for upholding these principles belongs to the church: 'Such a political philosophy implies that society is not an economic mechanism, but a community of wills which are often discordant, but which are capable of being inspired by devotion to common ends. It is, therefore, a religious one, and, if it is true, the proper bodies to propagate it are the Christian Churches.'[6] Tawney sees the church insisting on its members following these Christian principles, persuading society as a whole to follow them, and critiquing the actions of the state based on them: 'Like Missionary Churches in Africa today, it will have as its aim, not merely to convert the individual, but to make a new kind, and a Christian kind of civilization.'[7]

Samuel Keeble makes the same argument as Tawney, viewing it as the role of the church to 'cultivate a "divine discontent"', and outlining a 'Social Method' which 'consists first of a fearless, frank and constant criticism by Christians' of the faults in the capitalist system.[8] 'We dwell', wrote Keeble, 'in the midst of a civilization which is largely the creation of Christianity itself, and have, therefore, a potent, if not an authoritative voice in matters ethical, social, and even political.' 'In conversation, in public speech, in the home, from the desk, in day and Sunday schools, in the pulpit and in the Press, Christians should seek to create a strong public opinion against all unfair competition.'[9] Keeble concludes that 'the function of the Christian Church' is to aid Christians in working for the creation of a new society.[10]

William Temple reasons in the same way, arguing that '[t]he state must have some principles in which to guide its promotion of the good life for its citizens'.[11]

Temple's view is that 'there can be no Christian society unless there is a large body of convinced and devoted Christian people to establish it and keep it true to its own principles'.[12] This view echoes John Clifford's, who wrote that 'the churches can and ought to keep the minds of men alert to note every existing wrong in the framework of society'.[13] George Lansbury sought the 'preaching' of 'discontent', and he foresaw that very role for the church in post-revolutionary Russia, describing his belief – not, in the end, realized – that the Russian church would 'with whole-hearted purpose join Lenin and his comrades in recreating the moral and material life of the great nation'.[14]

Stewart Headlam often stated that the church should be the means by which socialism was brought about, his view that 'the Christian Church, and especially the Christian priesthood, might be, and ought to be, *the* great agency for human progress in religion, politics, society, customs, and institutions'.[15] The church could also help to 'make the State minister to the well-being of the people instead of maintaining the monopolies of the few'.[16] For Headlam 'the one main function of the Christian Church is to carry out the principles of Socialism, that the Church is intended to be a great instrument for Social Reform', and lest anyone should disagree '[i]t is for us to show that the reforms, the changes, which are needful for the well-being of the people, are fully sanctioned by Christian teaching'.[17] Wilfred Wellock agrees with Headlam on this latter point, arguing that social and economic change would only be a reality when people were aware that the spiritual arguments were in favour of it, with the church responsible for creating that awareness.[18] In this conception then, as socialism is morally superior to capitalism – an understanding based on morals derived from the Bible and the teaching of the church – it is therefore the church's role to make the moral case for socialism and uphold the Christian principles which will bring about the spiritual revolution and guide post-revolutionary life.

Part of Tawney's argument was that the social teaching of the church, while applying to society as a whole, should be enforced by the church on its own members. He goes so far as to say that the church 'will expect its adherents to face economic ruin for the sake of their principles'.[19] Keeble also sees this role for the church, writing that '[i]t is high time, then, that Christian teachers proclaimed that Christian business men, at least, are expected to respect the dignity of human nature in the humblest of their servants'.[20] For this reason Keeble desired to see Christian social principles preached from the pulpit.[21] While Tawney envisaged the church policing the actions of its members, he also believed that practising Christians were the most likely to be persuaded to practice socialism voluntarily; 'he sets', therefore, 'about the task of turning Christians into socialists'.[22]

Keeble also argued that 'Christian people must be enamoured of the vision of the true social order'.[23] He held 'that it is the business of the Christian Church fearlessly to teach such men their duty, and if they will not yield to the pleadings of love, to refuse to company with them as Christians. This would leave many churches crippled indeed, but also free from participation in disregard for human relationships, and in the oppression of the helpless'.[24] Headlam felt that Christians could be turned to socialism because of the unity of rich and poor within the body of the church: '[W]hen the people come to be united with [the rich] in common Churchmanship, they will be able to convince many of them that the necessary reforms, though they will make them poorer, will make them also happier, and will educate them so as to make them finer men and women'.[25] This was the aim of Henry Scott Holland's Christian Social Union, which was 'primarily an Anglican church society, concerned with propaganda among church folk'.[26] In this view then a large part of the church's role was to persuade and to some extent coerce its own members first and foremost.

The church's influence, however, was not to be limited to those who were already members. Lansbury, for instance, 'had come to believe that the individual capitalists could never be coerced into socialism by trade unions or a political party, but that they might be reformed by the power of Christ-like example'.[27] Similarly, Wellock 'placed his faith in the possibility of so arousing the public conscience that the capitalists would be compelled to see the error of their ways, realise the ruin they were causing and, thereby seek their salvation by satisfying the people's legitimate demands'.[28]

Holland felt that the Church of England as the established national church had a particular role, being 'a Church specially charged with national responsibilities'.[29] Headlam would probably have agreed insofar as the Church of England was a national church, but he felt that disestablishment would aid the church in fulfilling its role. 'A complete Christian Socialism', he wrote in a Fabian tract, 'cannot be brought about until the Church is free to use influence and discipline for the establishment of the Kingdom of Heaven upon earth'.[30] Headlam wanted as many people as possible to be active within the Church of England, but with the aim that 'as conscious Churchmen they will want to help set the Church free to manage her own affairs, to elect her own clergy, to be a real power to help bring about those secular reforms which are necessary'.[31] The Baptist John Clifford also felt that the Church of England should be disestablished, arguing that establishment 'tends to make the Church self-seeking instead of self-sacrificing, unprogressive and reactionary instead of leading the highest and best movements of mankind'.[32] The church, therefore, should 'be free in all its internal activities from the control of Princes and Parliaments, and from the interference of civic and political organisations of every kind'.[33]

It should be pointed out, however, that Christian Socialists did not necessarily see a role for the church in providing specific policies. William Temple includes a section of practical suggestions in *Christianity and the Social Order*, but these remain only suggestions as to how the principles the church proclaims could be carried out. Temple elsewhere explains the reason for this: '[I]t is the principle, and only the principle, which the Church as such has any right to proclaim. The rest is merely illustrative matter.'[34] The church, according to Temple, 'must point out conditions which flout Christian conscience. It cannot advocate specific remedies *qua* church, but it can stimulate those who respect its authority to find and apply for a remedy.'[35] This was also the position of Holland's CSU, which 'never declared itself for any given platform [. . .] practical reform suggestions were left to the individual consciences of members'.[36]

The prohibition that Temple places on the church as a whole is echoed by Keeble, who applied it to individual Christians. 'Nor should any Christian interfere in labour questions, either by word or deed, who has not had some practical industrial and business experience and read some political economy.'[37] Nevertheless, the church's role remained to proclaim those Christian principles in order that society as a whole, and especially the church's own members, would be persuaded of the need to replace capitalism with socialism, and be equipped to actually do it. Keeble concludes: 'A new public conscience needs forming, and this, as it is the business of, so only can it be accomplished by, the labours of the whole Christian Church, through her teachers, preachers and writers.'[38] To this end Keeble encourages 'discussion and conference [. . .] the publication of Christian social literature of every kind', and encourages Christians to pray, 'seeking divine light, and in intercession for society'.[39] Lansbury also encourages this, writing that 'our Labour movement wants men and women who will go down on their knees and pray for the success of the Labour movement'.[40] 'Still more Christians know', wrote Keeble, 'that "the grace of God" can and does change human nature.'[41]

The church however was not the exclusive means by which Christian Socialists sought to persuade society of the need to replace capitalism with socialism. Keir Hardie described how his 'work has consisted of trying to stir up divine discontent with wrong'.[42] Yet we have seen that Hardie was could be highly cynical about the church, writing that 'the rich and comfortable classes have annexed Jesus and perverted His Gospel', and adding that the 'modern Christian Church is a reflection of the modern business world'.⁴³ Hardie concludes that 'Christianity is no longer a reality. The religious form may still exist, but once again the spirit has passed away and found embodiment elsewhere.'⁴⁴ From this we may surmise that Hardie felt that the true spirit of Christianity was to be found in the labour movement, which would be why he suggested that Labour and various socialist movements were to offer 'constructive criticism, pointing out defects of capitalist legislation, and its inadequacy as a means of getting to the root of the social problem, and putting forward their own proposals'.⁴⁵ This, minus perhaps the putting forward of proposals, is the role that the other Christian Socialists seemed to envisage for the church.

George Lansbury also went through a period of disaffection from the church and during that time like Hardie saw the socialist movement as carrying out the role that Christian Socialists generally saw for the church. To that end he sought to model the SDF, of which he was then a member, on the church. He suggested that a branch of the SDF 'should never meet less than once a week', with that weekly meeting being 'the high festival of the week, never to be missed, and should be to us what Sunday is to the devout Christian'. He also called for a socialist Sunday school, which would include socialist songs and readings, and talks about the life and work of 'the prophets of Socialism'. Lansbury drew inspiration from the evangelism of the Nonconformist churches: '[T]he Dissenters go in for what is called tract distribution, and also the lending of small pamphlets [. . .] why should we not follow in their footsteps?' He suggested door-to-door socialist evangelism and open-air socialist preaching.⁴⁶ It is not surprising that he was later to describe how 'although for some period of my life I left the Church and Christianity on one side, I think it is only true to say this too, that all the time, at the back of my mind, I had the sort of feeling that you must have religious fervour and religious enthusiasm if you want to do anything'.⁴⁷

As noted, Samuel Keeble argued from the parable of the Good Samaritan that those who sought to help and support the working class were doing the work of God even if they were outside the church.⁴⁸ Margaret Bondfield declined to attend the King's Weigh House chapel of which she had been a member, having been rebuked by one of the deacons for missing a Sunday service in order to attend a trade union meeting. Bondfield 'chose the union without any hesitation, especially as she felt that her work was perfectly compatible with her Christianity, and indeed felt it was an extension of it'.⁴⁹ She returned to the chapel some twenty years later after a new minister, himself a Christian Socialist, had been appointed.⁵⁰ Ellen Wilkinson similarly went through a period of disaffection' from Methodism, focusing instead on political organizations and activities, though she was later to tell a meeting of the Left Book Club in 1939: 'I am still a Methodist – you can never get its special glow out of your blood.'[51]

Armstrong and Gray claim to see a similar way of thinking in the writing of Tawney. They argue that Tawney's work displays 'the gradual displacement of Christianity and the Church by socialism and the Labour Party, as the main architects of the Good Society'.[52] Tawney, according to Armstrong and Gray, believed that 'political doctrines' are capable of both setting out the ends to which society should aspire and the means of reaching them, and this 'reaffirms his abandonment of Christian exclusivity'.[53] Wright, however, argues that the secular arguments in Tawney's work do not reflect his own beliefs, but rather his desire to extend an argument for socialism beyond the adherents of the church. Tawney, according to Wright, was simply avoiding the necessity of arguing

> for the validity of Christian principles and their supernatural derivation [. . .] his aim is to persuade unbelievers of all kinds that the social problem is essentially a moral problem and that its solution is to be found in the realm of 'principles'. In undertaking this exercise in persuasion though, it was necessary to begin 'from the existing order' rather than from *a priori* positions.[54]

Again, Wright argues that 'he may have held privately that it was necessary to believe in God in order to believe in socialism, but this did not prevent him from constructing a public case for socialism in which God was conspicuous by his absence (except as an appendix for believers)'.[55] If Armstrong and Gray are correct that Tawney had begun to abandon the Christian basis of his socialism and his belief that the church would hold together a new society in 1918, it is hard to explain away that appendix – the final chapter of *The Acquisitive Society* – first published in 1920.[56] Beech and Hickson conclude that 'for Tawney democratic socialism is only possible because it flows from his Christian faith'.[57]

Tawney nevertheless sought to argue for socialism in a way that would also be persuasive to non-Christians, as did the other Christian Socialists. For this reason Stewart Headlam and John Clifford were both active members of the Fabian Society, with Jones describing Clifford as 'an energetic Fabian'.[58] Similarly, Holland's Christian Social Union 'was organized principally to study and to publicize social and economic problems'.[59] The aim of all this research and dissemination, whether carried out by Clifford and Headlam through the Fabian Society, Holland's CSU, Keeble's Wesleyan Methodist Union for Social Service, or any similar organization, was to persuade the population to see the problems with the existing system and seek to replace it. 'Our purpose is nothing if not practical', wrote Holland. 'All our study must issue in action [...] we cannot be so tangled and arrested in the intricacies of the study that we fail to carry it forward to the conclusion for which it exists.'[60]

Samuel Keeble, like Tawney, sought to persuade people that socialism was possible without reference to Christian theology. For example, in *The Ethics of Public Ownership* Keeble argues against those who would regard state control of industry as impractical. During the Great War, Keeble writes, 'we witnessed the Government organising practically the whole nation, not for a few months, but for five years; controlling and carrying on its financial, economic, industrial and commercial life'.[61] Keeble goes on to debate with those who would challenge the legality of public ownership, citing an act of Parliament which reserves the legal right for the government to purchase the railways; he then adds that, besides this, the only ultimate ownership of land in law is in the Crown, which in practice means Parliament.[62]

Tawney, Keeble and the other Christian Socialists made regular use of such arguments that would be accessible to both Christians and non-Christians. Headlam, for example, makes the case that 'the reason why so many have to work under such evil conditions for so long a time is because they have to produce not only sufficient for themselves and their families, but also sufficient for a large number of others who are themselves producing nothing, or nothing adequate, in return for what they consume'.[63] John Clifford describes collectivism: 'Here is the great business of industrial life; let us manage it so that all may share in the responsibility and share in the gains, and share fairly and justly as nearly as possible; not one doing all the work and another taking all the gains.'[64] Both Headlam's and Clifford's comments were made in Fabian tracts about religious socialism, yet even there many of the points are made without appeal to the scriptures or the teaching of the church. There were, therefore, several ways in which the Christian Socialists sought to bring society to the point where it accepted the need to replace capitalism with socialism.

Government

The second stage in our process is that, once thoroughly persuaded, the electorate would send the Labour Party into government, which would then be able to legislate for a socialist society; alternatively, the ranks of the convinced will include those in positions of power and authority, as well as those within the Liberal and

Conservative parties, and these would then bring about the necessary reforms to society. There was some division between Christian Socialists on this matter. Many were active Labour members, not least Margaret Bondfield, Keir Hardie, George Lansbury, R. H. Tawney, John Wheatley and Ellen Wilkinson, and it is therefore evident that these persons and others involved with the party believed that Labour would be the force to bring about a socialist society. 'For Parliament to do anything at all for the workers', declared Wilkinson, 'there must be a real majority of Labour – and that sustained over a good number of elections.'[65]

Hardie, according to one writer, wanted 'labour to capture the institutions of the State in order to emancipate itself from industrial serfdom'.[66] Hardie specifically wrote of the need for the Independent Labour Party to being about socialism, and argued that '[i]f Labour is to rule Labour members must be sent to the House of Commons'.[67] Hardie was clear that it was 'with the organisation of the enfranchised working class into a definite organisation of their own, industrial and political', which would initiate 'the final struggle for the freedom of the race'.[68] George Lansbury also wrote of the need for such an organization, as implied in his remark that 'our Labour movement wants men and women who will go down on their knees and pray for the success of the Labour movement'.[69] William Temple, at least earlier in his career, 'attacked competition and urged full Christian support for Labour'.[70]

Tawney's belief in Labour as the means of bringing about socialism is seen particularly clearly in his essay 'The Choice Before the Labour Party', in which he argues that Labour should be a properly socialist party, and 'an instrument for the establishment of a socialist commonwealth'.[71] 'The fundamental question', according to Tawney,

> as always, is: Who is to be master? Is the reality behind the decorous drapery of political democracy to continue to be the economic power wielded by a few thousand – or, if that be preferred, a few hundred thousand – bankers, industrialists and landowners? Or shall a serious effort be made [. . .] to create organs through which the nation can control, in cooperation with other nations, its own economic destinies; plan its business as it deems most conducive to the general well-being; override, for the sake of economic efficiency, the obstruction of vested interests; and distribute the product of its labours in accordance with some generally recognised principles of justice?[72]

Pointedly Tawney then adds: 'Capitalist parties presumably accept the first alternative. A socialist party chooses the second.'[73]

Wilfred Wellock makes a similar argument to Tawney about the need for Labour to be a genuinely socialist party. According to Wellock,

> The supreme danger of a Labour Government will be its fear of adopting and carrying through a revolutionary programme; and yet apart from such a programme it would have no *raison d'etre*. Were it to pursue a merely reformist policy it would court disaster, for it would thereby virtually accept the capitalist system, play into the hands of the capitalists and enable them to prove the 'failure of socialism'.[74]

Wilkinson argued that Labour's failure of 1931 came 'because it was not Socialist enough'.[75]

Wheatley appears to feel the same way, judging by the 'The Socialist's Evidence' given in Wheatley's fictional court case, in which two capitalists are tried for their 'robbery of the workers'. Here the socialist witness answers the magistrate:

> Mag. Why have your Liberal and Tory friends been silent on this matter?
>
> Wit. They belong to the class which fattens on the robbery of the workers, your honour.
>
> [. . .]
>
> Mag. How will you proceed?
>
> Wit. The first step is to have a majority of Labour Members in Parliament.[76]

'It would be political madness', wrote Wheatley, 'to leave the impression in the public mind that the Labour movement is not a menace to vested interests. These interests are keeping our people in the depths of poverty and are now actually threatening to throttle our national existence. We must destroy them rapidly in self-preservation.'[77]

At an Independent Labour Party (ILP) conference Wheatley echoed the words of Wellock, arguing that 'Labour should not again accept office as a minority. If Labour went back as a minority Government, it went back to administer a capitalist order of society that would only bring discredit to the party'.[78] He later warned the party against 'trying to administer a capitalist system in deepening crisis in which the working class would be the prime victims. Far better, he argued, to throw the responsibility on parties who professed to believe in the system'.[79] This was also the view of Wilkinson who criticized the Labour government for being satisfied to 'put patches on the social fabric', thereby leaving itself culpable for the failings of capitalism; a Labour majority was required to bring about socialism and 'no Labour government should ever take office again in a minority'.[80] Wheatley and Wilkinson here sound like Tawney, who concluded his essay:

> If capitalism is to be our future, then capitalists, who believe in it, are most likely to make it work, though at the moment they seem to have some difficulty in doing so. The Labour party will serve the world best, not by doing half-heartedly what they do with conviction, but by clarifying its own principles and acting in accordance with them.[81]

Not all the Christian Socialists, however, saw the election of Labour as the next stage on the way to socialism. Stewart Headlam, for example, 'had no time for the idea of a working-class political party'.[82] Headlam remained a member of the Liberal Party as a Liberal–Radical and reacted with disdain when the Fabian Society began to support Labour: 'To advocate the introduction of workingmen, as such, into Parliament, as the Fabians now seem to be doing, is utterly absurd.' Headlam feared that the ILP would steal votes from Liberal–Radical candidates and lead to the election of more Conservative MPs. He refused 'to vote for a man simply because he is a carpenter and will try to improve the carpenters' wages'.[83]

In *The Socialist's Church* Headlam drew a distinction between socialism and 'Labourism', which he characterized as 'an unnecessary challenge to the middle classes, who stand to gain largely by Socialism, but who for the most part do not know this, and who think they are attacking Socialism, while really what they are attacking is class legislation in the interests of "Labour"'.[84] For Headlam, a working-class party and working-class representation was wholly unnecessary, as 'the prophets of Socialism have been at work – telling forth the truth, bubbling over with enthusiasm – and the result is that the practical politicians are at last beginning to be alive to it'.[85] In Headlam's view persuading the people of socialism would not result in Labour coming to power, but those who already held power coming to accept socialism. Instead Headlam wanted socialists to support the Liberal Party, declaring: 'Yes, I am a Socialist, but I thank God that I am a Liberal as well.'[86]

We can discern a similar way of thinking from Henry Scott Holland, although he did not come out against Labour in the same way as Headlam. Holland and the Christian Social Union were almost completely separate from the working classes and Labour.[87] The 'official line' of the CSU was that 'Christians as such should never be absolutely committed to any political or economic system [...] it should always be possible for a sincere Christian to be either a good Tory or a good Radical, or even an honest Socialist or moral Individualist'.[88] In *Socialism*, published by the Oxford branch of the CSU, it was described how '[i]n most countries Socialism is a hostile movement of the lower classes against the upper; in England it is rather a benevolent movement of the upper classes towards the lower'.[89] This paternalistic attitude left little room for a working-class party gaining representation in Parliament for working-class men. Neither the CSU nor Holland was antagonistic to Labour; Holland was in regular correspondence with Labour leaders, while George Lansbury and Ramsay MacDonald were both contributors to the CSU's magazine.[90] The CSU nevertheless concentrated on acting as a pressure group on whoever had power, including Liberal and Conservative MPs.[91]

John Clifford straddles these two approaches, supporting the Liberals as well as Labour, along with other progressive elements. 'Socialism is not a class movement', he argued. 'Labour is in it; but so is science. The democrats of the streets proclaim its ideals, but so do the students of the universities. Agnostics confess its obligations, and orthodox Christians are eager to forward its aims.'[92] Clifford was aggrieved that 'many Liberals have been averse to any fellowship with Socialists; and the Independent Labour Wing of the Socialist party has exhibited the same repugnance to Liberals'; these opposing forces, suggested Clifford, must 'come together, and work together. Our ideas are the same. Our principles are the same. Our spirit is the same. Unity of method will make us triumphant.'[93] During the Boer War Clifford called for 'a new party [. . .] composed of the most level-headed of the Socialists and the most radical of the [Liberal] Radicals'.[94]

Hardie was opposed to a merger between Labour and the Liberals, arguing, first, that the Liberals were founded on capitalism while Labour were founded on socialism, and, secondly, that MPs who took the Liberal whip ended up voting against working-class interests. Hardie did make an approach to David Lloyd George, John Morely and John Burns, asking them to lead a Labour group in Parliament, but in this he was asking those men to leave the Liberal Party rather than Labour joining with the Liberals.[95] Despite this though, Hardie became party to a pact after the 1910 election which arranged Labour support for the Liberal government in order to keep the Conservatives from power. Lansbury, however, refused to accept the Liberal whip.[96] As far back as 1894, Lansbury had declared, in an article about the aforementioned John Burns leaving the SDF for the Liberals, that the 'ordinary workman does not understand the denunciation of the Liberal party one day and the glorification of it the next'.[97] In 1934, Edgar Lansbury would record that his father would not 'ever again become a member of a Labour Government which owes its tenure of office to the Liberal Party', the situation in which Labour had found itself in 1929–31.⁹⁸ This was a particularly significant view given that in 1934 Lansbury was party leader.

Hardie was in particular disagreement with Headlam over the need for a Labour Party and working-class representation. He may well have had in mind Headlam's comments in *The Socialist's Church* about 'Labourism' being 'an unnecessary challenge to the middle classes' when, in *My Confession of Faith in the Labour Alliance*, he denied that Labour 'shuts out the middle class'; by contrast, he argued,

> there are in the ranks of the I.L.P. thousands of what, without offence, I may describe as the lower middle class and a fair sprinkling of the middle class itself. The bulk of these are good comrades and their services to the party are invaluable. They very often bring into the movement a higher ideal of Socialism, and a much needed sense of business methods.⁹⁹

At the creation of the Scottish Labour Party, Hardie declared: 'If, therefore, any one, peasant or peer, is found willing to accept the programme and work with and for the Party, his help will be gladly accepted.'¹⁰⁰ Nor was Hardie blind to the fact that members of the working class will not necessarily fight for socialism. 'What difference will it make to me', he asked, 'that I have a working man representing me in parliament if he is a dumb dog who will not bark, and will follow the leader under any circumstances?'¹⁰¹ 'A working man can play the knave and act the fool as well as any other', he accepted, 'while the aristocracy may yield men prepared to sacrifice life itself, and all that is supposed to make life worth living, in order to help the workers.'¹⁰²

While, therefore, Headlam viewed Labour as a barrier to middle- and upper-class involvement with socialism, Hardie believed that such men would be more than welcome to join with Labour in fighting for socialism. This disagreement though was never solved, and Christian Socialists remained divided on whether it was necessary for Labour to form a government or simply for the existing politicians and holders of power to accept the need for socialism.

Socialism

The third stage towards socialism is that the state – now, one way or another, in the hands of those who see the need for socialism – will bring about the necessary reforms to transform society. This use of the state and its institutions to bring about socialism was to begin at a local level; for example, George

Lansbury stood for election as a Poor Law Guardian on a platform that included things like 'trade union rates [and] hours of Labour' and a call to 'lighten the burdens on the poorer parishes by compelling the richer ones to take share of the cost of finding suitable work on the land and in workshops for those out of employment'.[103] Holland urged people get involved: 'There are Leagues of Help to belong to; or Children's Care Committees; or the hundred and one civic activities for which the municipalities now put volunteers to use.'[104] 'The Municipality is sacred to us', wrote Holland. 'It is our only instrument by which to fulfil the commandment of our Lord – "You shall love your neighbour as yourself".'[105] Tawney also viewed local government as important, advocating something like devolution to cities and regions: 'When Birmingham and Manchester and Leeds are the little republics which they should be, there is not reason to anticipate that they will tremble at a whisper from Whitehall.'[106]

John Wheatley saw a similar role for local government, writing that 'democracy could raise a city which would be a worthy monument to the capture of civic power by the common people.'[107] Earlier in Wheatley's career 'his council work drew him to the belief that energetic municipal action by socialists could, if widely enough diffused, make the role of the state redundant. He could write with eloquence of a civic, decentralised socialist future, in the attainment of which Glasgow could lead the way'. For this reason, '[c]ontrol of a large elected local authority like Glasgow was always in his view a worthwhile socialist aim'.[108]

Lansbury was for a time the mayor of Poplar Borough Council, and during that time the council was responsible for such reforms as creating washing facilities, a library and leisure facilities, and the appointment of a full-time TB officer.[109] After his tenure as mayor Lansbury was one of the leaders of what has become known as the Poplar Rates Rebellion, in which the council withheld payment due to London County Council and various metropolitan services as in order to continue paying poor relief to the unemployed and a living wage to council employees. Wheatley, the minister with responsibility for local government in the 1924 Labour government, rescinded the order of his predecessor for Poplar Council to pay back the money it owed, citing administrative difficulties as his defence.[110] On leaving office, however, he made clear his 'great joy and pride in being associated with Poplarism', adding that 'only as the policy of Poplar permeated the country would they march towards a different order of society'.[111]

It was accepted that such reforms at a local level would not necessarily lead to socialism. Lansbury wrote that 'we are not going to end Capitalism by Poplar methods'.[112] Wellock also warned that 'if the capitalists do not accept Communism they will certainly prevent it from being established piecemeal fashion – that is, by means of "reforms", for they will undermine and neutralise everything that is done'.[113] Wheatley might have felt that local government could create, as it were, socialism in one city, but his later campaign for Parliament and time spent as a Labour minister indicate that he came to realize the limitations of local government.

What then was the point of such work at a local level? George Lansbury supplies three answers. First, as an act of persuasion and statement of intent: '[I]f we can once let men and women understand that our proposals are practical, and in all ways better than our opponents, it will not be long before they [. . .] join us in working, not to palliate but to sweep away commercialism with its workhouses and prisons.'[114] Secondly, that the people must not be crushed by capitalism, or they will never have the strength or ability to revolt: '[I]f we allow the condition of the people to get worse, there will be no material at all with which to work out social reform, to say nothing of social revolution.'[115] And thirdly, out of compassion and a desire to improve people's lives in the short term as well as the long term: 'I believe that the cure for industrial evils is to be found in the adoption of a Socialistic ideal. Until that time comes, however, I think that all of us ought to work and do what we can to palliate and alleviate the misery and distress which we see all around us.'[116] 'Lansbury and his friends had never equated Poplarism with Socialism. What they did believe was that as long as capitalism lasted, they must fight to alleviate the injustices. In so doing they would be demonstrating to the workers that Labour had something new to offer.'[117]

The key aim, however, remained taking control of the state itself. Henry Scott Holland identified municipality as the means by which the commandments of Christ could be carried out, but also recognized the limits of local government, and that being the case posed the question of 'what is the instrument, the medium, the method by which we can travel far outside the Municipal borders, and embrace those remote multitudes of our neighbours? There is but one answer possible – the State.'[118] Holland argues that only the state can control everything within its borders and seek to intervene in international matters; therefore the state is the only viable means for the creation of a reformed society. 'We invoke the State', he continues, 'We call upon it to relieve our individual conscience by doing for us what we are powerless to do for ourselves [. . .]. The State must take up the task of neighbourly responsibility, or it can never be taken up at all.'[119]

Holland's view of a powerful state can appear totalitarian – for example, his argument that 'Law is Liberty' – especially in light of the horrors of Nazi Germany and the Soviet Union which would follow in the half-century after his writing. Holland, however, has in mind, for example, factory legislation that frees the workers from the totalitarianism of their employers – a positive or 'effective' conception of liberty.[120] Hardie sought to refute those who equated state power with totalitarianism: 'The individualistic conception of the State as some external authority exercising a malign influence upon the life if the community is a travesty of fact. The State is that form of organised society which has evolved through the process of the ages, and represents the aptitude for freedom and self-government to which any people has attained.'[121]

Tawney likewise sought to reassure those who worried about the power of the state by suggesting that it was simply a neutral force – an 'instrument' which could be used by whoever possessed it: 'Fools will use it, when they can, for foolish ends, criminals for criminal ends. Sensible and decent men will use it for ends which are sensible and decent.'[122] Like Holland, Tawney viewed the state as the means by which society could be reorganized in a beneficial way. John Wheatley also 'presuppose[d] a benign and creative role for the British state', and, interestingly, 'he made no demand for the restructuring of its institutions before this role was asked of it'.[123] This reflects Tawney's view of the state as a neutral force; it did not need to be reshaped, merely redirected.

Christian Socialists were not blind though to the risks of an overly powerful state. Holland argued that municipal power would be a check on the ability of the state to act in a totalitarian way.[124] Similarly, we have already seen Tawney arguing that empowered cities like Birmingham and Manchester would not 'tremble at a whisper from Whitehall'. Samuel Keeble simply issued a warning: 'When the individual is nothing and the State everything, evils of all kinds arise.'[125]

What specific things did Christian Socialists want the state to do? We will examine this in more detail in Part Three, but for now we may note three things. The first was to create a new spirit within society, conducive to living a socialist life. Holland argued that the state was to 'create a social environment, a social atmosphere, which will enable any one, who wills, to make himself, by the help of God, good'.[126] Here Holland appears to be answering the perennial objection that the state cannot legislate for goodness or morality; according to Holland, the state could make men good indirectly by encouraging goodness. Keeble makes precisely the same point: 'You can make men good by Acts of Parliament which improve the environment, because men respond to them.'[127] Wilfred Wellock also calls for the state to create an environment 'wherein a new life and a new society can evolve'.[128]

Secondly, Christian Socialists wanted to see the state taking industries and land into public ownership; in the words of Keir Hardie, to make 'all capitalistic property public property'.[129] We have seen Keeble arguing for state ownership of the railways. In his diary Tawney calls for 'a large transference of property rights [. . .]. What I mean is (a) the municipalisation of urban land and the regular purchase of land by the state (b) the purchase of coal-mines and railways and licensed houses'.[130] Some Christian Socialists called for universal nationalization, while others sought only the nationalization of only key industries and land only where necessary.

Thirdly, there were several other reforms that Christian Socialists envisaged being carried out by the state. Tawney goes on to call for '(c) the creation of a really democratic system of higher education (d) heavy taxes on incomes from property'.[131] Keeble makes demands for 'a legal minimum wage', housing reforms, a shorter working day and a seventh day's rest, and taxation of the wealthy.[132] George Lansbury's policies in his 1900 Bow and Bromley Parliamentary campaign included maintenance of the elderly and public provision of housing, as well as the nationalization of land and railways. 'The object of these measures', he concludes, 'is to enable the people ultimately to obtain the Socialisation of the Means of Production, Distribution and Exchange, to be controlled by a Democratic State in the interests of the entire Community'.[133]

Occasionally introduction of a whole raft of socialist measures would be attempted in a single act of Parliament. Hardie introduced a private members' bill to inaugurate 'a Socialist Commonwealth founded upon the common ownership of land and capital, production for use and not for profit, and equality of opportunity for every citizen'.[134] Wheatley, along with James Maxton and others, tabled an amendment to the king's speech, demanding for every worker 'an income, including children's allowances, sufficient to meet the human needs of himself and his family, and measures aimed at the re-organization of the industrial system so that it shall provide for the needs of the community, by nationalizing the key sources of economic power'.[135] Both of these were defeated, and given that Hardie and Wheatley knew that would be the likely outcome, these were probably more of a statement of intent rather than a serious attempt to bring about socialism.

There does appear to be some disagreement among the Christian Socialists about which of these things, if any, actually constituted socialism. John Clifford, for example, regarded the Royal Mail as socialist, on the grounds that it was state-owned rather than privately owned.[136] Similarly, Samuel Keeble cited the Factory

Acts as an example of socialism.[137] However, R. H. Tawney viewed, for example, the welfare state as a step towards socialism rather than socialism itself.[138] He saw 'nationalization as a means to socialist ends such as equality and not an end in itself'.[139] In the same way Keir Hardie argued that state ownership 'is not an end, but only a means to that end. It is but the next stage in the evolution of a juster [*sic*] social order'.[140] 'Socialism means fraternity founded on justice, and the fact that in order to secure this it is necessary to transfer land and capital from private to public ownership is a mere incident in the crusade.'[141] Stewart Headlam went even further than this; the 'Factory Acts' were cited as an example of socialism by Keeble, but Headlam did not describe it as even a step towards socialism. 'The Factory Acts, valuable and necessary in our present condition, are no part of Socialism; they are only temporary expedients to make things a little better for the wage slaves until wage-slavery is abolished by abolition of the monopoly of the means of production.'[142] This was similar to Margaret Bondfield's view of the Royal Mail:

> The Post Office is quoted as an example of State Socialism. It should be called an example of State Capitalism, because it is run on capitalistic lines by a Capitalistic Government. It is a profit-making department which exploits the public and its employees in order to raise revenue for other less profitable government works. With all its faults, however, it will be admitted that from the wage-earner's point of view, this form of exploitation, checked as it is by public opinion, is a distinct advance upon private capitalism.[143]

To some, then, elements of socialism had already been introduced, and they desired the completion of this process; to others, though, socialism had yet to come about, and these things were merely stages that led to socialism, or temporary arrangements that would cease after the establishment of socialism. A good example of this latter viewpoint is John Wheatley's Housing Act (1924) which increased the amount of money available for local authorities to build houses for low-paid workers. Clifford or Keeble might have regarded this as socialism, but Wheatley did not. Before drafting the bill, he instructed his associate John Scanlan: 'Clear from your mind any ideas that you will get any Socialism. What can we do that will be worthwhile for the workers of Britain?'[144] At the third reading of the bill Wheatley explained this attitude: 'Why did I not introduce a Socialist measure? I was not in a position to introduce a Socialist measure. The country is not ready for Socialism. I wish it were ready for it. I will devote my life to an honest effort to prepare it for Socialism. Meanwhile I have to take things as I find them.'[145]

Conclusion

None of the Christian Socialists in this study set out a clear or precise method for bringing about socialism. We can, however, construct from their varied writings a process by which the non-violent revolution would be carried out. The Christian Socialist process can be characterized as having three stages: first, persuading people of the need for socialism, in order that they vote for socialist candidates and support a socialist government; secondly, the election of a Labour government, or the acceptance of socialism by those who already hold power; thirdly, the use of existing state institutions to create a socialist society, including the establishment of common ownership and a planned economy. These ideas, however, are not without their issues, and it is to these that we turn next.

6

Confusion and contradiction

In Part Two, we have so far concluded that Christian Socialism offers a synthesis of democratic and revolutionary socialism, and that Christian Socialists aimed at a peaceful revolution carried out by parliamentary means. This might be termed a spiritual revolution. We also concluded that this spiritual revolution was to be carried out in three stages. In this chapter we will consider some possible issues with and objections to these conclusions.

A democratic-revolutionary synthesis

There are a number of objections that might be made against the idea of a synthesis between democratic and revolutionary socialism. First, it may be suggested that the contradictions which appear in Christian Socialist texts are apparent because of individuals changing their minds over time. The scepticism, for example, of John Wheatley and Wilfred Wellock regarding Parliament only appeared after each had served in Parliament, so it may be argued that they first supported and then came to reject democratic socialism. Ellen Wilkinson appears to have moved in the opposite direction, replacing her belief in revolution with a commitment to parliamentary means.[1] George Lansbury followed the same path, stating in an interview in 1915 that 'I could not now take part in a revolution which meant the throwing up of barricades as once I thought I could'.[2] However, this interview came two years before Lansbury urged British supporters of Russia to emulate the revolutionaries; by contrast Lansbury's comments condemning violence whether in war or in revolution were made in 1892, more than twenty years before the interview. Wilkinson criticized the British Communist Party for rejecting parliamentary methods as early as 1924.[3] Wheatley advocated revolution prior to his stated disaffection with Parliament – indeed, while he was still in Parliament – while Wellock continued to advocate electoralism after his comments about Parliament. The explanation then that individuals simply changed their minds is insufficient to explain these contradictions.

Secondly, it might be argued, as opposed to there being a clear-cut change of mind, that what we find in the writings of Christian Socialists is merely evidence of confusion and imprecision of thought. This objection does carry more weight. For example, Lansbury declared his belief in pacifism, 'since I was a boy [. . .] my position personally has never shifted'. On visits to working-class areas, claimed Lansbury,

> I have said to them: 'No, you must not rise, you must have no violence, you must trust to the winning of this through public opinion.' I have never at any time said to the workers of this country: 'You must take up either arms, or sticks, or stones, in order to force you way to the end that you seek to attain.' [. . .] I have never under any circumstances said that I believe you could obtain Socialism by force.[4]

This statement is difficult to reconcile with Lansbury's comment that 'I could not now take part in a revolution which meant the throwing up of barricades as once I thought I could', implying as it does that at one time he would have been willing to take up arms. It is even more difficult to reconcile with his earlier comments: 'You have a right to rebel when you are tricked and deceived, it is the only course open to you [. . .] Burn and destroy property or anything you like.'[5] Wilkinson's biographer also suggests this possibility, citing the 'contradictory tensions between her beliefs in revolutionary transformation and her recognition of the need for parliamentary pragmatism.'[6]

This being the case, could it be that when Hardie speaks of 'the conquest of political power' or capturing the institutions of the state, he does mean by violent means rather than through the electoral system, and his other comments about electoralism represent simple confusion rather than any synthesis between to socialist methodologies?[7] It is possible, but this view does ignore that the idea of synthesis is not merely an inference from contradictions within Christian Socialist writings, but stated outright. Wellock called for 'Parliamentarianism [. . .] combined with a revolutionary spirit and method'; Headlam for 'a bloodless revolution'; Lansbury for 'a revolution of thought expressed in legislation'; Bondfield for 'peaceful revolution by mental processes – a revolution of the mind and heart'; Keeble for a revolution brought about by 'peaceful and if possible, evolutionary, means'; and Wheatley for a 'revolution' brought about 'peacefully'.[8] Hardie's biographer is therefore justified in concluding that he 'believed that workers could achieve a social revolution by democracy'.[9] We will, however, reconsider some of the confusions and, indeed, contradictions below, in reference to the three stages of the revolution.

A third objection might be that, despite the Christian Socialist use of revolutionary language, which they aimed at was not a revolution at all. This is a criticism made of other left-wing movements; Anthony Wright, for example, quotes Karl Kautsky from the German SDP: 'Social democracy is a revolutionary party, but not a revolution-making party. [. . .] We have no wish either to stir up revolution or to prepare the ground for one.' He concludes: 'Such formulations may now, with hindsight, appear to give the game away, reducing revolution to a metaphor and providing a rhetorical camouflage for political passivity.'[10] Could Christian Socialist talk of 'revolution' also be attacked in this way, being viewed as merely a 'metaphor'? For one thing, most Christian Socialists could not be described as demonstrating the 'political passivity' for which Wright feels Kautsky was seeking to provide 'rhetorical camouflage'. It is only Henry Scott Holland among those being examined here, who could possibly be viewed as politically passive, and Holland was never one to talk of revolution; those who did talk of revolution were those who were by any definition politically active. For another, the Christian Socialist use of revolution can only be viewed as metaphorical if we accept that a revolution necessarily means a forceful uprising against the existing system. On that definition, Christian Socialists are certainly being metaphorical. However, as Wilfred Wellock argued, 'widely different things are meant and conveyed by the word revolution', and violence is not 'the only revolutionary policy conceivable'.

A case in favour of the Christian Socialist synthesis of democratic and revolutionary socialism could be made by pointing out that Christian Socialists, unlike some other socialists who accepted the constitutional, parliamentary method, never came to abandon the goal of completely replacing capitalism with socialism.[11] Parliamentary socialism, says Wright, 'has certainly been prone to slacken its socialist resolve. [. . .] It has frequently shown a capacity for degeneration into mere electoralism and governmentalism, making it impossible to claim, except in the rhetorical sense, that its reforming endeavours were part of a wider strategy of social transformation.'[12]

An example of this is found in Eduard Bernstein, who, rejecting revolution in the sense of the forceful overthrow of capitalism, came to favour a more reformist policy. '[F]or Bernstein, violent or illegal acts implied a commitment to revolutionary ends, and, vice-versa, peaceful parliamentary activity implied a commitment to reform within the framework of the law'; the SPD should therefore, said Bernstein, 'make its mind up to appear what it is today, a democratic party of reform'.[13] 'I frankly admit', wrote Bernstein, 'that I have extraordinarily little feeling for, or interest in, what is usually termed "the final goal of socialism". This goal, whatever it may be, is nothing to me; but the movement is everything.' To other members of the SPD, Bernstein 'seemed to have rejected the final goal of the movement'; he was 'at least depicting political action as the day-to-day implementation of a general principle rather than the pursuit of a particular future objective'.[14] Rosa Luxembourg had Bernstein in mind when she wrote that

> people who pronounce themselves in favour of the method of legislative reform *in place of* and in *contradistinction* to the conquest of political power and social revolution, do not really choose a more tranquil, calmer and slower route to the *same* goal, but a *different* goal. Instead of taking a stand for the establishment of a new society, they take a stand for surface modifications of the old society. [. . .] Our programme becomes not the realisation of *socialism*, but the reform of *capitalism*.[15]

In this view then, a commitment to a democratic, parliamentary route to socialism leads to the aim of reforming society as already constituted rather than replacing capitalism with socialism.

This accusation, however, cannot be levelled at the Christian Socialists, who did seek the replacement of capitalism by socialism. Lansbury, for example, saw people working to 'establish a co-operative system of production and distribution to replace the present unsound order, based as it is on the subjection of the workers by means of the wages and profit-making system'.[16] Again Lansbury held that 'we should be able to transform Capitalism into socialism', and that it should be possible for this to be achieved 'in a peaceful, ordered manner'.[17] John Wheatley, in the same way, foresaw 'the end of the capitalist system'; Hardie, as we have seen above, called for the 'reconstruction of society on a Socialist basis' and endorsed the ruling of the 1893 conference in Bradford at which the ILP was founded, which 'declared for Socialism as the ultimate aim of the Party'.[18] Wilkinson concluded 'that reformism and Socialism are incompatible. [. . .] A compromise between capitalism and Socialism is impossible.'[19] Christian Socialists sought to bring about not just a reformed society, but a completely new and different order of society; in sum, a revolutionized society.[20] On this basis then we can conclude that Christian Socialism does offer a synthesis between democratic and revolutionary socialism.

The three-stage process

The characterization of the Christian Socialist method of revolution as a three-stage process, it might be argued, overlooks the evidence of lack of clarity and inconsistencies in Christian Socialist writing, some of which we have already noted. It has been argued that R. H. Tawney's philosophy lacked 'any practical proposals to realistically create the social basis of co-operation on which any social advances could be *permanently* based'; the same has been said of Keir Hardie, who, according to one writer, 'had no real policies to overcome these problems beyond the vague panacea of co-operation and state regulation. [...] The potential resistance to change by the capitalist class was never measured, and plans to counter this resistance were never seriously countenanced.'[21] One of Hardie's biographers writes that his 'ideological position could be confusing [...] Eleanor Marx, understandably, accused him of being "ideologically unstable"'.[22] 'Tawney himself', it has been argued, 'would have been the first to admit that he was not a systematic social thinker and that the construction of a philosophical system was never his aim.'[23] The same has been suggested of the movement as a whole: 'None of the Labour leaders were systematic "theologians", either in the sense of fully understanding or appropriating a Marxist analysis, or in developing a rounded Christian social vision. Rather, they drew organically, pragmatically and passionately on all available intellectual or moral resources to build their case for social change.'[24]

Hardie dismissed questions about such specifics by arguing that they belong 'to the future', and are 'a matter with which posterity alone can deal'; his simple belief was that '[o]nce the principle has been accepted, then experience and common sense will find the way to overcome every difficulty which may arise in connection with its working.'[25] A biographer of Tawney sees the same way of thinking in his 'argument that in principle socialism is superior to capitalism and that, once the battle of principle is won, then secondary matters of technique and machinery soon yield'.[26] This attitude could be characterized as 'where there's a will, there's a way'.

Wilfred Wellock's biographer identifies the same kind of uncertainty. 'Just how this revolution was to be carried through without physical violence and the forcible overthrow of the possessing and ruling class was something which Wellock left unclear'; there was 'very little in the way of a clear programme of action, a strategy for revolutionary change'.[27] This lack of clarity is evident in *Christian Communism*. 'Would it not be rather nice, think you', begins Wellock, 'if humanity woke up some morning and decided to consider itself a rather big family, and began to modify social policies accordingly?'[28] According to Wellock, 'Communism will be established by the declared will of the people', but he is vague when it comes to how the people will come to will the existence of communism: 'as a result of a vision which will come upon the people during an unexpected concurrence of events'.[29] This statement echoes a passage in *The Way Out*:

> I have a vision, which I cannot shake of, of a mighty campaign which will sweep through the land like a tornado, which will so quicken the conscience and fire the imagination of the people that the recalcitrant elements in the community will be cowed into submission by its sheer spiritual momentum. And apart from such a campaign, a period of spiritual illumination and moral exaltation wherein great social changes will be made, I see no hope, in this age of social decay and financial supremacy, of rescuing Western civilization and establishing it on a basis of service, fellowship and goodwill.[30]

We could point to not just the absence of practical proposals or clear thinking in Wellock's work, but also a major contradiction. At times, as in the earlier passage, Wellock suggested that a spiritual change would come, leading the people to desire communism and then implement it. This is in keeping with the three stages we identified in the previous section. Wellock argued that 'without a spiritual revolution – the perception of finer social values and ideas – an economic revolution will be impossible'.[31] In *Christian Communism* Wellock wrote: 'It is my firm conviction that no social revolution will be successfully carried through, and that no real social progress will be made until at least a very powerful minority possess a much clearer vision of the life they would live and the world they would see.'[32] However, this directly contradicts his statement earlier in the book that the 'Communist or Christian spirit, the willingness to share [. . .] cannot be generated to any extent in capitalist conditions, a Communist order of society being absolutely essential thereto'.[33] Here Wellock is arguing that a communist system must exist in order to bring about a communistic spirit, but elsewhere he argues that the communistic spirit must exist in order to bring about a communist system. The same argument had been made in *The Way Out*: '[U]ntil the social system has been radically modified, spiritual rightness must remain impossible to all but a very small minority.'[34] Wellock contradicts himself about whether spiritual change precedes economic and social change, or whether economic and social change must create the spiritual change; nor does he explain, if the latter is the case, what will bring about the social and economic change.

Wellock is perhaps most honest in *Christian Communism* when he writes that 'I do not think it is possible to say how the transition to Communism will be made'.[35] George Lansbury made the same confession in an article about his own socialism, admitting 'as to how it will be done eventually I do not know'.[36] In a possible attempt to cover up the lack of detail Wellock adds: 'More than that, I do not think we should greatly concern ourselves about that question: our business is to create a Christian Communist consciousness, and to let the revolution, or what there be, come out of that'.[37] This reflects the views expressed by Tawney and Hardie about the acceptance of principles leading to the practical solutions being found.

Even here though the contradiction emerges; we have already seen how a few pages earlier Wellock denied that such a consciousness can exist until the revolution is successfully carried out, unless we make the rather generous assumption that Wellock meant different things by 'Communist or Christian spirit' and 'Christian Communist consciousness'; but in any case such a difference is not made apparent. The result of this confusion was that Wellock gradually became disillusioned. On his time in the House of Commons as an Independent Labour MP Wellock wrote that 'I never felt so impotent. [. . .] I found that after a few years in the House of Commons, most Members seemed to lose their enthusiasm for idealistic objectives.'[38] Wellock eventually gave up on socialism itself: 'No longer could he believe that socialism was the pathway to the good society and world peace, for socialism had fallen victim to the materialism of the machine age.'[39] We can see then some of the vagueness and inconsistency in Christian Socialist thinking about how socialism would be brought about, and that in Wellock's case this in part led to his rejection of socialism.

It is these contradictions that are the most powerful counterargument to anything which may be concluded about Christian Socialist methods for bringing about a new society. We may disagree with the efficacy of seeking to bring about socialism through the existing structures of society and argue that the three-stage process of doing so would not work, but this does not mean that Christian Socialism is not internally logical. However, the contradictions of Wellock destroy the internal coherence of, at least, his plan for bringing about socialism and the vagueness identified in the work of Tawney, Hardie and Lansbury does not persuade us that they would have had any answer.

It is to be remembered that the three-stage model sketched out in Chapter 5 was never expressed in full by any of the Christian Socialists. It is instead that which has been constructed from various Christian Socialist texts and is therefore at best an imperfect representation of Christian Socialist thought, even without noting the above contradictions. Perhaps then it is best to conclude that the model is not to be taken as a firm expression of doctrine, but that it nevertheless does have some validity in describing the methods of Christian Socialism to the extent to which they were expressed.

Given this validity, perhaps it is overly harsh to say that, for example, Tawney lacked 'any practical proposals to realistically create the social basis of co-operation on which any social advances could be *permanently* based', or that Hardie 'had no real policies to overcome these problems'.[40] Hardie and Tawney both sought to create a strong body of socialist opinion in all classes of society, which would not only bring Labour to power but also sustain them as they used the state and its institutions to bring about socialism. There is no reason to doubt that a socialist government in a country almost wholly persuaded of socialism could have established socialism. This was the Christian Socialist view of how a new society would be established. Neither did they sit back and wait for this to happen but worked to make it happen.

The criticism perhaps also overlooks the spiritual quality of Christian Socialism. There was a belief that God would bring about a new society, His Kingdom on Earth. For this reason Tawney sought to persuade Christians, who already possessed 'so revolutionary a basis' to their thinking, Clifford and Headlam believed in the inevitability of socialism because it was being brought about by God, and Lansbury pointed to Christ, who 'lives now to give men and women the revolutionary spirit'.[41] From a purely political perspective these things hardly add up to practical proposals; we can, for example, dismiss Keeble's belief in prayer as a way of creating a socialist society. Yet to do so ignores that these men were Christians as well as socialists and overlooks a large part of the makeup of their political thought. Lansbury concludes that 'if we get God behind us in spirit and in truth we will revolutionize the whole face of England'.[42]

Conclusion

The attempts in the previous chapters to systematize Christian Socialist thinking on bringing about a new society can be objected to. In terms of a synthesis between revolutionary and evolutionary socialism – a 'revolution' by peaceful means – it might be asserted that the texts reflect nothing more than changes over time, a simple confusion or 'revolution' used merely as a rhetorical device. These objections though are not fully persuasive: the chronology of statements do not allow for changes in perspective across time; the argument regarding confusion does not take into account the clear statements, such as Headlam's 'bloodless revolution' or Wellock's 'Parliamentarianism [. . .] combined with a revolutionary spirit and method'; Christian Socialists, at least in this period, did not turn to reformism. The three-stage process in turn may be regarded as an artificial construction, yet it does have some explanatory power. We do have to note confusion and potential contradiction in Christian Socialist texts, but this in part may be excused by the religious rather than 'scientific' character of Christian Socialism as political ideology.

Part Three

A Christian Socialist society

7

Collectivism and the role of the state

Having considered how Christian Socialists sought to bring about socialism, we turn to question of what they were aiming for. What did a Christian Socialist imagine that society would be like once socialism had been brought into being? In this chapter we shall examine the Christian Socialist commitment to collectivism and cooperation and consider whether this required a large and powerful socialist state. In later chapters we will examine some principles that would be enshrined in a Christian Socialist society – such as democracy, equality and pacifism – as well as the utopian element of Christian Socialist visions of the future.

Difficulties

There are two difficulties in trying to set out the Christian Socialist vision of a new society. The first is the extent to which Christian Socialists consciously avoided giving firm and definite proposals or policies. Peter d'A Jones writes of Henry Scott Holland's Christian Social Union that 'practical reform suggestions were left to the individual consciences of members' rather than set out by the organization itself. Jones then adds that '[t]his was a condition that characterised many "Christian socialist" groups'.[1] William Temple consistently argued that it was not for the church to suggest specific policies, but rather to proclaim Christian principles which would guide political decision-making.[2] Stewart Headlam made the same argument in a sermon, saying: 'It is not my business, speaking to you from the pulpit, to deal with details, or to suggest definite action on the social and political problems, but it *is* my business to suggest, as I have done, the principles, and warn you, as I do now, as to what prevents those principles from being carried out.'[3] Similarly, Samuel Keeble wrote that the ideal situation was for the church to be 'declaring social duties, and pointing out social perils and evils', leaving the work of making specific changes to society to others.[4]

However, it was not just clergymen who disavowed themselves from making specific proposals or definite predictions; Keir Hardie took a similar attitude, writing:

> To dogmatise about the form which the Socialist State shall take is to play the fool. That is a matter with which we have nothing whatever to do. It belongs to the future, and is a matter which posterity alone can decide. The most we can hope to do is to make the coming of Socialism possible in the full assurance that it will shape itself aright when it does come.[5]

Fortunately, this does not mean that these men contributed absolutely nothing of what they hoped to see in a socialist society. Temple, for example, added an appendix of practical proposals to *Christianity and the Social Order* in order to illustrate the principles he expounded in the rest of the book. Holland, Headlam, Keeble and Hardie all made suggestions as to what they hoped would be the case in a new society. However, this reticence to make firm proposals or set out a definite vision casts some doubt over whatever the Christian Socialists say about the potential future (is it a practical suggestion or simply an illustration of a principle?) and leads to predictions, policies and ideas being much more vague than perhaps ought to be the case.

The second difficulty comes of the fact that it is not always clear whether a policy suggested or supported is one that the Christian Socialist imagines will be part of a socialist society, or one which they view as a necessity in the current capitalist society. Are the Christian Socialists arguing for something that will be part of a new world, or simply a reform to the existing one? As an example, Keeble regarded the Factory Acts and municipal ownership of utilities as part of 'state socialism'.[6] Stewart Headlam, by contrast argued that '[t]he Factory Acts, valuable and necessary in our present anarchic condition, are no part of Socialism; they are only temporary expedients to make things a little better for the wage slaves until wage-slavery is abolished by abolition of the monopoly in the means of production'.[7] Headlam, however, does concede that 'the ownership and management by the State or the Municipality of certain great industries and enterprises – what has contemptuously been termed Gas and Water Socialism – is genuine Socialism so far as it goes, and will probably still be necessary when the ideal of Socialism has been reached'.[8] Here Headlam makes a distinction between two things – factory legislation and municipal ownership of utilities – regarding the latter as part of socialism but the former as not; Keeble, however, identifies both as being part of socialism.

The difficulty here is that Christian Socialists viewed certain things as necessary reforms under capitalism, others as part of the establishment of socialism and perhaps some things as being both at the same time; and that this is not always made clear. For example, George Lansbury's policies as an SDF member in 1894 included 'trade union rates [and] hours of labour' for workhouse inmates, a commitment to 'lighten the burdens on poorer parishes by compelling the richer ones to take their share of the cost of finding suitable work on the land and in workshops for those out of employment', as well as 'socialisation of the means of production [. . .] to be controlled by a democratic state in the interests of the entire community, and the complete emancipation of labour from the domination of capitalism'.[9] It might be assumed that the latter demand is a description of socialism, while the former are reforms to capitalism – after all, there would presumably be no workhouse inmates or unemployed after 'the complete emancipation of labour' – but nowhere is this made explicit.

Sometimes this distinction is made clear, or at least hinted at. In suggesting some reforms pertaining to unemployment in 1929, Lansbury wrote: 'I am still a Socialist, but I am also a realist, and as such I am not prepared to sit silent and see the manhood of our nation perish because a theory of life I hold is not at the moment practicable.'[10] Lansbury's ideas in this instance must then be reforms to capitalist rather than socialist proposals. Similarly, even though Keeble argued that '[w]e are not ready for an entirely non-competitive form of society', he held that 'we must do what we can, not what we should like. [. . .] Certainly, if we be wise, we shall not refuse to do anything at all because we cannot secure all we want.'[11]

Another example is afforded by John Wheatley's housing bill. Wheatley declared that his proposals were 'real capitalism – an attempt to patch up, in the interests of humanity, a capital ordered society. [. . .] I am not submitting to the House proposals for changing the capitalist order of society. I am merely submitting proposals of a limited character.'[12] Wheatley here is likely overstating his position in order to disarm opposition to the bill, but nevertheless the housing bill is an act of reform rather than the introduction of socialism. However, even when this is the case we can find – as in the example of Keeble and Headlam earlier – that what one Christian Socialist regarded as socialistic, another did not.

Keir Hardie is particularly confusing when he defines socialism as meaning 'that land and industrial capital shall be held as common property to be administered by the community in the interests of the whole of its members; and that industry shall be organised on the basis of Production for Use rather than Production for Profit', because he then argues that this 'is not an end, but only a means to an end. It is but the next stage in the evolution of a juster [sic] social order'.[13] Does Hardie mean that the common ownership of 'land and industrial capital' does not constitute socialism? Perhaps this is explained in the following statement by Hardie:

> Socialism we believe to be the next step in the evolution of that form of State which will give the individual the fullest and freest room for expansion and development. State Socialism, with all its drawbacks, and these I frankly admit, will prepare the way for free Communism in which the rule, not merely the law of the State, but the rule of life will be – From each according to his ability, to each according to his needs.[14]

Hardie, in a similar way to Marx, believes that once capitalism has been replaced by socialism, socialism would then be replaced by communism. However, this explanation does not assist in alleviating confusion: most Christian Socialists have two forms of society in mind – capitalist society and its necessary reforms and socialist society and its necessary components. Hardie confuses things further by adding a third: communism. This difficulty is exacerbated as other Christian Socialists – such as Headlam and Wilfred Wellock – also write about communism, but there is no indication that they mean, like Hardie, that communism will follow socialism; it appears more that they are using the terms socialism and communism synonymously.

Despite these two difficulties – the shying away from specific policies and the difficulty of knowing whether those policies which are put forward are reforms to capitalism or part of socialism (or, indeed, whether socialism is the final stage or itself an intermediate stage) – it is still possible to draw some broad conclusions about the kind of society envisaged by Christian Socialists. Even if only principles are put forward, with actual proposals lacking in specifics and relegated to the status of illustrations, or if we cannot always tell whether the proposals are reforms to capitalism or components of socialism, we can still grasp from this something of what the Christian Socialists were aiming for and working towards.

Cooperation and collectivism

Like other socialists, Christian Socialists envisaged a society run cooperatively and collectively. For example, Keir Hardie's private member's bill called for 'a Socialist Commonwealth founded upon the common ownership of land and capital'.[15] As early as 1888, Hardie called for 'a new economic departure in which our entire industrial society shall be worked on the principle of one vast co-operative'.[16] The ILP, under Hardie's influence, stood for 'collective ownership of the means of production'.[17] Years later, R. H. Tawney, having become committed to some form of public ownership during his investigations into the coal industry, would oppose Hugh Gaitskell's attempt to remove Clause IV from the Labour Party constitution.[18] Margaret Bondfield argued: 'The ownership of land and the large basic industries should be placed in the hands of Parliament. [. . .] It is vitally important that the banking system should be nationalised and the power of credit placed under national control, in order that the fullest success should attend the development of public ownership.'[19] In a manner similar to Tawney, Bondfield wanted a situation in which 'the administration and control of industry will be in the hands of those who are actually engaged in it, in conjunction with representatives of the public, instead of, as now, on behalf of those who have merely invested capital in it'.[20]

Lansbury, as we have already seen, called for the 'socialisation of the means of production [. . .] to be controlled by a democratic state in the interests of the entire community'. John Wheatley, alongside James Maxton and others, tabled an amendment to the king's Speech which called for 'measures aimed at the re-organization of the industrial system so that it shall provide for the needs of the community, by nationalizing the key sources of economic power'.[21] 'Britain', according to Wheatley, 'should be treated as a National Workshop. No industry should be regarded as self-contained. Every industry must be looked upon and treated as a department of one workshop.'[22]

This was not just the view of Labour politicians in this study, but also of those engaged in Christian ministry; Stewart Headlam, for example, despite his liberalism, 'became a champion' of 'collectivist solutions'.[23] At the Christian Socialist Society in 1887, 'Headlam endorsed a resolution calling for "the establishment of a system of National Cooperation under which land and capital being vested collectively in the whole people, it will be impossible for anyone to live on the labour of others"'.[24] The platform set out by Headlam's Guild of St Matthew sought 'to restore to the people the value which they give to the land' and 'to bring about a better distribution of the wealth created by labour'.[25] William Temple also favoured some measure of cooperation, arguing that 'the Christian is called on to assent to great steps in the direction of collectivism'.[26]

Samuel Keeble, similarly, criticized 'sweating', 'reduction of wages and unemployment', and 'those fluctuations of the market most of which might be avoided under a rational system of industry'. This 'rational system' in

Keeble's view was one 'which adjusted supply to demand, produced primarily for use and not profit, and kept a stern hand on the Stock Exchange'.[27] For John Clifford, socialism was 'an endeavour to displace the fierce and disastrous competitive methods of industrial life, by the introduction of co-operative and organized action based on justice and intended to promote the general welfare'.[28] Clifford also summarizes collectivism or cooperation like this: 'Here is the great business of industrial life; let us manage it so that all may share in the responsibility and share in the gains, and share fairly and justly as nearly as possible; not one doing all the work and another taking all the gains'.[29] The Declaration of Clifford's Free Church Socialist League held 'that the principle of Brotherhood as taught by Jesus Christ [. . .] must result in the Socialization of all natural resources, as well as the instruments of production, distribution and exchange'.[30]

We can therefore see that Christian Socialists sought in general a society which was managed in such a way as to provide for the needs of the whole community, rather than the laissez-faire society that exists under capitalism. This implies the nationalization of both land and industry. As Hardie viewed it: 'Make the worker his own employer and his own landlord and then he receives all which his toil creates. This is Socialism.'[31]

Christian Socialists foresaw a society in which land would no longer be a private monopoly; in Chapter 3 we observed support – especially by Stewart Headlam, but also by others – for the Single Tax proposed by Henry George in *Progress and Poverty* which would serve to abolish peacefully private ownership of land.[32] According to Jones, 'Headlam declared private property in land to be in ethical opposition both to the Ten Commandments and to the teaching and life of Jesus Christ'.[33] Another suggests that 'to Headlam and the Guild [of St Matthew], private ownership of the land was the fundamental cause of social evil, for it embodied that individualism and isolation from God which was the effect of the Fall'.[34]

George Lansbury's view was that there were 'no means for dealing effectually with the land question as a whole except by making all those who wish to use land pay, not to private individuals, but to the State, for the use of such land'.[35] Tawney wrote in his diary of the need for 'a large transference in property rights', which among other things would include 'the municipalisation of urban land and the regular purchase of land by the state'.[36] Hardie argued for 'a Co-operative Commonwealth in which land [. . .] shall be the property of the community'.[37] William Temple suggested in the latter part of *Christianity and the Social Order* that the government should acquire land for the building of houses, writing that '[i]f well-established vested interests are disturbed there should be compensation; but in no case should speculation in land values or vested interests be allowed to interfere with the use of land to the best public advantage'.[38] John Wheatley has his fictional 'Socialist' declare before the 'Magistrate' that a Labour government 'would take over the land and thus by one stroke save to the workers the amount of wealth the Duke takes'.[39]

As well as land, Christian Socialists envisaged the common ownership of industry. Wheatley has his 'Socialist' continue: '[T]hey would take over the mines and save the wealth taken by the colliery shareholders. [. . .] They would take over the railways and again save what railway shareholders pocket. They would also cheapen house property by the amount which now goes in ground rents, and profits. They would organise industry so as to abolish all useless labour.'[40] For Lansbury, this was necessary for land reform to be at all effective: 'I should support the taxation of ground values up to 20s in the £, though that is not going to improve the condition of the workers so long as they are compelled to labour for wages for the benefit of the employing classes.'[41] 'The only possible remedy', according to Lansbury, 'is for you to obtain control of that upon which your lives depend, viz., the means and instruments of production and distribution, or, in other words, the land, machinery, tools, buildings, etc., and see that they are administered for the benefit of all, instead of, at the present time, for the interest of the few.'[42]

Hardie wrote that 'in addition to the land, the pits, and railways, and docks, and ironworks, and steelworks, and tinworks, should also belong to the people, and not to a few only'.[43] In Hardie's view therefore, as well as collective ownership of the land itself, there should be collective ownership of all manner of industry. Stewart Headlam expressed the same view, arguing that 'the main thing at which Socialism aims is that the great means of production shall be in the hands of the whole community, and therefore shall be taken out of the hands of private individuals'.[44] Samuel Keeble foresaw the 'possession by the community of all the instruments of production and distribution – land, machinery, railways and all means of transport or communication'.[45] John Clifford hinted at holding to the same view, asking 'if society is always a necessary factor in the production of the results of Labour, how can it be intrinsically unjust that society should ask to be heard as to the ownership and control, both of the instruments and the results of labour?'[46] Finally, Tawney's view was that 'industry should be subordinated to the community in such a way as to render the best service technically possible'.[47]

However, the Christian Socialist view of collectivism is not as straightforward as might initially appear. While it might fairly be stated that Hardie, Lansbury and Headlam all favoured the nationalization of industry and land, the same is not necessarily true of all the Christian Socialists. For example, we saw William Temple's idea that the state should purchase land in order to build houses; however, Temple did not believe that full nationalization of land was necessary, writing:

> [I]t seems to me, we have been far too tender towards the claims that have been made by the owners of land and water as compared with the interests of the public, who need that land and water for the ordinary purposes of human life. I am not myself at all persuaded that the solution of this problem is to be found in the nationalization of land; but I am persuaded that we need to find ways of asserting the rights of the public over the interests of the private owners; and we come back here to the great Christian principle that the right which attaches to ownership is a right of administration, but should never be a right to exclusive use.[48]

Temple then adds to this: 'Over land and water we must establish a social control, whether or not this carries with it national ownership. (Personally, I believe that it need not and hope that it will not; but the control is essential.)'[49] Temple's view is that the confiscation of property was a last resort. A man who owns land, he writes, must own it 'not as a possessor of so much material resources, but as a steward and trustee for the community. Land not beneficially used should involve liability to fine, or, in extreme cases, to forfeiture.'[50] Temple, therefore, sought a way in which the community as a whole could assert its interests over private property, but without necessarily taking that private property into collective ownership.

This was also the view of Samuel Keeble, who argued that 'every property-owner, though he possesses a certain moral right to "his own", and is granted full legal control, is yet not absolute owner, *but the steward of society*'.[51] Keeble did not necessarily want all industries to be nationalized, writing that 'the natural grievances and injustices' felt by the labouring class could be remedied by 'making the labourer master of his product, whether by systems of technical education, co-operative production, industrial partnership, municipal Socialism, or by other practicable methods'.[52] This suggests that he is not necessarily committed to nationalization in every circumstance. In *Towards the New Era* Keeble argues for 'State ownership of the *vital* industries and *some* of the national sources of wealth which should not be in private hands'.[53] The railways and coal mines are noted as industries which ought to be nationalized, but Keeble only goes far as to say that '[l]and nationalization or the taxation of ground values is a matter for careful discussion'.[54] Therefore, while committed to a measure of collectivization, Keeble did not see full nationalization as a necessity nor as the only solution.

Tawney shares Keeble's view that nationalization is not always necessary. In *The Acquisitive Society* Tawney sets out his view of what a 'Functional Society' ought to be like, arguing that the principle of function is a 'standard for discriminating between those types of property which are legitimate and those which are not'.[55] Tawney, therefore, is not opposed to all forms of private ownership of industry or land; only in those situations in which the owners perform no function is the ownership of land or industry illegitimate. Indeed, Tawney goes on to say that 'the idea of some Socialists that private property in land or capital is necessarily mischievous is a piece of scholastic pedantry as absurd as that of those Conservatives who would invest all property with kind of mysterious sanctity. It all depends on what sort of property it is and for what purpose it is used.'[56]

Part of Tawney's argument is that nationalization does not necessarily mean state management:

> The merits of nationalization do not stand or fall with the efficiency or inefficiency of existing state departments as administrators of industry. For nationalization, which means public ownership, does not involve placing industry under the machinery of the political state, with its civil servants controlled, or nominally controlled, by Cabinet Ministers, and is compatible with several types of management. [. . .] The authorities to whom it is entrusted may be composed of representatives of the consumers, or of representatives of professional associations, or of state officials, or of all three in several different proportions. Executive work may be placed in the hands of civil servants, trained, recruited, and promoted as in the existing state departments, or a new service may be created with a procedure and standards of its own. The industry may be subject to Treasury control, or it may be financially autonomous.[57]

Similarly, in *Equality* Tawney argued that '[w]hether control should take the form of regulation, or of their acquisition by the State and management by a public body, is a question of expediency, to be answered differently in different cases'.[58]

However, Tawney also argues for what he terms 'professionalization' of industry as an alternative to public ownership, describing

> the difference between the existing industrial order, collectivism and the organization of industry as a profession. [. . .] The first involves the utilization of human beings for the purposes of private gain; the second their utilization

for the purpose of public service; the third the association in the service of the public for their professional pride, solidarity and organization.[59]

In this conception, industry is made to serve the public not by being nationalized, but by being run voluntarily according to a professional ethic which demands certain standards of service. As Tawney continues, 'the alternative to the discipline which Capitalism exercised through its instruments of unemployment and starvation is the self-discipline of responsibility and professional pride'.[60] This is not to suggest that Tawney was against nationalization – in *Equality* he called for the Labour Party to nationalize key industries in order to begin dismantling capitalism – but rather that, like Keeble, he did not view it as a necessity in every case. Tawney did envisage some industries remaining in private hands, but – as well as the introduction of a professional ethic – Tawney suggested a government department to ensure that industries remaining in private hands were conducted with due regard to the public interest.[61] Therefore, the principle of society being run cooperatively was still to be established with or without nationalization.

Even those Christian Socialists most committed to collective ownership of land and industry did not foresee a society in which all property was abolished. In 'Labour and Christianity' Keir Hardie argued that 'Christ in His Gospels denounced property in all its forms. [...] Christianity on its social side can never be realized – if it is to be interpreted in the light of Christ's teaching – until there is full, free Communism, and the very idea of private property has disappeared from men's minds.'[62] Yet, in *The I.L.P. and All About It*, published around the same time, Hardie's view on first consideration seems to be rather different:

> Neither does Socialism propose, to take away anyone's private possessions. Not only a man's tooth pick, but also his personal attire, his household goods and effects, and where he so desired it, his house, would all under Socialism still remain his personal private property. So too with his books, his pictures, and his money. He would be just as free to hoard his savings then as he is now, and just as free to spend them in any way his taste might dictate.[63]

However, Hardie continues:

> One thing alone he would not be able to do under Socialism; he would not be able to buy a tract of land, and say to all the rest of the earth, 'No matter what your needs or necessities, this is mine, and you shall not be allowed to use it, save with my permission and on condition that you pay me tribute.' Neither would he be able to use capital for the enslavement of the worker, nor to live in idleness all the rest of his life upon interest extorted from the forced labour of others. With land and capital transferred from individual to communal ownership, industry

would be organised for the purpose of supplying the means for a healthy and fully developed life for the whole of the community.[64]

Hardie therefore draws a distinction between different kinds of property: first, private property in the means of production, which ought to be owned communally; secondly, personal property – clothes, household goods and even the house itself. The latter is perfectly acceptable, while it is the former which is denounced.

John Wheatley made a similar argument writing that 'Socialism is defined as the public ownership of land and capital. This does not mean the abolition of all private property', and again that '[o]ur Socialism is not confiscation or robbery. [. . .] It differs from the Socialism condemned by the Pope in that it retains the right to own private property. It is simply a scheme to abolish poverty.'[65] The same is true of Samuel Keeble, who 'never envisaged the disappearance of private property in the era of public ownership of basic industries and services. Christianity, he believed, favoured both jointly.'[66]

We have already seen that Tawney did not imagine all property being abolished, because he divided property into two classes – legitimate and illegitimate – with the test of legitimacy being whether the ownership of any given piece of property corresponded with a function or not; 'it is not private ownership', he reminded readers in *The Acquisitive Society*, 'but private ownership divorced from work, which is corrupting to the principle of industry'.[67] Like Hardie, Tawney does not even consider that socialism would remove the right to personal property, writing that 'if by "Property" is meant the personal possessions which the word suggests to nine-tenths of the population, the object of Socialists is not to undermine property, but to protect and increase it'.[68] Far from its abolition, Tawney wished to see a wider diffusion of property, with legitimate property rights being held by more people than were able to do so under capitalism.[69]

Temple viewed the existence of property as being a result of human sin. This might cause us to imagine that he sought its abolition; instead, he regarded it as a necessity. 'The institution of property is rooted in sin', Temple explained, 'for if all men loved God with all their hearts and their neighbours as themselves, they would cheerfully labour for the common good. But men are sinful, so property rights are needed, not so much for the satisfaction of the rich as for the protection of the poor.'[70] In *The Church Looks Forward* he expands on this:

> Now, if we did all love God with all our hearts and our neighbours as ourselves, we should work our hardest to produce what the whole fellowship needed: we should take our own reasonable share of it and no more; and we should be eager

that everybody else should have what he needed also, and there would be no need for property rights. And, in consequence, the early theologians are always quite clear that property rights are rooted in sin. They don't say that property is wicked: they say that the whole business is rooted in sin: that is, in the failure of man to rise to the height of his calling, and rights are needed, not for the security of the great property owners, but for the protection of the small property owners: because in a world in which people do not love God with all their hearts, and their neighbours as themselves the strong are going to take advantage of the weak and you need to protect the weaker members in such rights as they have been able to establish.[71]

For Temple, the existence of legal rights to property was a source of protection to vulnerable property owners in a world of sinners. Temple also states his belief in 'voluntary communism', based on the example of the church as recorded in Acts of the Apostles: 'And all that believed were together, and had all things common; and sold their possessions and goods, and parted them to all men, as every man had need.'[72] Temple's view is that this 'is as different from what is ordinarily called communism as anything can be; it is, indeed, its polar opposite. Modern communism abolishes legal ownership by private persons; under it no one has property to give away', adding that '[t]o renounce property is a conspicuously vivid act of personal freedom; to have no property or be forcibly deprived of it is a serious infringement of personal freedom.'[73]

However, this stress on the voluntary nature of relinquishing property does not mean that Temple was simply seeking more charity from the better off. 'If the present order is taken for granted or assumed to be sacrosanct, charity from the more or less fortunate would seem virtuous or commendable.' However, 'to those for whom the order itself is suspect or worse, such charity is blood-money. Why should some be in the position to dispense and others to need that kind of charity?'[74] Temple, then, called for a change in the way society was organized, rather than mere charity. He also reminded those who did give charity that theology regards 'almsgiving' not as a 'kindness' or act of 'mercy', but as an act of 'justice'.[75] Therefore, the reorganized society envisaged by Temple was not just one that encouraged charity, but one which sought to establish justice.

This same view was held by other Christian Socialists. Stewart Headlam wrote of the charity of the upper classes, asserting that 'these monopolists will do almost anything for the people except one thing, and that is, they won't get off their back.'[76] In a sermon at Westminster Abbey, 'Headlam told the well-to-do congregation that their almsgiving would be worthless unless they were also working "to get rid of the miserable class divisions with which England is cursed'".[77] Samuel Keeble wanted '[t]hose in positions of power, rich men, capitalists, managers, and employers [to] never forget that justice precedes charity. Donations and great subscriptions to church, public, or party funds, whilst donors are sweating the workers, or appropriating more than their share of the wealth produced, can no longer be endured in professing Christian men.'[78] John Clifford also spoke of justice, declaring that '[c]ollectivism approximates more closely to universal justice than the wage system'.[79] Similarly to Keeble, Clifford suggests that '[i]t is easier [. . .] to bestow a donation on a hospital than pay a fair wage to a toiler', but that this was not sufficient. 'Charity is good [. . .] but far to be preferred is the justice which quenches the need for it.'[80] Finally, George Lansbury made the distinction between charity and socialism in discussion with Simon Montagu, who sought to persuade Lansbury to remain within the Liberal Party:

> I told him I had become a socialist and wanted to preach socialism. He replied: 'Don't be silly, I am a socialist, a better socialist than you. I give a tenth of my riches each year to the poor'. I said: 'Yes, I know how good you are and respect you more than it is possible to say, but, my dear friend, we socialists want to prevent you from getting the nine-tenths. We do not believe in rich and poor and charity. We want to create wealth and all the means of life and share them equally among the people.'[81]

For Christian Socialists then, charity was not a bad thing in itself, except insofar as it was used in such a way as to argue against the establishment of justice or socialism.

The role of the state

It might be supposed, given the commitment to collectivism, that Christian Socialists envisaged a society governed by a large and powerful state. Keir Hardie, for example, foresaw a society in which 'land and machinery is socially owned [. . .] with the entire nation organised so as to turn each individual's service to the most profitable account'.[82] George Lansbury sought 'to replace the present system of society, the dominant features of which are ruthless competition and production for profit, by a society where the wealth of the community shall be equitably distributed'.[83] These aspirations would suggest the existence of a state large and powerful enough to carry them out. John Wheatley, for example, believed that public ownership necessitated state control of wages and prices.[84]

Stewart Headlam is described as calling for 'an expansive role for the state in social regulation', 'a redistribution of wealth by state action, and a full programme of educational and welfare provision by government'.[85] Even those not necessarily committed to state ownership of industry made proposals that seem to rely on a powerful state. We have already seen William Temple suggesting that the government should be able to acquire land from private ownership in order to build new houses, while as a means of reforming the education system R. H. Tawney suggested a central authority which would govern all schools.[86]

In Part Two we sketched out a three-part process by which Christian Socialists believed socialism would be brought about: first, persuasion of the deficiencies of capitalism and the need for a socialist alternative; secondly, the election of Labour to a position of power (or the 'conversion' of those already in power to socialism); thirdly, with convinced socialists now in power, the reorganization of society by a socialist state. This presupposes the existence of a powerful state to bring socialism into being, and very little in Christian Socialist writing suggests that this state would fade away after the establishment of socialism.

However, Paul Bickley argues that 'the Christian Socialist tradition has tended towards a strong view of the diffusion of power and the redemption of social relationships through non-statist means. [. . .] The Christian tradition, like other ethical socialisms, is therefore disposed towards non-statist responses to the problem of economic and political disadvantage.'[87] He cites the example of Tawney, who was suspicious of the idea of a benign state ruling over the people, writing that '[h]owever the socialist ideal may be expressed, few things could be more remote from it than a herd of tame animals with wise rulers in command'.[88] Bickley argues that 'Tawney could never be at one with the Fabians or the Marxists, both of whom proposed to create social change through the agency of a powerful, "scientific" state. Tawney's vision was of human liberty and dignity in the context of accountability to a conception of the [common] good.'[89] This fits with Tawney's view that nationalization was not always a necessity, and that the important factor in industry was a sense of professional obligation.

There does seem to be some tension in Christian Socialist thought between ideas about the role of the state and ideas about the freedom of the individual. For example, John Clifford sets out five 'chief functions of the ideal state':

> (*a*) It should give liberty for the full utterance and development of the personality of every sane citizen of the commonwealth; (*b*) secure justice between man and man, and between all organisations of men within the State, so that there shall be fair play for each, and not the slightest shade of favouritism for any man as against another, or for any organisation as against another; (*c*) it should educate

and drill every child of the commonwealth for *citizenship*, so that the life of the State may be continued in health and prosperity, and the future well-being of the State may be continued in health and prosperity, and the future well-being of the State secured; (*d*) it should neutralise, and as far as may be destroy, everything that makes for strife and division in the commonwealth, and seek to unify the life of the citizens; and (*e*) it will show mercy to the poor and needy.[90]

Here Clifford sets out a vision which some might interpret as being a large and domineering state, powerful enough to 'educate and drill every child' in order to secure its own 'health and prosperity'. He also argues that Christians ought to 'seek with passionate ardour to incarnate a collective rather than an individualistic idea in society', and that socialism involves 'a State which shall exist for all and be served by all'.[91] However, Clifford's first 'chief function' is the liberty of individuals, and the state which is to 'be served by all' is also one which 'exist[s] for all'. Clifford argues that collectivism 'does not advocate the absorption of the individual by the State', and that the principles of collectivism 'must not be permitted to obliterate, or overwhelm, or fetter, the *freedom of the individual*'.[92] It was not that Clifford advocated a totalitarian state, but that – in Catterall's phrasing – he regarded the state as 'every bit as divinely ordained as the church'.[93]

The same tension is evident in the work of William Temple. According to Matthew Grimley, 'Henry Scott Holland and the young William Temple both drew on [Bernard] Bosanquet's idea that the individual only found full development in the state.' He then quotes Temple in *The Education of Citizens*: 'A man has no right to have his talents developed apart from his intention to devote them to the state, because his whole being is comprised in the fact that he is a member of the state. [. . .] The man is essentially and before all else a member of the state.'[94] The older William Temple still regarded the state as representing the community, and put forward as illustrations proposals which involved much state intervention; for example, 'Family allowances – perhaps in the form of food and clothes coupons having the value of money – should be paid by the State to the mother for every child after the first two'; and 'The State should maintain a certain number of works beneficial to the community, from which private enterprise should be excluded, which it would expand and contract according to the general demand for labour at any time'.[95]

However, in discussing the overreaction to capitalist individualism, Temple's view is that 'there was a tendency to swing over and lay all the emphasis upon the other note: community. Value was to be found in the whole society alone, not in its individual members, and this has found in the modern world two main expressions: Communism and Fascism, both of which are totalitarian.'[96] Elsewhere Temple declared: 'Man is the child of God [. . .] for whom, therefore, the State exists and not he for the State.'[97] This was also the view of Samuel Keeble, who argued that '[t]he State must act for the benefit of the citizens as a whole; if necessary at the expense of a few', but also that '[w]hen the individual is nothing and the State is everything, evils of all kinds arise.'[98]

Returning to Henry Scott Holland, he saw a reformed society as being that in which the state ensures freedom and justice, saying that '[w]e must have all we can get of State order, of State machinery'.[99] This is reflected in *Our Neighbours* in which Holland – quite at odds with Bickley's suggestion that Christian Socialism is 'disposed towards non-statist responses to the problem of economic and political disadvantage' – argues passionately for the acceptance of state power and authority. We have already seen Holland's view of the state as the means by which socialism can be carried out: 'We invoke the State, then. We call upon it to relieve our individual conscience by doing for us what we are powerless to do for ourselves.'[100] Holland foresaw a society in which the state is responsible for the creation of 'a social environment, a social atmosphere' conducive to justice and morality, as well as, more concretely, replacing the laissez-faire free market with a market which will, for instance, provide all workers with an adequate income.[101] Holland did not view the regulation that this would require as an imposition; rather, it provided freedom to those for whom free-market capitalism was an imposition. 'Law is Liberty', declared Holland, adding, 'Law will move forward so that it may slowly take up every corner of our social life and organise it according to the mind and interpretation of the brotherhood.'[102]

Holland's view of the state, however, was perhaps softened in later years; in a lecture during the early months of the First World War he spoke of being 'face to face with the notion of an absolute State that sweeps up all individual liberty', adding that the state is 'too huge, too remote, too abstract to allow us to find freedom in it'.[103] According to Wilkinson, Holland came to believe in smaller communities within the state that would help to sustain freedom and liberty.[104]

Keir Hardie also foresaw a key role for the state in a socialist society. Hardie's view was that the state represented the interests of the workers: 'To the Socialist, the State always means the People, and the People are the workers.'[105] From this we can conclude that when Hardie writes of 'land and industrial capital' being 'common property', in practice this requires state ownership. For example, Hardie argues that there is only 'one solution' to industrial disputes between railway owners and the workers: '[T]he State must own the railways.'[106] This is in keeping with the view that Hardie 'was a collectivist who wanted the state to run essential industries'.[107]

The same view could be attributed to George Lansbury. Lansbury sought 'the full control, by the whole people, over the means of creating and distributing wealth', but saw this role as belonging to the state: '[T]he whole evil is summed up in the word "profit", and that can only be wiped out by the State taking over all industries and working them not for profit, but to produce the things we need.'[108] It has been argued that Lansbury was 'an ardent supporter of state supremacy, and he went so far as to endorse the system of compulsion that was beginning to emerge in the Soviet Union'.[109]

Like Holland, Hardie saw the state as the provider of justice: 'Much may be left to the energy of the individual and the municipalities, but there is a minimum of humane living which it is in the interests of society to claim for every one of its members at the hands of the Central Government.'[110] Hardie and Lansbury therefore envisaged a state powerful enough to own land and industry, and provide 'a minimum of humane living' to all the people that it represented.

Finally, despite Bickley's description of Tawney as being suspicious of state power, he did not fear the state. Indeed, according to Anthony Wright, Tawney argued against both the Marxist claim that the state is essentially capitalist and Friedrich Hayek's claim that the state is essentially totalitarian.[111] As we have already seen, Tawney's view was that the state was simply a neutral force – an 'instrument, and nothing more' which could be used by whoever possessed it: 'Fools will use it, when they can, for foolish ends, criminals for criminal ends. Sensible and decent men will use it for ends which are sensible and decent.'[112] Tawney goes on to describe the state in the following terms:

> The faithful animal [which] will run our errands; fetch and carry for us; convey us on our journeys; attend our sick-beds; mind our children; show, on the rare occasions that we tell him, a handsome mouthful of sharp teeth, and generally behave like a useful and well-conducted cur. If he does not do his tricks nicely, we are quite capable of beating our own dog ourselves, as – to do him justice – he is well aware. It is really too much to expect us, at this time of day, to relapse into hysterics because some nervous professor has decided, on the grounds of high theory, that the harmless and obedient creatures, whom we have cursed, kicked and fondled all our lives, is in reality, not a dog at all, but a ferocious species of Siberian wolf.[113]

In this metaphor, Tawney views the state as able to perform a number of functions, including coercive functions – the dog's 'sharp teeth'. The state is also subject to control by the people, which fits in with the importance Tawney gives to democracy. Therefore, while Bickley is correct insofar as Tawney did not see the need for hands-on control by the state in every sphere of life, neither was Tawney opposed to the idea of a relatively powerful socialist state.

Conclusion

There is some difficulty in setting out the Christian Socialist vision of the state. For one thing, Christian Socialists – particularly but not necessarily those who were ministers of religion rather than politicians – appear reticent to commit themselves to clear and precise proposals. For another, even where such proposals are set out, it is not always obvious whether they are intended as reforms to capitalist society or as components of a future socialist society. Nevertheless, it is clear that – despite differences of emphasis on matters such as state control of industry – Christian Socialists were committed to cooperation and collectivism. While these may require a large and powerful state, Christian Socialists were not authoritarians who relegated the worth of the individual to the needs of the state. The state was merely an instrument which could represent the community.

8

Democracy, equality and conservatism

In the previous chapter we examined the nature of the cooperation and collectivism sought after by the Christian Socialists. In this chapter we shall consider some other elements of the imagined socialist society, observing that Christian Socialists sought to establish the principles of democracy and equality. We will also consider some of the conservative elements of Christian Socialist thought and whether Christian Socialism should be regarded as ideologically conservative.

Democracy

We have already seen that Christian Socialists, despite their revolutionary language, in practice sought a democratic route to socialism. However, democracy was not just the means by which socialism would be brought about, but would also be a feature of a socialist society. As R. H. Tawney put it:

> The question for Socialists is not merely whether the state owns and controls the means of production. It is also, and even more important, who owns and controls the state. Democracy, in one form or another, is, in short, not merely one of several alternative methods of establishing a Socialist commonwealth. It is an essential condition of such a commonwealth's existence.[1]

Tawney argued that undemocratic socialism would never gain enough support to be workable, writing that socialists 'must face the fact that, if the public, and particularly the working-class public, is confronted with the choice between capitalist democracy, with all its nauseous insincerities, and undemocratic socialism they will choose the former every time. They must make it clear beyond the possibility of doubt that the socialist commonwealth which they preach will be built on democratic foundations.'[2]

Not all the Christian Socialists offer an extensive discussion of democracy in their work, but a commitment to democratic principles is implied in what they say and do. John Shepherd points to George Lansbury's 'unbridled passion for social justice and unshakable belief in democracy'.[3] This can be seen in, for example, Lansbury's desire to see self-rule given to India and Ireland as well as his support for the abolition of the hereditary House of Lords. Lansbury foresaw the extension of democracy via the creation of separate parliaments for England, Wales and Scotland, as well as Ireland.[4] Lansbury's support for female suffrage, a topic to which we shall return, also points to his high view of democracy; the same can be said of Margaret Bondfield and Ellen Wilkinson. Stewart Headlam also called for the abolition of the House of Lords, while John Clifford was a critic of the upper chamber, arguing against the Lords' veto.[5] This was also the view of Wilkinson: 'In a country that calls itself a democracy it is scandalous that an unelected revising chamber can be tolerated in which the Conservative Party has such a permanent and overwhelming majority.'[6]

In a similar way, James Keir Hardie's favourable view of democracy is implied by his opposition to the undemocratic institution of monarchy.[7] On the birth of the future Edward VIII, Hardie made clear his opposition in the House of Commons:

> We are asked to rejoice because this child has been born, and that one day he will be called upon to rule over this great Empire. Up to the present time we have no means of knowing what his qualifications or fitness for that task may be. It certainly strikes me – I do not know how it strikes others – as rather strange that those who have so much to say about the hereditary element in another place should be so willing to endorse it in this particular instance. It seems to me that if it is a good argument to say that the hereditary element is bad in one case, it is an equally good argument to say that it is bad in the other.[8]

Here Hardie makes the point that the future ruler of the country may not be qualified to do so, and argues that if the hereditary House of Lords is to be opposed on the grounds of being undemocratic, then the monarchy must logically be opposed on the same grounds. The commitment to democracy of Lansbury, Clifford, Wilkinson and Hardie is therefore evident.

Why did Christian Socialists commit themselves to democracy? Henry Scott Holland viewed it as an important safeguard if more and more power was to be left in the hands of the state:

> [T]he only safety and resource lies in trusting a nation to make its own Laws [. . .] only under democracy can we afford to put out the amount of Legislation

which our industrial situation necessitates. Any such minute regulation of the incessant details of daily labour would appear as an intolerable tyranny if any other authority than the workers' own attempted to impose it.[9]

Holland's view was that the 'Government, which actually legislates and administers, through chosen representatives and qualified experts, must find its authoritative momentum in the living beings who lie behind it – in those very multitudes to whom its legislation is applied and whose interests it is to serve. Then, there will be nothing imposed; there will be no ideal dictated: there will be no artificial forcing.'[10]

William Temple did not accept that democracy was a result of the people's sovereignty, as only God is and should be considered sovereign.[11] However, he nevertheless did believe that democracy was the best system; by calling upon everybody to take a share in the responsibility of government democracy encouraged fellowship within society.[12] Democracy, though, must exist in subservience to the revealed will of God and be governed by Christian principles.[13] This was also the view of Samuel Keeble, who favoured democracy but also argued that 'all forms of government should endeavour to become theocratic, in the sense that they explicitly acknowledge, by deed and not merely word, the ultimate authority of the moral law and the revealed will of God'.[14]

R. H Tawney's commitment to democracy went deeper, insofar as he viewed democracy not just as a political system but a principle which should pervade the whole of society. Tawney 'did not – first and foremost – advocate extensive public ownership or welfarism, but the extension of democracy into areas of life that had hitherto escaped its influence'.[15] This was the point Tawney made in a lecture in 1941 in the United States, telling his audience that socialism meant 'the extension of democracy from the sphere of government and law to that of economic life. Arbitrary economic power, exercised for purposes of personal profit is as incompatible with democracy as arbitrary political power.'[16] Tawney elsewhere made the related argument that 'democracy is unstable as a political system, as long as it remains a political system and nothing more, instead of being, as it should be, not only a form of government, but a type of society, and a manner of life which is in harmony with that type'.[17]

This included the extension of democracy into industrial life, and – in one form or another – workers having control over their own industry. Tawney therefore argues that industries ought to have 'a constitution securing [their] members an effective voice in its government', and that '[w]hat is required is not simply to limit the power of Capital to impose terms upon Labour, but to make the workers, not the capitalist, the centre of industrial authority', albeit 'subject to such limitations upon their sovereignty as may be imposed in the interests of the community as a whole'.[18] This was also the view of Bondfield, who argued:

> Socialism involves the re-organisation of society on the basis of both political and industrial democracy. [. . .] The public ownership of industry, without democratic administration by the workers engaged therein, whilst superior to the existing system of private ownership and control, would not of itself provide that intelligent co-operation in the new social order or that sense of freedom which Socialism involves.[19]

Bondfield and Tawney therefore foresaw a situation in which organizations within democracy were themselves democratic.

Equality

Christian Socialists, as might be expected, foresaw a society in which the principle of equality was enshrined. As George Lansbury explained, 'true social co-operation means that we each give our very best, whether of brain power or manual power, for the service of mankind, and thus by equal service make it possible, so far as material things are concerned, equality of life for all'.[20] Keir Hardie's socialism, for example, has been described as 'egalitarian':[21]

> Hardie's socialism was essentially about equality. All people had a right to help shape a new kind of society. They could use their powers to achieve a more equal society by the public ownership of essential industries and just redistribution of goods between individuals. This material equality would occur when members were bound to each other by a commitment to the common good. This mutuality, this caring for each other, this fraternity, was the heart of socialism. And it extended to other races and so promoted peace.[22]

Hardie imagined that '[u]nder Socialism there would be no exploiting class, no tyranny of one sex or race over another. Socialism would give reality to the claim so often insisted upon from the Christian pulpit, and yet so universally belied by our every day deeds, that God hath made of one blood all nations of the earth to dwell together in unity.'[23]

Hardie here suggests that human equality is based on a common status as God's created beings. R. H. Tawney's view was similar, described as being that '[s]ince all men were the children of God, each of infinitely precious, an end not a means, rich in the possibilities for self-development, brothers and sisters in a shared humanity and a common civilisation. This is what is described here as Tawney's principle of equal worth.'[24] Samuel Keeble made the same argument: 'Men are brothers, whether rich or poor, masters or men, high or low, white or coloured [sic]. They are equally the children of the heavenly father.'[25] Bondfield 'saw all humanity as the children of God, equal in His eyes'.[26] This was also the view of William Temple, who wrote that

> apart from faith in God there is really nothing to be said for the notion of human equality. Men do not seem to be equal in any respect, if we judge by available evidence. But if all are children of one Father, then all are equal heirs of a status in comparison with which the apparent differences of quality and capacity are unimportant; in the deepest and most important of all – their relationship to God – all are equal.[27]

Hardie explained that socialism 'does not assume that all are alike, but only that all are equal'.[28] This was the same view expressed by Tawney in *Equality*:

> When the French [. . .] set [equality] side by side with liberty and fraternity as the motto of a new world, they did not mean that all men are equally intelligent or equally virtuous, any more than they are equally tall or equally fat, but that the unity of their national life should no longer be torn to pieces by obsolete property rights and meaningless juristic distinctions. [. . .] When Arnold [. . .] wrote 'choose equality', he did not suggest, it may be suspected, that all children appeared to him to be equally clever, but that a nation acts unwisely in stressing heavily distinctions based on birth or money.[29]

Equality, therefore, does not mean that everything or everyone must be the same. Lansbury, for example, writes: 'I do not mean "equality" in the sense of everybody having to do the same kind of work, but I do mean that men and women who toil shall receive the full fruits of their toil.'[30] Tawney imagines society in the same way:

> It is possible to conceive a community in which the necessary diversity of economic functions existed side by side with a large measure of economic and social equality. In such a community, while the occupations and incomes of individuals varied, they would live, nevertheless, in much the same environment, would enjoy similar standards of health and education, would find different positions, according to their varying abilities, equally accessible to them, would intermarry freely with each other, would be equally immune from the more degrading forms of poverty, and equally secure against economic oppression.[31]

Tawney also argued, not for strict equality of incomes, but rather for 'the pooling of [the nation's] surplus resources by means of taxation, and the use of the funds thus obtained to make accessible to all, irrespective of their income'.[32] The Christian Socialist notion of equality was therefore one of formal or legal equality based on equal worth, alongside policies to diminish the extent of inequality of outcome.

Tawney argued for the former, suggesting that '[t]he true meaning of equality, in short, is uniformity of legal rights. In this sense, and in this sense alone, is it proper to seek, or possible, to obtain it'.[33] Similarly, Keeble called for '[e]quality before the law, equal freedom, equal opportunities in the vital things of civilization', as well as 'equality of consideration, and equality of privilege'.[34] Tawney and Keeble may have disagreed over Keeble's phrase 'equal opportunities'. Tawney felt that 'equality of opportunity' was meaningless in a society without equality: 'As though opportunities for talent to rise could be equalized in a society where the circumstances surrounding from birth are themselves unequal!'[35] However, despite his phrasing here it is not evident that Keeble sought merely equality of opportunity without seeking greater equality of outcome.

Most Christian Socialist calls for equality can be divided into three areas: sexual equality; racial and international equality; and class equality. John Clifford wrote that

> the false idea of the inequality of the sexes has wrought incalculable mischief to the world through the injustice it has inflicted on women, refusing to them an equal share in the legislation and administrative activities of the State, holding back equal pay for equal work with men; refusing equal marriage and divorce laws, and equal municipal and political responsibilities and privileges.[36]

Keir Hardie argued that '[o]urs is the one political movement where women stand on terms of perfect equality with men'.[37] Stewart Headlam wrote of his concern that Labour would provide only for the needs of the male working class, thereby excluding women and their needs.[38] Keir Hardie, for one, would presumably have disagreed with Headlam; both would agree that socialism should result in sexual equality, but while Hardie saw the Labour Party as the vehicle for socialism, Headlam made a distinction between socialism and 'Labourism'.

Hardie saw in socialism a call for sexual equality and argued that socialism would free women by removing their financial dependence upon men.[39] George Lansbury argued against any view of women as being inferior to men: 'We must also set our faces against all theories of inferiority where women are concerned: we must declare with unceasing insistence that motherhood and home-making are great services; above all, that women's life and work together with man's shall be recognised as of value to the State.'[40] Both Hardie and Lansbury expressed their view of sexual equality by campaigning in support of female suffrage. Hardie argued for the importance of women having the right to vote within the ILP, and both 'Hardie and Lansbury criticized Labour's failure unanimously to support the women's cause or condemn the force-feeding of women'.[41] Lansbury argued that 'political power should be in the hands of women as well as men'.[42] In 1912 he resigned his Bow and Bromley Parliamentary seat in order to fight a by-election on the issue of enfranchising women, and the following year was imprisoned following a speech made in support of suffragette tactics.[43] Hardie resigned from the Labour Party executive in order to fight for Lansbury in the 1912 by-election.[44]

Margaret Bondfield and Ellen Wilkinson were of course both suffragist campaigners – Wilkinson early in her career was a full-time organizer for the National Union of Women's Suffrage Societies and Bondfield was the president of the Adult Suffrage Society.[45] Both, however, saw suffrage campaigns as part of a wider struggle for equality and social change; in Bondfield's case this caused a division between her and Sylvia Pankhurst.[46] 'Bondfield', it is argued, 'was not a feminist in the modern sense, nor even in the sense it was understood at the time. She was opposed to all forms of gender discrimination, not just because it was aimed at women but because it also affected everyone within the working class.'[47] Wilkinson, described as a 'class-conscious feminist', argued on being elected to Parliament that 'I have women's interests to look after, but I do not want to be regarded purely as a woman's MP [. . .] men voters predominate in Middlesbrough East, thousands are unemployed, and I mean to stand up to the gruelling work for all their sakes'.[48] Nevertheless,

> Nothing affecting women was too insignificant for Ellen's attention. She exposed the iniquitous decision refusing pensions to nursing staff who had suffered mental breakdowns from war service; derided the illogicality of women being barred from the diplomatic corps on grounds of their alleged inability to keep a secret as 'a relic of masculine prejudice'; conducted a protracted, ultimately triumphant, campaign to enable British women who married aliens to retain their British citizenship; chided the government for not appointing a working-class woman to serve on the Food Committee; and attacked Winston Churchill, when Chancellor of the Exchequer, for taxing cheap artificial silk 'on which working class girls so greatly relied for their clothing'.[49]

Nor were they only ones to support women's rights and female suffrage. John Clifford, for one, 'was always on the side of enfranchisement of women'.[50] Samuel Keeble, for another, called for 'full civic and legal recognition' for women, for

> they are equally important members of the community with men, and have their own rights and duties in relation to the community as such. They are under its laws, and profit or suffer by civic development and change quite as much as, if not more than, men. They are, as sisters, wives, and mothers, as well as workers, and often property-owners, a vital portion of the civic community, and should be legally recognised as such, with the full rights of citizenship. There certainly cannot now be any healthy and progressive civic life where women do not claim, receive, and exercise equal civic rights and duties with men.[51]

Elsewhere Keeble called for 'Justice to Women', pointing to

> legal injustices in matters of divorce and property; political injustices, in matters of citizen rights and duties, and the franchise; industrial injustices, in sweating, defective factory laws and inspection, in the employment of married women, especially mothers, in the denial of equal remuneration with men for absolutely equal services; social injustices, in the prevalence of two standards of morality for the sexes – the more lenient for the not less guilty sinner, the man.[52]

However, it is not certain that all Christian Socialists viewed sexual equality as being of such great importance. R. H. Tawney has been criticized for the lack of references to women in his work. Tawney wrote of an imaginary 'Henry Dubb', the archetypal working-class man, a reference played upon by his biographer Anthony Wright: 'Where, by the way, is the female Dubb in Tawney's universe? There are far too many "men" in his socialist argument [. . .] and a conspicuous absence of women (except, when needed, as wives, mothers and children). No doubt he meant to write about human beings, but he actually wrote about men.'[53] This criticism is echoed by Alan Wilkinson.[54] However, it would be wrong to argue from silence that Tawney was not in favour of sexual equality.

Another biographer points to a letter Tawney wrote to a friend from Baliol, in which he wrote that he was 'plagued with old ladies' who ask him his views on female suffrage, 'which are that women are all fools, that all women over 30 are damned fools, & that anyhow injustice is the best policy'. This, however, is defended as 'knockabout student stuff, a display of bravado and self-mockery, and probably of no consequence in a political context'.[55] It is probably fair to say that a genuine argument against female suffrage would not refer to 'injustice' being 'the best policy'. It should be noted that Tawney 'protested in 1933 when the University of Liverpool slipped into women's contracts the stipulation that they must resign from the teaching staff on marriage'. He also 'gave support to a campaign to raise funds for Hillcroft, the women's adult education college in Surbiton'.⁵⁶ Tawney's calls for equality can certainly be interpreted as including women; for example, Tawney's picture of a 'society which [. . .] holds that the most important aspect of *human beings* is not the external differences of income and circumstance that divide them, *but the common humanity that unites them*, and which strives, therefore, to reduce such differences to the position of insignificance that rightly belongs to them'. This, according to Tawney, is the 'society which British socialists are labouring to create', as evidenced by the campaigning of Hardie and Lansbury.⁵⁷

It is also evident that Christian Socialists believed in racial and national equality. George Lansbury argued: 'This Labour Movement of ours stands in a very real sense for the uplifting of the people of all races and classes.'⁵⁸ To Lansbury, 'the mere accident of being born in a special part of the globe should not confer any special privilege or power upon anyone'.⁵⁹ Keir Hardie explained that the 'exploitation of the coloured [*sic*] races by the whites is just as obnoxious to the Socialist as is the exploitation of the poor by the rich'.⁶⁰ 'When Indian can meet European as a fully enfranchised equal', wrote Hardie, 'and compel that respect which is his due, then, and not before, will race prejudice begin to die out and finally to disappear'.⁶¹ Samuel Keeble described a true, Christian patriotism, which involved 'the love of other countries, as much as is the love of one's own home'.⁶² John Clifford, similarly, declared in stark language that 'I do not care for the brotherliness that goes out to Timbuctoo and forgets the starving poor in Paddington; nor do I value highly the patriotism that talks incessantly of the workless in London, and is dumb as death about the atrocities in Armenia, and the lynching of negroes in the Southern States of America'.⁶³ Wilkinson argued that it should be made an offence for hotels to refuse 'coloured [*sic*] guests' while Bondfield declared: 'Today our outlook is international. We have many close friendships in all parts of the world with workers whose hopes and aspirations are the same as ours.'⁶⁴

Peter d'A Jones describes the Christian Socialist attitude to the British Empire: 'Colonial expansion was the one object of censure common to almost all Christian socialists' who, like other socialists and liberals, viewed the Empire as an instrument of capitalist oppression.⁶⁵ However, Christian Socialists did not seek to abolish the Empire as such; rather, they sought to convert it into a Socialist Commonwealth: 'In relation to the Empire leading Leftists such as George Lansbury and John Wheatley now argued that Labour should seek to transform the area under British protection into a commonwealth based on socialist principles which, in contrast to the competitive, bellicose world of capitalism, would represent a new co-operative idea of international relations.'[66] As George Lansbury explained:

> It is true we do not desire to maintain an Empire built on force, domination and exploitation: every such Empire of the past has perished. We love our own land and mean to rule ourselves: we think other peoples who love their land should enjoy the same right. Therefore we urge the workers of Britain, now they have the power, to transform the Empire into a commonwealth within which the so-called subject races shall become partners and comrades.[67]

'There is no reason for breaking up the British Empire', argued Lansbury, 'any more than there is reason for smashing our own national institutions. Our duty is to transform the British Empire of Domination into a Commonwealth of free nations, including within this Commonwealth those people who desire to join with us.'[68] Similar views were held by Hardie, who, 'was not opposed to imperialism as such, merely to its militarist and undemocratic form'.[69]

Lansbury went a step further in arguing for a commonwealth, not just of those countries within the British Empire, but also of 'a commonwealth of all the nations of the world, in which shall cease not merely ugly war, but also the internecine strife of competitive commercialism'.[70] Similarly, Keeble – criticizing the League of Nations as a 'League of Victors' – argued that the League ought to be reformed, allowing all countries to be a part of it.[71] William Temple also sought an international commonwealth, but based more explicitly on Christianity; Temple's 'aim was for the voluntary acceptance of a kind of ecumenical Christian commonwealth on a national and international scale'.[72] Lansbury's view – expressed in the memorandum for a meeting with Adolf Hitler as part of his ill-fated peace campaign, to which we shall return – is that 'an effort must be made to treat the world as an economic unity, all nations understanding that the prosperity of each means the prosperity of all'.[73] We can therefore conclude that the vision of a Christian Socialist future was one of racial equality and international cooperation.

While it might be imagined that Christian Socialists argued for the supremacy of the working class, it seems instead that they argued for class equality. This was a theme in the work of Stewart Headlam, especially in *The Socialist's Church*. Headlam argued that the working class and the middle class were both wage slaves, and that as such working-class and middle-class interests are 'identical'; the word 'worker' should therefore refer to 'all those who with brain or hand are producing something adequate in return for what they consume'.[74] Headlam foresaw 'a Society which knows no class distinction'.[75] It could be assumed that Headlam's views derive from his own middle-class background and his opposition to the Labour Party. Here he points to 'the danger of exalting the working class above the other workers who do not belong to the "working class"', adding that 'Labourism, for instance, is an unnecessary challenge to the middle classes, who stand to gain largely by Socialism, but who for the most part do not know this, and who think they are attacking Socialism, while really what they are attacking is class legislation in the interest of "Labour"'.[76]

However, the same sentiments are shared by other Christian Socialists. Catterall points out that 'Free Churchmen in the [Labour] party were generally happier emphasizing love, goodwill, and common humanity than class or nation', adding that 'This was not least true of Independent Methodists like Wellock'.[77] Keir Hardie's view was that 'Socialism makes war upon a system, not upon a class'.[78] According to James Maxton, Hardie 'wrote critically of the conception of the class struggle as a motive for social change'.[79] It is certainly true that, like Headlam, Hardie argued that '[t]he term "working class" is not used in any restricted sense, but includes all who by head or hand are rendering useful service to the community'.[80] Like Headlam, Hardie foresaw a classless society, writing that socialism 'will one day abolish class distinctions'.[81] This was for two reasons. First, there would be no private ownership of property: 'When the property-less working class has made all capitalistic property public property, then classes will have disappeared , since that which now divides a community into classes, the private ownership of property, will have disappeared.'[82] Secondly, everybody would be engaged in 'useful service to the community', and therefore everybody would be part of the working class: 'When the modern industrial movement reaches fruition, land, capital, and the State itself shall be owned and controlled by the useful classes. There shall no longer be an exploiting class left to reduce the workers again to penury and want.'[83] Hardie even agreed with Headlam's view of the middle class as being oppressed by capital, going still further by including the 'upper classes':

> The poverty of the poorer, the business of the middle, and the wealth of the upper classes, are but different forms of bondage. Socialism has its message of freedom for all three, To the poor it offers release from the bondage of thankless toil and harassing poverty; to the middle class it promises freedom from the tyranny of the market, and to the rich it holds out the hope of joy in life in exchange for the burden of property.[84]

To Hardie then, just as much as to Headlam, socialism meant good news to all classes and sections of society. For this reason Hardie happily reports that 'men and women from all ranks and classes of society are casting their lot in with the workers'.[85]

R. H. Tawney agrees with Headlam and Hardie that there should not be a narrow understanding of who was and was not a worker. Tawney regarded manual workers and managers as being 'different grades of workers', adding that 'an equilibrium between worker and manager is possible, because both are workers'.[86] This, however, was not the case for owners who performed no workplace function; because he performed no function, such an owner should not be considered a worker: 'Joint councils between workers and managers may succeed, but joint councils between workers and owners or agents of owners [. . .] will not, because the necessity for the mere owner is itself one of the points in dispute'.[87] Tawney's vision of society is one in which there would be no functionless owners or masters, but those who worked at management and organization would take their 'proper place as one worker among others'.[88] In 'The Choice before the Labour Party' Tawney argued that the business of the party ought not to be 'the passage of a series of reforms in the interests of different sections of the working classes'. In this he would have found the agreement of Stewart Headlam. 'It is', Tawney continues, 'to abolish all advantages and disabilities which have their source, not in differences of personal quality, but in disparities of wealth, opportunity, social position and economic power. It is, in short – it is absurd that at this time of day the statement should be necessary – a classless society'.[89]

For Tawney, the equality of people regardless of class meant that there should be no inequality in education, and that all children should be able to attend the same schools. Tawney argued that the 'English educational system will never be one worthy of a civilized society until the children of all classes in the nation attend the same schools'.[90] This view was shared by William Temple, who argued that the existence of private schools 'makes a cleavage in the educational and social life of the country as a whole', adding that 'it should be possible for children from every kind of home to come into any kind of school provided that they are qualified by mental, physical and personal talents'.[91]

Wilfred Wellock was another who made this equality of classes a key theme in his work, and 'saw the basic evil of capital as a moral or spiritual one, shared by capitalists and workers alike'.[92] In *Christian Communism* Wellock argued that '[i]t ought not to be forgotten that for the most part [capitalists] are the victims of circumstances, of a fatally false view of life, inculcated in the home, the church, in school and college, in consequence of which they have, though in a quite different way, as much to gain by resort to Communism as have the workers'.

'Communism', he declared, 'is the condition of well-being to the capitalists no less than the workers'.[93] Wellock believed that capitalists would eventually come to accept the immorality of capitalism and would therefore assist in the creation of a new society and their part in it.[94]

This was also the view of Samuel Keeble, who argued that 'the interests of Capital and Labour are identical – certainly all their permanent interests are, if their temporary interests are not, and therefore their strife is suicidal as well as fratricidal'.[95] Yet, like Wellock, Keeble was optimistic that this strife would pass, for the labourer 'has friends even among the capitalists themselves [. . .] this is perhaps the most hopeful sign of all, for when there are searchings of heart in the very camp of the enemy, victory is not distant'.[96] George Lansbury sought 'to rouse an entirely different spirit, that recognises our common brotherhood and the unity of all life, rather than insist upon the rights and righteousness of one's own class as against the others'.[97] Lansbury perhaps sums up the Christian Socialist attitude to class equality: 'Our Party is not a class or a sect. It comprises the whole mass of the nation. For to our ranks we welcome all who work, whether by hand or brain: the only test of membership is willingness to serve.'[98]

Conservatism

There are elements of conservatism in Christian Socialist thinking. These relate to family, marriage and sexuality; alcohol; and in some instances the poor and unemployed. Margaret Bondfield, for example, is described as having a social conservatism – albeit, 'social conservatism allied to political radicalism' – derived from her Congregationalist upbringing; she 'could not abide alcohol or drunkenness, or behaviour deemed immoral in any form'.[99] In some cases the tag of conservative could be applied simply due to moderation, from, as an example, Henry Scott Holland's CSU. Jones points out that 'the CSU fell far short of what is traditionally regarded as socialism'.[100] This may not have been by design, but rather because of a focus on theological issues and matters such as religious education rather than on economics. Chris Bryant suggests this was a difference between the CSU and Stewart Headlam's Guild of St Matthew, 'with the Union far less certain than the Guild about any direct commitment to redistribution or economic socialism'.[101]

In 1897 John Carter, the secretary of the CSU, described the union's position as being that 'it should always be possible for a sincere Christian to be either a good Tory or a good radical, or even an honest Socialist or a moral

Individualist'.[102] In 1905 a CSU pamphlet on *Socialism* argued that '[i]n most countries, Socialism is a hostile movement of the lower classes against the upper; in England it is rather a benevolent movement of the upper classes towards the lower'.[103] In 1906 the CSU's executive included both a Liberal and a Tory MP, but no representative from the Labour Party.[104] By 1909 'rival Christian socialists were complaining of the Union's conservatism'.[105] In 1911 Henry Scott Holland wrote that 'we have not got to take a Competitive Society to pieces and reconstruct it on Co-operative lines. All that is needed is that we should emphasise again, and release into full play, the Co-operative powers which are already and always in action.'[106]

According to Alan Wilkinson, '[t]he CSU envisaged society as a partnership in which consumers would exercise ethical discrimination in purchasing; management would cooperate for the common good; and the state or city would act to regulate conditions and in some cases provide services'.[107] On the face of it this seems a similar vision that that imagined by R. H. Tawney. However, Tawney wanted to identify and remove those owners of property who provided no service and performed no function, leaving only 'managers' who actually worked for a living; there is no evidence that the CSU sought to do likewise. Perhaps then Tawney's vision can be defended as socialist, but the CSU's, as Jones puts it, falls short. Wilkinson, however, makes the case for the CSU's 'right to be included in the socialist tradition'.[108] Nevertheless, there was a conservative element in the thought of Holland and the CSU which prevented a full and unflinching commitment to socialism.

The same could be said of Stewart Headlam and the Guild of St Matthew, though in Bryant's view the Guild made more of a commitment to socialism than the CSU. If anything Headlam was more bitterly opposed to Labour than the CSU, who were open to different political parties. However, as we have seen, Headlam's opposition was not because he was opposed to economic socialism, but because he differentiated between socialism and that which was proposed for the benefit of trade unions and working-class men. Samuel Keeble helped to found the Wesleyan Methodist Union of Social Service, one of a number of organizations influenced by the CSU. Similarly, the Methodist Union aimed at 'social reform without socialism', and while it 'continued to influence the Church towards a social outlook, it was one increasingly divorced from that of the Christian Socialism that Keeble championed'.[109] However, we will see that Keeble himself demonstrated some conservative traits in his thinking.

Christian Socialists often had conservative ideas about marriage and sexuality. In this is shown most clearly the influence of religious belief: John Wheatley, for example, as a devout Roman Catholic refused to support a campaign to improve education about and supply of contraceptives.[110] Ellen Wilkinson despite her feminism did not become involved in the campaign – though this may have been out of sensitivity to the views of her Roman Catholic constituents rather than out of personal religious convictions.[111] William Temple argued that venereal disease would be almost completely eliminated if men and women ceased to practice 'illicit sexual intercourse' or 'fornication', adding that this behaviour ought to be 'something that arouses the condemnation of all decent citizens'.[112] Temple stated plainly that '[a]ll sexual indulgence outside matrimony is contrary to God's law and is sin'.[113] Samuel Keeble records that one of the resolutions to come from Temple's Conference on Christian Politics, Economics and Citizenship was that 'young people should receive instruction in the matters of sex, and in the nature of Christian marriage'.[114]

Keeble's view was that while 'Socialism threatens the family and the Church, and through them morality and religion, Christian Socialism cleaves close to them both'.[115] Keeble argued that 'Christians can never support those who extend the doctrine of all things in common to wives', adding: '"Free love", or unions and separations at will [. . .] mean the reign of animal passion and vice, the degradation of women and the abolition of family life.'[116] However, Keeble also suggested that capitalism was just as much an enemy to family life, Christian marriage and the status of women as non-Christian socialism.[117] Stewart Headlam argued that under capitalism it was as hard to make a good marriage as Ruskin and Morris had pointed out it was to make a good chair. Marriage, however, 'cannot be conveniently socialized, while Chairmaking might be'. According to Headlam, 'free love' had 'nothing at all to do with Socialism, which simply aims at the tremendous revolution of getting the great means of production out of the Monopolists and into the hands of the people'.[118]

George Lansbury was willing to countenance the possibility of legal divorce in Russia and elsewhere, but only, it seems, with great reluctance, re-affirming his personal belief in the sanctity of marriage:

> The longer I live the more convinced monogamist I am, but, and it is a very big but, I have seen so much downright misery, so much deceit and lying makebelieve by married people trying to make the outside world believe they love one another, when indeed they detest each other, that I support any rational means whereby such people may secure freedom from a tie which only degrades them both. [. . .] In Russia and elsewhere the Church considers marriage a sacrament and binding for life; so do I, but this cannot be imposed by a law or a Church ordinance or a priest saying it is.[119]

Keir Hardie also 'stressed the values of family life'.[120] There may well be a hint of Hardie's conservatism when he wrote of Stewart Headlam that '[a]s a Scotsman and a Nonconformist, I well remember the shock it gave me that the leading member of the Guild divided his attention fairly evenly between socialism and the ballet'.[121] Headlam caused a great deal of controversy when he assisted in posting bail for Oscar Wilde. In this he demonstrated his own liberalism, but also the conservatism of the other members of the Guild. One called for a new leader who 'would make it very clear that the Guild rejected doctrines subversive of Christian marriage'.[122] Another, Charles Marson, mocked Headlam, declaring that it should be possible to build a new Jerusalem 'without wading through Gomorrah first'.[123]

Another area in which Christian Socialists displayed quite a conservative attitude was alcohol. Bondfield, as noted earlier, did not drink. Keir Hardie was a lifelong teetotaller, who entered politics by campaigning for temperance: 'When a man is so lost to moral control and to decency as to become a slave to a degrading influence in liquor he thereby forfeits his claim to be regarded as a responsible being fit to be entrusted with the duties of citizenship.'[124] Hardie also wanted 'the community' to have 'the right to declare the liquor trade a public nuisance, and as such to be voted out of existence'.[125] Hardie's ideas about drinking did change slightly; originally he regarded drinking as a cause of poverty, but later came to regard both as symptomatic of capitalism – 'drunkenness, like gambling, immorality, and profligacy generally, is but a symptom of a more deeply-seated disease [. . .] the cause is unnatural, anti-human, respect-destroying conditions by which man is surrounded and, if the diagnosis be correct, the true remedy is to be found in cleansing our moral sewers of the poisons which selfishness and Mammon-worship have tainted them'.[126]

John Wheatley was also an abstainer from alcohol, and while an MP voted in favour of prohibition.[127] Keeble was another fierce opponent of drinking, arguing that 'it is utterly immoral to waste money required for necessities in drink' and that 'working men should avoid drink as an enemy'.[128] Keeble did not call for absolute prohibition, but came very close to it: 'Drink reform should occupy a very prominent place in the workers' programme. It should begin with the work of moral suasion. [. . .] Then the movement should work up to the most desirable end of reducing the number of legalized temptations to drink and strictly controlling the drink-trade.'[129] Keeble also makes the startling argument that '[i]f the resources already wasted in drink and gambling had been used by the working classes for the amelioration of their own condition and the strengthening of their own social and industrial position, they would have been in a state of prosperity today'.[130] This is the kind of argument that Hardie might have made early in his career, but later rejected.

Other Christian Socialists were not quite as stern regarding the consumption of alcohol. Lansbury was himself a teetotaller for most of his life and included in one of his early election platforms a commitment to public control of liquor traffic.[131] He also sought – unsuccessfully – to revive a pledge first introduced by Hardie by which Labour MPs committed to abstaining from alcohol during the sitting of Parliament.[132] Lansbury, however, was also criticized for allowing as the First Commissioner for Works the serving of alcohol at Hyde Park Lido, and late in life drank occasional glasses of wine for medical purposes.[133] R. H. Tawney's view was that the socialist society should not be

> a herd of tame, well-nourished animals, with wise keepers in command. It is a community of responsible men and women working without fear in comradeship for common ends, all of whom can grow to their full stature, develop to the utmost limit the varying capacities with which nature has endowed them, and – since virtue should not be too austere – have their fling when they feel like it.[134]

The church pastored by John Clifford ran a temperance bar known as Clifford's Inn, and Clifford himself was an advocate of temperance. However, he was also critical of those whose moral code consisted solely of 'a series of negative commandments, such as "Don't bet", "Don't drink", "Don't cheat", "Don't swear"', and who seemed to suggest that 'on these and their like hangs all the law of human safety and progress'.[135] Stewart Headlam believed that men could be encouraged to drink less – for example, by making work healthy and pleasurable – but that full prohibition was 'unchristian'.[136] 'People drink too much', argued Headlam,

> because they have failed to realise how many and various are the delightful pleasures to be got out of life: yet only a few years ago there were serious religious people who told you that you must not dance, you must not play cards, you must not go to theatres, except perhaps for one or two, that you must certainly never go to music halls.[137]

Not all Christian Socialists, therefore, were completely opposed to the consumption of alcohol, or prioritized their opposition to it.

Christian Socialists could also demonstrate conservative attitudes towards the poor and unemployed. We have already seen Keeble arguing that the working class might have improved its position had men not given themselves so much to alcohol. For Keeble this was true not only of drinking, but also of other vices.

'Much of the poverty of the lower labouring classes is self-caused', he declared, 'caused by sheer laziness, by drink, gambling, and vicious living.' Keeble argued that this applied to what he termed the 'idle class', a group distinct from the presumably more virtuous working class.[138] It is perhaps surprising to hear this from one who has been identified as a socialist, who professed some admiration for Marx, and who in the same book called for 'the elevation of the working classes by putting them in full possession of the product of their labours, and therefore of themselves'.[139] However, Keeble's views were more balanced than the above may suggest. Poverty, he suggested, also 'comes to many who have no bad and many good habits, who are literally the *victims* of poverty'. Keeble complained that 'honest, willing, industrious men cannot earn their bread because they find no work to do', adding that of the 'million of the unemployed amongst us, only a small proportion are "wastrels"', and that due to research into the causes of poverty 'the old cry that the unemployed are drinkers, idlers, loafers, inefficient, and ne'er-do-wells is finally silenced'.[140]

If some of Keeble's views are surprising then it is still more surprising to see similar sentiments expressed by George Lansbury. Lansbury argued that there should be 'no sympathy either with the rich loafer or the poor loafer. We want all men of the country to do their share of the work of the community.'[141] Lansbury favoured the setting up of labour colonies for the long-term unemployed, succeeding in setting up two of these at Laindon and Hollesey Bay, and suggesting that, in the labour colony, 'the man or woman refusing to work should simply not eat'.[142] Keir Hardie was also a supporter of this idea.[143] Again, Lansbury wrote that 'if each county or town had its labour colony, all tramps should be sent there [. . .] in every case no penal task should be enforced, simply ordinary work under ordinary conditions, and for punishment I should say, "No work, no food"'.[144] Lansbury applied a similar principle in his own business. When men came seeking employment they would be offered an immediate start, and if they sought to delay beginning work Lansbury would not employ them; a reporter explained that 'he never believes a man wanted work unless he was willing to start at once'.[145] Lansbury, however, did not believe that most men would refuse work, pointing to the example of around one hundred men who were sent from the Poplar Workhouse to work in Essex: 'Of the whole number sent, only some half a dozen proved wasters.'[146] Nevertheless, both Lansbury and Keeble demonstrate some conservative views about the poor and unemployed: that in at least some cases their problems were self-caused, the result of laziness and immoral living. It should be noted here that such statements may not fully reflect the views of Keeble, Lansbury or Hardie; it may be that such was a rhetorical device to allay accusation from opponents that socialism served to support those who refused to work, support themselves or contribute to society.

Should we conclude that Christian Socialism is a conservative ideology? Sometimes it is presented as such, perhaps most recently by the 'Blue Labour' movement. One of the leaders of Blue Labour, Jon Cruddas, regards George Lansbury as Labour's greatest ever leader; an executive member of Christians of the Left (formerly the Christian Socialist Movement), Ian Geary, is co-convenor of the Blue Labour Midlands seminar and co-editor of *Blue Labour: Forging a New Politics*; and Christian Socialist Frank Field makes a contribution to the book. In his chapter Field argues that Blue Labour values such as 'country, loyalty [...] the belief that duties beget rights' as being Christian values.[147]

In some ways the connection is justified: 'Blue Labour blends a "progressive" commitment to greater economic equality with a more "conservative" disposition emphasising personal loyalty, family, community and locality', and to an extent this fits in with what we have seen of the conservative element of Christian Socialist thought.[148] However, while a mere 'commitment to greater economic equality' may well be a fair definition of what Scott Holland was aiming for, it certainly does not do justice to the radical changes imagined by Keir Hardie, Lansbury, Wheatley, Tawney, Wilkinson or Headlam. They all foresaw the replacement of capitalism by socialism, rather than the Blue Labour approach of simply managing capitalism in a fairer way.

An analysis into non-Christian and Christian socialism does not 'correspond in any way to an analysis into Left and Right, into moderate and extreme'. 'Christian Socialists in parliament have generally been on the left of the Labour Party and advocated a thorough-going Socialism. [...] [T]hey have resisted the temptation to compromise with a capitalist system they have regarded as fundamentally unjust.'[149] The words of Conrad Noel provide an appropriate answer: 'Christian Socialism [...] is not, as some appear to think, a particular variety of Socialism, milder than the secular brand, but economic Socialism come to by the road of the Christian faith and inspired by the ideas of the Gospel.'[150]

Conclusion

Christian Socialism was committed to democracy, not just as the means for achieving socialism but as a component of any socialist society. Democracy was a necessity to preserve rights and freedoms in an economic system which would require a more powerful state. In the view of Tawney, cooperation in industry required the extension of democracy into the workplace. Democracy also reflected the equal status of all people in the eyes of God, and this links to the Christian Socialist argument for legal or formal equality. This though was not the extent of the equality aimed at; Christian Socialism was committed to, if not full equality, then to achieving a reduction of inequality of outcome. Christian Socialists could certainly demonstrate conservative view in matters of sexuality, the use of alcohol, and towards the unemployed. This, however, was not a major theme in Christian Socialism, and we should not automatically think of it as being more conservative or moderate than other forms of socialism.

9

Pacifism and utopianism

So far in this section we have looked at some principles – collectivism, democracy and equality, for example – which Christian Socialists envisaged being part of a new socialist society. In this chapter we will examine Christian Socialist pacifism. While most of the Christian Socialists discussed in the book espoused pacifism to some extent, they were not all absolute pacifists, with particularly the Second World War being regarded as a just and necessary war. Most seemed to share the belief that the world would one day be free from war. This will lead us to consider the utopian elements of Christian Socialist thinking about the nature of the new society, in which a world was imagined free not only of war but also of poverty, disease and all forms of exploitation. These views reflect the Christian Socialist view that the socialist society would be the realization of the Kingdom of Heaven on Earth.

Pacifism

One of the most pronounced aspects of Christian Socialism is pacifism. Jones describes Christian Socialists as being 'bitterly opposed' to the Boer War, adding that 'Christian socialists preserved more of a united front against colonial war than did British socialists in general'.[1] Keir Hardie and John Wheatley, among others, were opposed to the First World War, while George Lansbury – a convinced pacifist – embarked upon a major campaign to try and prevent the Second World War.[2] However, we will see that not all Christian Socialists were pacifists, and even the opposition of those who were was not always absolute.

Henry Scott Holland was a fierce opponent of the Boer War; in a sermon at St Paul's Cathedral he spoke of his disbelief 'that we could fall so far from the very memory of Jesus Christ', adding: 'We should humiliate ourselves for the blundering recklessness with which we entered on the war, and the insolence and arrogance which blinded us so utterly.'[3] Jones describes John Clifford as an 'avowed pacifist' who was 'bitterly against the Boer War'.[4] Clifford persuaded a group of Nonconformist ministers to join him in calling for

1. the immediate surrender of all arms;
2. unlimited amnesty;
3. a federation of South African states, with autonomy for each guaranteed;
4. equality for all races; and
5. protection of the African natives and their rights as workingmen to be secured.[5]

Clifford's view was that

> [t]he war of man upon man is totally alien to the spirit and genius of the religion of Christ. His teaching condemns it. His example is against it. His cross forbids it [...] It is not because of Christianity, but against it; against its express teaching, and in direct opposition to the will of its Creator and Lord, that States and Churches have gone to war, and still prepare for war.[6]

Clifford imagined the 'abolition of the idolatry of military leaders, and the extinction of the love of war', in order 'that misguided nations may stand together in the interests of peace'.[7]

As might be expected, Samuel Keeble, Wilfred Wellock and Ellen Wilkinson – all Methodists – were opponents of war. 'War is wholly un-Christian', wrote Keeble, 'The resort to force is unbrotherly, contrary to love; it is irrational, contrary to reason; brutal, contrary to humanity. It cannot determine the question of justice, it merely determines that of strength.'[8] In Keeble's view 'Socialism is infinitely truer to Christianity when it condemns war and armaments, and advocates universal disarmament and peace, than is that bastard imperialism and false nationalism which cultivates in a Christian country militarism, international strife and bitterness, and an exclusive arrogant patriotism'.[9] Keeble's *Methodist Times* newspaper was 'strongly opposed to the Anglo-Boer war'; he wrote, for example, that those responsible for setting up concentration camps in South Africa were 'traitors to the religion of Jesus Christ'.[10] For Keeble, writes his biographer, 'the Gospel and war were mutually incompatible'.[11] Wilkinson, a member of the Women's International League for Peace and Freedom, advocated disarmament, arguing that if 'Great Britain and the United States together should disarm, the cause of world peace would be tremendously advanced', and 'nothing stands in the way of disarmament but willingness to start it'.[12]

John Wheatley also argued for the incompatibility of war and Christianity, noting sarcastically during the First World War: 'We are assured that if Christ lived today he would don the patriotic khaki and place his services unreservedly at the disposal of Kitchener.'[13] Keir Hardie agreed with this assessment, arguing that 'war is of the Devil, not of Christ', and adding that Christ 'taught the doctrine of non-resistance even when attacked, as an integral part of his philosophy of life.'[14] During the Boer War Hardie argued that '[w]hen clergymen advocate or support a war like the one now being waged they but proclaim themselves infidels who do not believe the gospel'.[15] In this we can see that Hardie was a committed pacifist. As Maxton puts it, Hardie's 'opposition to war was a deep and fundamental part of his political faith [. . .] he saw in it nothing but a greedy capitalism using the lives of man to extend its power and to increase its range of profit-making'.[16]

George Lansbury was perhaps the most committed pacifist of all these individuals, 'an absolute Christian pacifist'.[17] His son Edgar quotes him thus: 'I would close every recruiting station, disband the Army, dismantle the Navy, and dismiss the Air Force. I would abolish the whole dreadful equipment of war, and say to the world: "Do your worst".'[18] In perhaps his most famous stand for pacifism, the 1935 Labour Party conference, Lansbury told delegates: 'If mine were the only voice in the conference, I would say, in the name of the faith I hold, the belief that God intends us to live peacefully and quietly with one another.'[19]

Lansbury's pacifism forced him to resign as leader of a party that was willing to go to war against Germany and Italy. Afterwards in his own constituency election he campaigned on a pacifist platform and embarked upon a remarkable global peace campaign in which he travelled to meet a number of world leaders.[20] This included a meeting with Adolf Hitler in 1937, who was told by Lansbury: 'I come to you solely in the cause of peace, peace secured not by war or force but by each nation agreeing to pool knowledge and resources for the service of one another.'[21] In a telegram to Hitler, sent in April 1939, Lansbury reminded him that '[a]ll mankind is looking to you and Signor Mussolini for such a response as will lead all nations away from war and along the road to peace through cooperation and sharing territories, markets and resources for the service of each other'.[22] Despite the failure of his campaign, Lansbury, in an article written less than a month before his death, confirmed that, '[a]s for myself, I remain an unashamed, solid-as-a-rock-of-granite pacifist'.[23]

However, Lansbury's enduring commitment to pacifism in its full extent was not the norm among Christian Socialists. A stark contrast is found in Ellen Wilkinson, who in spite of her earlier pacifism called for the provision of arms to the Spanish Popular Front in order to support the fight against fascism. The threat of fascism was such that Wilkinson was convinced of the impracticality of pacifism, and resigned from the Peace Pledge Union, of which she had been a founder member.[24] Having only a few years earlier called for global disarmament, she declared in 1937: 'If you want peace, be a realist. Don't let us disarm this country – that's nonsense.' 'You may be troubled', she acknowledged, 'because it seems that the Labour Party is going back on the pacifist programme preached since the days of Keir Hardie, but Labour today is faced with the new menace of fascism.'[25] In 1940, responding to those who called for peace, Wilkinson retorted: 'Can they tell me how it is to be done except on such terms which would mean a complete Hitler victory? If they had seen fascism at such close quarters as I have, they would not talk so complacently as some of them are doing.'[26]

While Henry Scott Holland was a vocal opponent of the Boer War, his Christian Social Union accepted the First World War as 'a necessary evil'.[27] The same is true of Stewart Headlam, who opposed the Boer War, but 'the German invasion of Belgium, his long-standing dislike of Prussianism, and the self-sacrifice of British soldiers, many of them from the East End, persuaded him that the nation was right to take up the sword'.[28] According to Headlam, 'it was only when those who [. . .] worked for Peace were convinced that there was a spiritual idea to be maintained and that Liberty, national and individual Liberty, was at stake, that the nation was convinced it must take its share in this most righteous War'.[29]

John Clifford, another who denounced the Boer War, 'supported the [First World] war because the "progress of humanity" depended on it'.[30] 'Opposed uncompromisingly to the Boer War, he was wholly on the side of Britain in the Great War. And it is necessary, because he has been misrepresented, to make his position and reasons clear.'[31]

> While Dr. Clifford's convictions led him to oppose the Boer War, he upheld the European War, but there was nothing inconsistent in this. From first to last his reasons were to himself perfectly justified. Oppression against the weak, come from whom it might, he felt bound to resist, and where wrong was inflicted he was ready to throw himself with every fibre of his being into means for remedying that wrong. In the Great War a smaller nation was ruthlessly trampled upon, and common humanity demanded that aid should be given.[32]

Clifford was nevertheless sympathetic towards conscientious objectors, arguing, 'It is altogether a mistake to imagine that these men are cowards. They are showing a courage such as witnesses to the stuff, the fibre, of which they are made.'[33]

Some Christian Socialists, therefore, who espoused pacifism were convinced of the necessity of entering the First World War. Even Keir Hardie, while he did not support the First World War, chose not to actively oppose it, writing, 'A nation at war must be united, especially when its existence is at stake. With the boom of the enemy's guns within earshot, the lads who have gone forth to fight their country's battles must not be disheartened by any discordant notes at home.'[34] Margaret Bondfield opposed the First World War, but agreed with Wilkinson in viewing the Second World War as a just and necessary conflict:

> We have made the choice between two evils – for we hold war to be an evil way of settling our national differences; yet the greater evil would be to refuse to resist a policy which uses power so ruthlessly, for that would make us accomplices to the crime. That is why the British Labour movement, which for generations inscribed Peace upon its banners, is now supporting the war.[35]

There were also some Christian Socialists who did not hold any commitment to pacifism. For example, R. H. Tawney enlisted in the Manchester Regiment and fought in the First World War, believing that it was a duty to resist Germany and, such being the case, it was wrong for an individual to stay at home while others did the actual fighting.[36] He also resigned from the ILP due to its opposition to the war.[37] Although he later spoke of his shame at having enjoyed shooting at and killing the enemy, he nevertheless rejected pacifism as being utopian.[38] Tawney's views regarding the Second World War were that 'the war is a catastrophe, though in the circumstances we were, I think, right to go in', and he served as a member of the Home Guard and Civil Defence Warden. In the post-war period he was opposed to unilateral nuclear disarmament. Tawney disagreed with other Christian Socialists, concluding as he did, 'I do not believe that capitalism is the sole cause of wars', nor that 'there is a distinctively socialist policy which at all times can be pursued'.[39]

William Temple's views agreed with those of Tawney. 'Confronted twice with world war, Temple was no pacifist. He subscribed to just war theory, and considered pacifism as a universal principle to be heretical in tendency.'[40] Temple argued that the Nazis posed such a great threat that '[i]t is our duty as Christian citizens to do our utmost towards winning the war.'[41] Temple argued that having peace as the goal had two different effects:

> It will lead either that form of pacifism which is ready to welcome pain and death, even of loved ones, rather than have recourse to the infliction of those, or else to the dedication of force to the maintenance of law between the nations as well as within them. Between those two I will not state the argument, but only

record my own conviction that the latter, the subordination of force to law and to that end the endowing of law with force, is the more truly Christian way.[42]

This conviction led Temple to support the controversial Allied bombing of German cities.[43] Stewart Headlam, similarly, was, according to a biographer, 'no pacifist and warned against what he considered hasty generalizations from the Sermon on the Mount'.[44]

Christian Socialism, therefore, tended towards pacifism, but it was not so absolute as might be supposed. Men such as George Lansbury and Wilfred Wellock stood out for their utter commitment to pacifism, as opposed to the qualified commitment to pacifism of John Clifford or even Keir Hardie. Meanwhile, men such as R. H. Tawney and William Temple were statedly not pacifists. Therefore, it would be wrong to conclude that a commitment to pacifism is a necessary part of Christian Socialist thought or a prerequisite for being considered a Christian Socialist.

Utopianism

The Christian Socialist idea of a new socialist society is a highly utopian one. Often descriptions of this society to come are fantastic, otherworldly visions of a time when all manner of ills would be banished and all people would enjoy material and spiritual fulfilment. Most Christian Socialists seemed to identify this with the 'Kingdom of God' or 'Kingdom of Heaven' on Earth. Both R. H. Tawney and William Temple argued against this tendency, emphasizing instead man's imperfectability; however, in this realism they were very much in the minority, most Christian Socialists were lured on by a vision of a perfect world.

Part of the utopian Christian Socialist vision is that pacifism would finally triumph. Keir Hardie imagines a world of 'kindly brotherhood' in which 'wars would cease', and writes of a future 'triumph over war' that would be brought about by socialism.[45] George Lansbury spoke of his 'belief in the fatherhood of God, in the Brotherhood of Man, and in the fact that men and women can co-operate, if they will, so that there need be neither wars abroad nor class wars at home'.[46] In a very moving article from Christmas 1914 aimed at children, Lansbury expressed the hope that war would one day be a thing of the past:

> Just how many of us are mourning and in sorrow because we have lost some loved one in the war? Well, all of us must remember there are millions of mothers and children in France and Belgium, in Germany and in Austria, all

suffering just the same. When you are grown-up and are men and women like your fathers and mothers, you will manage the world differently.⁴⁷

Wellock foresaw a society in which everyone accepted the principles of pacifism and non-resistance and therefore had abolished war and military force, taking it as an irrefutable fact that war would no longer exist under socialism: 'Obviously a society which orders its life on the principle of co-operation and mutual service has solved the problem of war, having gone right behind the principle of greed, which is the source alike of fear and war, to the fundamental unity of human nature.'⁴⁸

It was, however, not only war that would be vanquished under Christian Socialism. While suggesting that 'wars would cease', Hardie also argued that socialism 'could more than double the production of real wealth, reduce toil to a mere incident, abolish all poverty, and dethrone the brute god mammon'.⁴⁹ John Clifford envisaged a future in which brotherhood could 'heal our diseased world, remove its woes, lead it in right paths, get rid of drunkenness and the money lust', as well as making 'wars cease to the ends of the earth'.⁵⁰ George Lansbury spoke of 'a commonwealth of all the nations of the world, in which shall cease not merely ugly war, but also the internecine strife of competitive commercialism. And men and women, learning what love means, shall translate their love into actual deeds'.⁵¹ Even as the Second World War drew ever nearer, Lansbury held out the belief that '[t]here is yet time to transform our civilization from a competitive mass of competing countries into a co-operative unity working with each other for the good of all'.⁵²

Samuel Keeble hoped for an 'ethicized economy', that would lead to 'perfect industrial justice, mercy, and peace, and therefore into paths of industrial prosperity'.⁵³ Keeble described a society in which 'distribution of the products of joint industry is scientific and universal. The new political economy [. . .] has made distribution as careful a study as that of the nineteenth century did production for profit.' All people are well educated, there is no army or war, nor is there any crime: 'Everyone controls himself'. Society has been transformed, for, 'the motive [. . .] is not self but service.'⁵⁴ Catterall argues that 'Keeble, one of Marx's earliest English readers, thus went further than Marx himself ever did in trying to offer a vision of a social order following the withering away of the state'.⁵⁵

Stewart Headlam wrote that under socialism 'all the men and women and children of England shall be fed and clothed beautifully', and that 'the soul of man would be able to expand, the body would become beautiful, and disease and premature death would be conquered'.[56] Headlam imagined a renewed spiritual life; for example, in the new society

> the Christian Sunday will be as a rule a day on which you hear Mass in the morning and from time to time make your Communion, a day for genuine healthy mental and bodily recreation, a day on which, as far as may be, no work shall be done except for such work as is necessary for the worship and recreation of the people.[57]

Keir Hardie had a similar vision, imagining that a people freed from toiling under capitalism 'would be set free for conflict with the powers of darkness in the higher spheres of mind and spirit. Art, science, literature, would flourish under Socialism as they have never done in any age of the world's history [...] mankind would rise to heights which hitherto have only existed in the rapt vision of the seer or the poet'.[58]

John Wheatley aimed at 'the elimination of landlordism, private profit, interest privilege, poverty, disease and ignorance from human society and the fostering of international brotherhood'.[59] Clifford foresaw the end of theft and all manner of crime, sexism and unemployment.[60] Lansbury wanted that 'society should be organised from top to bottom so as to bring every man, woman and child full, free, happy lives'.[61] Wilfred Wellock believed that 'a state of society is possible where everybody will be able to live after his or her own heart'.[62] Society would consist of small, rural communities of around 500 people spending their time on arts and crafts, devoting just a few hours a day working in the cities.[63] Wellock's vision was of

> A community where none are in want, where all are able to develop freely, are decently and comfortably housed, and are equal as individuals one with another! A world where nothing counts but worth, real soul worth, and where fear is extinct, even the fear of poverty, which is the source of nearly all fear! A world where freedom to live, to do and be is the heritage of all, and where life stands before every individual waiting to be won![64]

'What is Socialism?', asked Margaret Bondfield:

> An economic system, which many believe to be the next, and rapidly approaching, phase of social evolution. A system under which poverty of mind and body will not be made obligatory by external surroundings. The creation of an environment which will enable human nature to grow finer, more true, more heroic. [...] [M]en and women engaged in this service to the community would have the opportunity to acquire new dignity and purpose in life. Their

work for the State would occupy less than a third of their time, starting, perhaps, with an eight-hour day, and coming down gradually to six, or maybe four, hours per day as scientific organisation of labour and supplies became more complex. There would be time for reading, for thinking, for friendship, for laughter, and for love. There would be the opportunity to become citizens, musicians, poets, philosophers.[65]

Examples of this utopian way of thinking could be multiplied, but it is clear enough that the Christian Socialist view of a new society was not one rooted in reality, but rather a vision of an entirely new and perfect world.

One writer suggests that 'Socialism, in these hands, then, was little more than a word used to express approval for good things and a yearning for better things to come'.[66] Another criticizes ethical socialism in a way that could be applied to here, arguing that their

> political thought [...] was utopian in the worst sense of the word. It was basically a withdrawal from the world and, as such, it was impossible to translate into the practical policies of government. [...] It had no answer to the problem of budget deficits, mass unemployment [...] it had no answer to the real world.[67]

The accusation here would be that Christians Socialists lacked solid proposals for how their society would function. Their utopian vision was so disengaged from the world around them that it was simply a fantasy which could not become a reality. However, the Christian Socialist would respond that the new socialist society was not a concept of their own making, but rather the 'Kingdom of God' on Earth.

For many Christian Socialists, the new socialist society is synonymous with the Kingdom of Heaven or Kingdom of God. As Paul Bickley explains:

> The New Testament announcement of the Kingdom of God looks like a profound reversal of the social order, where the first shall be last and the last shall be first, where those who care for the 'least of these brothers of mine' will be recognised by God. This is not an idle eschatological vision – pie in the sky when we die – but one which its proponents have often sought to realise within the present political order.[68]

There are multiple examples of Christian Socialists referring to a future socialist society in this way. In his tract written for the Fabian Society, John Clifford writes that socialism is that 'by which the Kingdoms of this world are becoming the Kingdoms of our God and of His Christ', as well as being 'that full redemption and regeneration of the individual and of the world which Jesus Christ came to effect'.[69] For Keir Hardie, the Lord's Prayer, in which Jesus teaches His disciples to pray 'Thy Kingdom Come', was evidence that God's Kingdom was to be set up on Earth.[70] 'The Kingdom in Christ's mind', wrote Hardie, 'did not refer to a heaven in the future: The Kingdom of God meant the establishment right here upon earth of a condition of things in which human life would be beautiful and would be free to develop upon Godlike lines'.[71]

The same view was expressed by Stewart Headlam, who wrote that those who studied the teachings of Christ 'will find that He said hardly anything at all about life after death, but a great deal about the Kingdom of Heaven, or the righteous society to be established on earth', and that this earthly Kingdom of Heaven was to be 'a righteous Communistic society'.[72] It is reported that the Bishop of Newcastle, after listening to Headlam, exclaimed, 'Why, you talk as if you believe that Christ's Kingdom was coming here on earth!' 'What else should I believe?', Headlam responded, 'Of course I do.'[73] Henry Scott Holland, likewise, envisaged 'a Kingdom of earthly righteousness and social happiness. [. . .] The Holy Jerusalem descends from heaven to Earth: the City of God.'[74]

Samuel Keeble also suggested that Christ had taught that His 'Kingdom is to take visible shape upon the earth', and that this would be a society 'where the Lord Jesus is crowned its actual King, controlling by consent all the processes of production, distribution, and exchange, and the possession, use, and consumption of all material things'.[75] Elsewhere he wrote of 'the kingdom of God', 'the grand and glorious setting up of a new social order on earth – the City of God, a "new earth wherein dwelleth righteousness"'.[76] 'The future commonwealth', in this view, was to 'be a real theocracy; it will be "the father's kingdom" – the kingdom of God'.[77]

George Lansbury declared that 'the Kingdom of God is attainable here on earth', and that men and women should be 'determined in very deed to fight against the devil and all his works, and by God's good grace to establish the Kingdom of Heaven on earth'.[78] Wilfred Wellock urged 'a passionate endeavour to make earth like heaven', and the bringing about of 'a Communist Society, in which alone the teaching of the Sermon on the Mount is capable of being carried out – a society where there are neither privileges nor classes, but where the meek inherit the earth and the cardinal sin is the laying up of riches'.[79] For Bondfield, 'the basis of her Christian socialism [was] loving your neighbour inspired by love of God, and in this way playing a part in helping to build the City of God on earth'.[80] Once again examples could be multiplied, but the above is sufficient to show that for the Christian Socialist, a socialist society was synonymous with the Kingdom of God or the Kingdom of Heaven on Earth. The charge that Christian

Socialists had no idea how such a society would function or be sustained might then be answered that God would sustain His own Kingdom; that this was no man-made utopia, but rather the everlasting Kingdom of Heaven.

This, however, is not the view of all Christian Socialists. Of the men in this study R. H. Tawney and William Temple opposed the view that such a heavenly Kingdom is to be established on Earth. Matt Beech and Kevin Hickson argue that 'Tawney's Christian socialism meant that he believed that humans could not make a perfect society, nor remove the sinfulness present in the human character'.[81] Anthony Wright makes the same point, arguing that Tawney's belief in original sin gave him a more realistic view of human nature and the ability of men and women to form and function within a socialist society.[82] This view, however, is at odds with that of R. H. Preston, who has argued, according to Lawrence Goldman, that Tawney does not fully take into account man's sinfulness; on this basis Goldman argues that '[w]here human nature was concerned, Tawney was too much the optimist and utopian', and again that in focusing on abstract moral improvements rather than tangible material improvements Tawney 'verges on the utopian, or at least the unreal'.[83] It seems difficult to maintain, however, that Tawney did not fully grasp the sinfulness of human nature. Take, for example, Tawney's view of original sin, being 'that what goodness we have reached is a house built on piles driven into black slime and always slipping down into it unless we are building day and night'.[84] Neither is it fair to describe Tawney as utopian because his focus was on intangible justice rather than strict material equality. Hardie's view that socialism 'could more than double the production of real wealth, reduce toil to a mere incident [and] abolish all poverty' is altogether focused on the material, but it is far more pie in the sky than Tawney's thoughts about the future. It seems that Wright along with Beech and Hickson are correct in viewing Tawney as a realist.

William Temple was also a realist, arguing that the 'assertion of Original Sin should make the church intensely realistic, and conspicuously free from Utopianism'.[85] Temple wrote,

> [I]t is our duty as Christians to think out that kind of action which is practicable in the world we know with such human nature as ours and that of our neighbours as its agent; not to dream of what would be a perfect world if everyone already were a perfect Christian. Even then if we should be successful in establishing it for a moment we should break it into pieces in a fortnight.[86]

The basis on which Tawney and Temple disagree with the others is not whether or not human beings were sinful, but rather whether or not that sinfulness could prevent the establishment of socialism. Headlam, for example, writes that people must 'face the fact of sin', and suggests that sin would not disappear under socialism; however, he nowhere suggests that this prevents the 'righteous Communistic society' from being established.[87] Keeble wrote that a 'New Theology which denies sin, grace, redeeming love, and the new birth cannot suffice for the spiritual needs of the Labour Movement', but still maintained that God's Kingdom could be established on Earth.[88] Lansbury argued that 'we must smash the notion that original sin is so firmly embedded in us it cannot by the Grace of God and the humility of men's minds be changed'.[89]

It seems that William Temple originally held the same view as other Christian Socialists. In a report on COPEC, which took place in 1924, Samuel Keeble quotes, as we have seen, Temple's view that the conference represented 'a great movement within the Church for the Kingdom of God on earth'.[90] At some point Temple came to reject this viewpoint. In 1941 he argued that '[h]istory is not leading us to any form of perfected civilisation which, once established, will abide. It is a process of preparing the way for something *outside history altogether* – the perfected Kingdom of God'.[91] In 1942 he reiterated that 'we cannot hope to see the Kingdom of God established in its perfection in this mortal life. That belongs to eternity.'[92] In an address that same year Temple declared: 'The Christian religion gives us no assurance that there will ever be upon this earth a society of perfect love, indeed it gives us many reasons to believe there never will be [...] Certainly it cannot be completely fulfilled on this planet.'[93] 'We may not hope for the Kingdom of God in its completeness here', Temple concludes, 'but we are to pray for its coming and to live even now as its citizens.'[94] It seems though that Temple and Tawney are the exceptions here. The weight of evidence suggests that Christian Socialism can be fairly characterized as utopian, and that Christian Socialists saw the socialist utopia as the establishment of the Kingdom of God or the Kingdom of Heaven on Earth.

Conclusion

Christian Socialists were in general favourable towards pacifism and reluctant to countenance war. While, however, it has sometimes been assumed that Christian Socialism is an inherently pacifist ideological position, this does not seem to be the case. The absolute pacifism of Lansbury, for example, contrasts sharply not only with the realist views of Tawney and Temple but also with the just war arguments of those who had been pacifists such as Bondfield and

Wilkinson. Most Christian Socialists nevertheless foresaw a time in which war and conflict would be ended, and this is one element of the utopian aspect of Christian Socialism which envisaged a society free from exploitation, poverty, even sickness and premature death. While this may strike us unrealistic, it is nevertheless consistent with the conflation between a socialist society and the Kingdom of God or Kingdom of Heaven on Earth.

Conclusion

Despite the more ready association between Christianity and the political right and the assumption that religion in general favours political conservatism and free-market capitalism, we have been able to go into some depth describing and analysing a tradition of left-wing Christianity in Britain. These Christian Socialists have made a full and lasting contribution to socialist theory, the labour movement and Christian theology. Here we have considered the theoretical basis of this Christian Socialism, the proposed method of bringing about a new society and the vision of what that society would look like, and we are now in a position to consider in summary the answers to the questions posed at the outset:

(1) What does Christian Socialist ideology consist of? What principles and concepts are common to Christian Socialists?
(2) To what extent does Christian Socialism draw its ideas from theology or religious teaching, and to what extent from other sources?
(3) What kind of society – if any – do Christian Socialists seek to create? How do they seek to create it – by revolutionary or democratic means?
(4) Is Christian Socialism necessarily distinctive from other kinds of socialism?

Christian Socialism is here under consideration as political ideology, and we should bear in mind the definitions of ideology which we have already encountered. An ideology is, in effect, a belief system consisting of a structure of political ideas or concepts. 'An ideology', explains Robert Leach, 'involves firstly an interconnected set of ideas which form a perspective on the world.'[1] Michael Freeden adds that ideologies are 'configurations of political concepts', and described the purpose of studying an ideology as 'identifying, describing, and analysing the building blocks that constitute it and the relationships among them'.[2] In response to question 1, we can begin to consider the conceptual structure of Christian Socialism – the concept at the core of Christian Socialism as that of brotherhood. This concept in a sense sits at the intersection of Christian theology and political theory, as it is derived from the theological concept of God's Fatherhood and results in a commitment to the political theoretical concepts of equality, cooperation and democracy.

This core concept of brotherhood is drawn in part from the teaching of Christ in the Gospel of Matthew: 'But be ye not called Rabbi: for one is your Master, even Christ; and all ye are brethren. And call no man your father upon the earth: for one is your Father, which is in heaven.'[3] The Christian Socialist understood the Bible to teach, as George Lansbury put it, God's 'Fatherhood and the consequent Brotherhood of man', and believed that Christians were sent forth with, in James Keir Hardie's words, a 'Gospel [. . .] proclaiming all men sons of God and brethren one with another'.[4]

The idea of universal brotherhood was used as a powerful argument against capitalism. Samuel Keeble identified 'the great Christian principles of the Fatherhood of God and the Brotherhood of Man' as in tension with the inherent selfishness and individualism of capitalism. Competition, according to Keeble, 'is contrary [. . .] to the teaching of the Christian religion, which [. . .] condemns selfishness, and demands that men love their neighbour as themselves. It is contrary, because Christianity proclaims the brotherhood men'.[5] John Wheatley made the point even more strongly in the letter, 'A Catholic Defence of Socialism', to the *Glasgow Observer*, asking: '[I]n a society which is one of swindler versus the swindled, how can there be brotherly love?'[6] Capitalism therefore stood condemned, for it ignored and made impossible to practice the familial relations which the Bible declared existed between all people.

This negative argument – that capitalism was contrary to the brotherly existence urged by scripture – was also accompanied by a positive one – that socialism was the system by which brotherly love could be practised. According to Keeble, a 'great cry of Socialism' was 'for brotherhood – the most Christian of cries'. 'The Socialist', in Keeble's opinion, 'who demands brotherhood in industry is far nearer the mind of Christ than the economist who clamours for "free" competition.'[7] This view was also expressed in the declaration of John Clifford's Free Church Socialist League:

> Believing that the principle of Brotherhood as taught by Jesus Christ cannot adequately be wrought out under existing industrial and commercial conditions, and that the faithful and commonplace application of this principle must result in the Socialization of all natural resources, as well as the instruments of production, distribution and exchange, the League exists to assist in the work of eliminating the former by building the latter Social Order.[8]

For the Christian Socialist, therefore, socialism is the natural and rightful outworking of biblical Christianity; the Bible teaches that God is the Father, and socialism is that system whereby the people of the world, or of a particular society, can live as brothers and sisters.

The concept of brotherhood therefore underpins the Christian Socialist commitment to equality, cooperation and democracy. The concept of equality flows naturally from the concept of brotherhood, as William Temple explained:

> Apart from faith in God there is really nothing to be said for the notion of human equality. Men do not seem to be equal in any respect, if we judge by the available evidence. But if all are children of one Father, then all are equal heirs of a status in comparison with which the apparent differences of quality and capacity are unimportant; in the deepest and most important of all – their relationship with God – all are equal.[9]

Keeble, as we have seen, maintained that all people were the children of God, and on that basis equal regardless of ethnicity, nationality or social class.[10] The Christian Socialist did not equate equality with uniformity, but could not see how discrimination on the grounds of race or sex, or an economic system which enshrined inequality could be compatible with brotherhood. Tawney, for example, sought 'a society which [. . .] holds that the most important aspect of human beings is not the external differences of income and circumstance that divide them, but the common humanity that unites them, and which strives therefore, to reduce such differences to the position of insignificance that rightly belongs to them'.[11]

The concept of cooperation in economic and industrial matters is also drawn from the concept of brotherhood, for those who were, on this interpretation, part of one family should work together rather than competing against each other. 'A well-conducted family', declared R. H. Tawney, 'does not, when in low water, encourage some of its members to grab all they can, while leaving others to go short. On the contrary, it endeavours to ensure that its diminished resources shall be used to the best advantage in the interests of all.'[12] Keeble agrees with this, writing that 'if Christ came to teach anything, and if reason and God's Word have any validity, then all we are brethren, the human race is God's family, and mutual service is the only true law of human or industrial society'.[13] Margaret Bondfield 'saw all humanity as the children of God, equal in his eyes', and this faith 'opened the door to a belief in co-operative effort'.[14] It was therefore on the basis of brotherhood that Headlam could favour a system in which 'the great means of production shall be in the hands of the whole community, and therefore shall be taken out of the hands of private individuals', and Keir Hardie declared: 'Make the worker his own employer and his own landlord and then he receives all which his toil creates. This is Socialism.'[15]

While of course equality and cooperation are staples of socialist thought, the Christian Socialist commitment to democracy is not necessarily shared by all variants of socialism. It may not be immediately obvious that the concept of democracy is drawn from the concept of brotherhood; if, however, democracy is viewed as that system which allows each individual to take part in the governance of society, then it makes sense from a perspective which views humanity as a family that each family member should have their say and their part in the political process. 'Man is created for fellowship in the family of God', argued Temple, 'fellowship first with God, and through that with all God's other children. And that is the primary test that must be applied to every system that is constructed and every change in the system that is proposed. Does it help us nearer towards the fullness and richness of personal fellowship?' From this Temple argued that democracy was the best system, for by including everybody in the political process it led to the greater expression of fellowship, and 'gives the highest value, higher than any other political scheme to the personality and the personal relationships of all the citizens of the community'.[16] Democracy was not just the preferred method of establishing socialism – as we shall consider below – but was also to be a vital part of a socialist society; as Tawney puts it: 'Democracy, in one form or another, is, in short, not merely one of several alternative methods of establishing a Socialist commonwealth. It is an essential condition of such a commonwealth's existence.'[17] 'Socialism, argued Bondfield, 'involves the re-organisation of society on the basis of both political and industrial democracy'.[18]

Recognition of this conceptual structure also leads us towards an answer to question 2: Christian Socialism appears to draw its ideas far more from theology and religious teaching than any other source. We have already summarized, earlier, the arguments regarding the brotherhood of man and Fatherhood of God. Apart from this Christian Socialists appealed to a wide variety of scriptural ideas and proof texts. Many of these, as well as the concept of brotherhood, were drawn from the teaching and example of Christ; Keir Hardie went so far as to declare that 'the impetus which drove me first of all into the Labour movement, and the inspiration which has carried me on in it, has been derived more from the teaching of Jesus of Nazareth, than from all other sources combined'.[19] The view of Stewart Headlam was that '[a]ll those ideas which we now express vaguely under the terms solidarity, brotherhood, co-operation, socialism, seem to have been vividly present in Jesus Christ's teaching'.[20]

Christ's Sermon on the Mount as we have seen was a particular influence on Christian Socialists with 'its message of hope for the poor and forgotten'.[21] Hardie, for example, declared: 'Socialism is the application to industry of the teachings contained in the Sermon on the Mount', which is 'a consistent and powerful argument against property'.[22] The teaching in the Sermon about Mammon was also influential for Christian Socialists, who attacked capitalism for enshrining the worship of Mammon, in the form of material wealth, rather than Christ. Christian Socialists pointed to other of Christ's denunciations of wealth; Headlam, for example, referring to the account of the rich man and Lazarus, argued that 'the rich man was in Hell simply because he allowed the contrast between rich and poor to go on as a matter of course, day after day, without taking any pains to stop it'.[23]

The parables were also employed as arguments for socialism. It was the parable of the sheep and the goats which, to Headlam, 'seems to compel every Christian to be a socialist'.[24] Keeble made the Parable of the Workers in the Vineyard into an argument for a government-mandated minimum wage, suggesting that, a denarius per day being a sufficient amount on which to live, each of the workers in the parable received a living wage, even those who had not been hired for a full day.[25] Christ was also, at times, viewed by the Christian Socialists as Himself a political revolutionary. For Headlam, Christ was 'a radical reformer', 'a Socialistic carpenter' and a 'revolutionary Socialist from Galilee'.[26] Lansbury viewed Christ as 'the greatest revolutionary force of His times', 'the lonely Galilean – Communist, agitator, martyr – crucified as one who stirred up the people and set class against class'.[27]

Other parts of scripture, Old and New Testaments, were advanced as part of the socialist cause. The words of Paul in 2 Thessalonians – 'if any would not work, neither should he eat' – could be used to argue against provision for the unemployed; Christian Socialists reversed that interpretation by making the verse refer to a capitalist class which exploited the labouring class and lived without having to work. Such an argument was made by Headlam, Hardie, Wheatley and Keeble.[28] Headlam and Hardie pointed to the condemnation of the rich in the

> Epistle of James: 'Go to now ye rich men, weep and howl for your miseries that shall come upon you. Your riches are corrupted [. . .] Behold, the hire of the labourers who have reaped down your fields, which is of you kept back by fraud, crieth: and the cries of them which have reaped are entered into the ears of the Lord of sabaoth.'[29]

The Acts of the Apostles, in which Luke records that 'all that believed were together, and had all things in common; and sold their possessions and goods, and parted them to all men, as every man had need', were also used to argue for a collectivist, cooperative order of society.[30] In the words of Headlam: 'The first Christians were, as you well know, in the simplest sense of the word communists – they put all their goods into a common fund and distribution was made to every man according to his need.'[31]

The main arguments advanced from the Old Testament were drawn from the doctrine of creation and from the land laws given to Israel. Christian Socialism's core concept of brotherhood is clearly linked to the idea of all people having been created equal by God; Tawney, for example, viewed the consequences of capitalism as 'an odious outrage on the image of God'.[32] The same argument was advanced by Wilfred Wellock, who declared that the issue of whether society should be capitalist or socialist 'depends upon whether we are going to regard man as a beast or a soul, a collection of physical appetites or a spiritual being made in the image of God'.[33] Another implication of the doctrine of creation was that the land, being created by God, ought not to be privately or exclusively owned. Lansbury's view was that 'land was not made by man but by God, and belongs to the whole people, for the use of mankind and not for the profit of the idle few'.[34] Similarly, Wheatley told a working-class audience, that the 'gifts of God' in creation 'have been stolen from you'.[35]

Keeble makes just the same argument from the laws given to Israel regulating the use of land: 'The Hebrew regulations concerning the Sabbatic year, land-debts, rural housing, the pledge, and the year of Jubilee, all declare that "the earth is the Lord's", and not the landlord's, and they all aim at preserving the economic freedom of the worker and his family. There is no absolute property in land in the Bible.'[36] According to Headlam 'a study of Hebrew polity shows that careful arrangements were made, by the Jubilee laws especially, to deal righteously with the land, to see that the whole community enjoyed its value'.[37] Likewise, Hardie writes that 'land could neither be sold outright nor held for more than a limited period as security for debt; even the debtor was freed from all obligations when the year of Jubilee came round'.[38] Temple argued that the year of Jubilee should be reinstated in order to prevent monopoly of land.[39] Again, we can see that Christian Socialists made extensive use of the scripture in defending and advancing their political programme.

We have also noted the significance of church teaching, past and present, for Christian Socialism. One example of this is the social teaching of the Roman Catholic Church; for example, Pope Leo XIII's *Rerum novarum* or *On the*

Condition of Labour of 1891, an encyclical written in response to the problems caused by the Industrial Revolution. It is not difficult to see why such a document could be used by socialists such as John Wheatley to argue for socialism, or as a basis or their personal socialist beliefs. For instance, Leo writes: 'But all agree, and there can be no question whatever, that some remedy must be found, and quickly found, for the misery and wretchedness which press so heavily at this moment on the large majority of the very poor.'[40] Again Leo refers to 'the cruelty of grasping speculators who use human beings as mere instruments for making money' and calls for rulers to ensure that the poor are 'housed, clothed and enabled to support life'.[41] Here Pope Leo seems to be supportive of socialist ideas.

The sacraments have been identified as a key aspect of Christian Socialism. The foremost sacramental socialist, Stewart Headlam, saw both sacraments as of equal significance: 'Baptism, the Sacrament of Equality, and Holy Communion, the Sacrament of Brotherhood: these two are fundamental, the one abolishing all class distinctions, and admitting all into the Christian Church, simply on the ground of humanity; the other pledging and enabling all to live the life of brotherhood.'[42] This view was shared by Henry Scott Holland, who linked the 'social solidarity of man' with 'the essential solidarity of Church fellowship' as expressed in the Eucharist.[43] Holland's CSU passed a resolution that its members should be those who had a 'bond of union in the Sacrament of Christ's body', on the grounds that this allowed the CSU to 'demand from Communicants that social service to which their Communion pledges them'.[44] William Temple, similarly, viewed the Eucharist as 'the perfect picture of the Christian society'.[45] George Lansbury also speaks of the meaning of this sacrament, writing that 'the Communion service to me is not only the sacrifice again of Christ but a reminder of all the good men and women who have made their sacrifices in order to make the world better'.[46] Headlam reportedly declared that 'those who come to Holy Communion must be holy communists'.[47]

This is not to minimize other influences. The Christian Socialists of this period openly acknowledged their debt to their predecessors in the movement, such as F. D. Maurice and Charles Kingsley. Headlam, in a lecture titled 'Maurice and Kingsley: Theologians and Socialists', credits those men with 'revealing the theological basis of Socialism, by showing how essentially Christian it was', adding elsewhere that his own work is 'an earnest attempt to apply [Maurice's] principles and teaching to the needs of our time'.[48] We have seen though that the Christian Socialists of this period tended to be far more radical – arguably, more socialist – than Maurice and his contemporaries, and those who were primarily politicians rather than churchmen were more likely to cite the influence of secular socialist thought. Tawney, for example, writes of the 'genius of Marx' in predicting and analysing the division of 'what might have been a community into contending classes'; Keir Hardie views Marx and Engels' *Communist Manifesto* as 'the birth certificate of the modern Socialist movement'; Ellen Wilkinson engaged in Marxist analysis of economics and war ad was a co-founder of the British Communist Party.[49] None of this was accepted uncritically – Keeble for example wrote of *Das Kapital* that '[i]t is a wonderful book, full of genuine learning, passion, and love for the people', yet also 'much marred by materialistic philosophy, Hegelian jargon, and economic errors'[50] – but the influence is undoubted.

We have – in response to question 3 – set out a three-stage process by which Christian Socialists believed their favoured form of society could be brought about:

(1) persuading the people of the need for socialism;
(2) electing a Labour government, or those already in power becoming socialists; and
(3) establishing socialism by the state, acting in accordance with the will of the people.

This approach appears to be a synthesis of revolutionary and democratic socialism: revolutionary insofar as society was to be completely changed, with capitalism overthrown and socialism established; democratic insofar as this was to be achieved via peaceful, parliamentary means. '[W]idely different things are meant and conveyed by the word revolution', argued Wilfred Wellock. 'Communism does not supply the only revolutionary policy conceivable, nor is there any reason why Parliamentarism should not be combined with a revolutionary spirit and method.'[51] 'It is true that Christians are not red revolutionaries', argued Keeble, 'but they are revolutionaries. They seek to revolutionize, by peaceful, and if possible, evolutionary means.'[52]

The society envisaged by Christian Socialists would be one of equality, cooperation and democracy, as noted earlier. Yet it was also highly utopian: the new society would include not only the abolition of poverty, overwork, discrimination and prejudice, competition and injustice, but also an end to sickness, premature death and spiritual dissatisfaction. While Tawney and Temple warned against this tendency, most Christian Socialists appeared committed to this vision of a perfect world. Stewart Headlam wrote that under socialism 'all the men and women and children of England shall be fed and clothed beautifully', and that 'the soul of man would be able to expand, the body would become beautiful, and disease and premature death would be conquered'.[53] Headlam imagined a renewed spiritual life; for example, in the new society

> the Christian Sunday will be as a rule a day on which you hear Mass in the morning and from time to time make your Communion, a day for genuine healthy mental and bodily recreation, a day on which, as far as may be, no work shall be done except for such work as is necessary for the worship and recreation of the people.[54]

Keir Hardie had a similar vision, imagining that a people freed from toiling under capitalism

> would be set free for conflict with the powers of darkness in the higher spheres of mind and spirit. Art, science, literature, would flourish under Socialism as they have never done in any age of the world's history [. . .] mankind would rise to heights which hitherto have only existed in the rapt vision of the seer or the poet.[55]

If such a society appeared unrealistic and beyond the reach of humanity, the Christian Socialists might respond that it was to be the Kingdom of God on Earth; this was no mere political or economic change, but a spiritual renewal or recreation brought about by God Himself. John Clifford writes that socialism is that 'by which the Kingdoms of this world are becoming the Kingdoms of our God and of His Christ'.[56] 'The Kingdom in Christ's mind', wrote Hardie, 'did not refer to a heaven in the future: The Kingdom of God meant the establishment right here upon earth of a condition of things in which human life would be beautiful and would be free to develop upon Godlike lines.'[57] The same view was expressed by Headlam, who wrote that those who studied the teachings of Christ 'will find that He said hardly anything at all about life after death, but a great deal about the Kingdom of Heaven, or the righteous society to be established on earth', and that this earthly Kingdom of Heaven was to be 'a righteous Communistic society'.[58] Henry Scott Holland, likewise, envisaged 'a Kingdom of earthly righteousness and social happiness. [. . .] The Holy Jerusalem descends from heaven to Earth: the City of God.'[59]

To the final question – is Christian Socialism necessarily distinct from other branches of socialism? – the answer is, in some ways, no. The commitment to equality and cooperation is fairly standard across socialism; indeed, equality has been identified by both Anthony Wright and Michael Freeden as being common to all forms of socialism.[60] The commitment to democracy – whether as a means of bringing about a new society or as a principle of that society – is not necessarily one shared by all forms of socialism, but neither is it unique to Christian Socialism. Utopianism, likewise, is not a necessary component of socialism, but there are forms of ethical socialism distinct from Christian Socialism which held to such a view of the future.

Christian Socialism may be distinct insofar as it aimed as a revolution by democratic means and in the three-stage method of establishing socialism which we have outlined earlier. Other forms of socialism can be characterized as either democratic or revolutionary. Not so Christian Socialism, it offers a synthesis of the two. That being said, it is perhaps overstating the case to argue that all other forms of socialism fit into one category or another. We have already quoted Hardie arguing for an evolutionary approach on the basis that 'Marx only knew of one way; the organisation of a working-class movement, which would in process of time evolve the Socialist state'.[61] By the same token, we have seen that democratic socialists – such as Eduard Bernstein and Karl Kautsky – also talked of their aims in the same manner. Here though we could argue that by adopting a democratic method the democratic socialists lost their revolutionary aims, Bernstein instead committing himself to 'reform'.[62] We may argue that democratic socialists such as Bernstein therefore became social democrats rather than socialists; this was not the case for the Christian Socialists of this period who remained committed to the overthrow of capitalism. Lansbury, for example, saw people working to 'establish a co-operative system of production and distribution to *replace* the present unsound order, based as it is on the subjection of the workers by means of the wages and profit-making system'.[63] Again Lansbury held that 'we should be able to transform Capitalism into socialism', and that it should be possible for this to be achieved 'in a peaceful, ordered manner'.[64] The extent though to which this is a distinctive of Christian Socialism is nevertheless called into question, especially if we expand the scope of analysis to the present day and pose the question of whether contemporary Christian Socialists have retained a revolutionary commitment.

Where Christian Socialism is undoubtedly unique is in its basis for all these things. The concepts of equality, cooperation and democracy might be staples of socialist thought, but their derivation from a concept of brotherhood rooted in the Fatherhood of God is distinctive to Christian Socialism. Again, the idea of a change of a God-wrought change of spirit in order to facilitate the transition to socialism – admittedly something of a cover for the potential unwieldiness of the three-stage process – is unique to Christian Socialism. Finally, while other forms of ethical socialism exist, none other associate their vision of socialism with a Christian eschatological vision of the Kingdom of God or Kingdom of

Heaven on Earth. As one writer puts it, Christian Socialism is 'rightly bracketed with other "ethical" socialisms. But although it has fed from them and into them, it rests on unique foundations.'[65] Christian Socialism is then far from just secular socialism with a religious facade; it is at every point derived from and underpinned by Christian theology.

Criticisms

While we have established the fact that Christian Socialism is built on Christian theological foundations, we have yet to consider whether this is fully justified. If not, then this is only one of a number of criticisms which can be made of Christian Socialism. Making such criticisms can be tricky in such a context; this book has largely taken an interpretivist rather than normative perspective in its treatment of Christian Socialism, making no value judgements about the arguments, tactics or aims of Christian Socialism (except, as in the case of how socialism will be brought about, where an internal logic is lacking). It is nevertheless fair to pose questions of Christian Socialism and to, while treading carefully, consider a potential critique of the movement.

The religious basis of Christian Socialism is doubtless one which non-Christian socialists would find off-putting. The idea that Christianity is the basis for socialism is laughable from a Marxist perspective, in which all religion is but a form of false consciousness generated by the material conditions of society. 'All religion', writes Engels, 'is nothing but the fantastic reflection of in men's minds of those external forces which control their daily life, a reflection in which terrestrial forces assume the form of supernatural forces.' For Engels, 'God' is no more than 'the alien domination of the capitalist mode of production'.[66] On this basis Marx writes:

> Man makes religion, religion does not make man. In other words, religion is the self-consciousness and self-feeling of man who has either not yet found himself or has already lost himself again. [. . .] Religion is the sigh of the oppressed creature, the heart of a heartless world, just as it is the spirit of a spiritless situation. It is the opium of the people. The abolition of religion as the illusory happiness of the people is required for their real happiness.[67]

Similar criticisms were levelled by non-Marxist socialists. The attitude expressed in the *Syndicalist* newspaper attests to this: Christianity is 'a religion which pays no heed to anything except the Soul', and James Larkin's activism in Dublin is criticized on the grounds that 'his mind is warped by clericalism. Where the wealth is, there will the priest also be. So long as the wage-slaves of Dublin or anywhere else respect priests their servitude is hopeless.'[68] Jack Radcliffe, a contributor to the *Syndicalist*, opines:

> It would be curious to know, if it were possible, why Catholics (or Anglicans, or Nonconformist Christians, for that matter) interest themselves in Socialism. In the mind of a Christian,of course, the welfare of the soul is an infinitely more important matter than the welfare of the body. But Socialism has no interest save the improvement of purely material conditions. Hence, what do these good Christian 'souls' want with Socialism. God is their master, and His heaven is their reward. Let them look to that [. . .] 'God' is always on the side of the rich and powerful.[69]

Radcliffe's distinction between body and soul might be something of a false dichotomy, and his description of 'the mind of a Christian' an unfair characterization. Nevertheless, on this reading Christianity is but a reflection of capitalism and a means of support for the capitalist class. So much on this reading for the Christian basis of socialism.

While Fabian thought was varied, and the Fabian Society included Christian Socialists such as Headlam and Clifford, it does not appear that the Fabians routinely accepted the idea that Christianity provided a theoretical underpinning for socialism; a section in *Fabian Essays in Socialism* on 'The Basis of Socialism' speaks very little of religion. Sidney Olivier, writing on the moral basis of socialism, takes an approach which simply assumes the existence of objective morality, declining to outline where exactly those morals come from; such an approach is designed to 'avoid the certainty of losing, at the very outset of our attempted demonstration, the company of all but that minority who might assent to our fundamental propositions'.[70] For Olivier the growth of collectivism will provide a basis for socialism; similarly for Sidney Webb, the emergence of democracy was the basis for socialism.[71] This runs counter to the conceptual structure outlined above, in which collectivism and democracy are concepts drawn from a moral or spiritual basis for socialism.

There are a few hints at hostility to organized religion in the *Fabian Essays*. For Olivier, the pre-Reformation Roman Catholic Church could be a basis for socialism, but Protestantism – being individualistic and denying the universal application of God's love – could not be.[72] Doubtless Headlam would agree, provided that the Church of England was considered part of Catholicism rather than Protestantism; equally doubtless is that Clifford would disagree with

Oliver's assessment. William Clarke criticizes the spiritual rhetoric of Maurice and Kingsley, including the denunciation of 'Mammon' in place of any more rigorous economic analysis.[73] Far from a basis for socialism, George Bernard Shaw views the commandments of scripture as more a means of bolstering the individual property rights of the capitalist system.[74]

Christians might also object – and in considerably more detail – to the theological interpretations of Christian Socialism. We have noted earlier that brotherhood – a concept derived from the Fatherhood of God – is the very core of Christian Socialism, yet not all Christians would accept that the Fatherhood of God is universal. A key text is found in Gospel of John:

> Then said they to [Jesus], We be not born of fornication; we have one Father, even God. Jesus said unto them, If God were your Father, ye would love me: for I proceeded forth and came from God; neither came I of myself, but he sent me. [. . .] Ye are of your father the devil, and the lusts of your father ye will do.[75]

We may also point to the words of the writer to the Hebrews: 'It is for discipline that you have to endure. God is treating you as sons. For what son is there whom his father does not discipline? If you are left without discipline, in which all have participated, then you are illegitimate children and not sons.'[76] Both passages indicate that those who are not Christians do not have God as their Father, and if God's Fatherhood is not universal then neither is humanity's brotherhood; there is then no familial basis for equality, cooperation or democracy.

We have also seen that Christian Socialists used the doctrine of creation as a basis for human brotherhood. While in some ways this is a stronger argument it does not necessarily resolve the issue. It is correct to say that all people are God's children in the sense that they are His creation, but in a fallen world they do not all relate to Him on that basis; Christ clearly states that those who oppose Him cannot claim to have God as their Father. The Christian Socialist vision of a collectivist society requires unity of vision and purpose; this unity could potentially exist between those who share brotherhood on the basis of a common Christian faith, but cannot exist between those who share no such brotherhood, even if it is accepted that they share brotherhood on the basis of a common creation. All of mankind is linked insofar as they are all created by God, but, again, in this fallen world, mankind consists of believers and unbelievers, and these two groups will have different aims, objectives and priorities.

Questions may also be raised over other Christian Socialist uses of scripture, as a few examples will illustrate. Keir Hardie's view of the Sermon on the Mount as 'a consistent and powerful argument against property' cannot be sustained. Hardie might have had in mind Christ's instruction 'Lay not up for yourselves treasures upon earth', yet we are not to understand from this verse that private property must be collectivized, but rather that we ought to concentrate more on eternal and spiritual things than temporal and materialistic things.[77] The Christian might well argue that socialism is no less focused on the materialistic than capitalism; it is not evident that the creation of a socialist society would remove the Mammon worship which the Christian Socialists opposed. Criticisms may also be applied to Samuel Keeble's interpretation of the Parable of the Workers in the Vineyard as an argument for the government-mandated minimum wage. Christ taught that parables spoke of 'the mysteries of the kingdom of heaven', rather than earthly issues; in this case the parable refers to the common reward that each believer will receive – eternal salvation – regardless the stage of life at which they are saved.[78]

We may also take issue with the application of Paul's discussion of 'the body' in 1 Corinthians 12 to the right ordering of society. The 'body' referred to is not the society but the church; Paul writes that 'by one Spirit are we all baptized into one body', and that this body is 'the body of Christ', 'the church'.[79] The description of common ownership in Acts of the Apostles does not compel a socialist order of society as this generous giving and sharing of resources took place solely within the church rather than throughout society.[80] The same applies to Israel's land laws; these laws were given to the community of Old Testament believers, and today point to the free sharing of resources within the church, as exampled in Acts. Finally, though not a biblical reference, Roman Catholics might object to the use of Catholic social teaching as a basis for socialism given Pope Leo XIII's clear statements in *Rerum novarum* that 'the main tenet of socialism, the community of goods, must be utterly rejected', and that '[e]very human being has by nature the right to possess private property as one's own'.[81]

The Christian Socialist interpretation of the sacraments may also be queried from a number of Christian perspectives. Stewart Headlam's view of baptism as a 'Sacrament of Equality' is easily dismissed from a Baptist perspective, as stated in the 1689 Confession of Faith: 'Those who do actually profess repentance towards God, faith in, and obedience to, our Lord Jesus Christ, are the only proper subjects of this ordinance.'[82] It is, however, not even necessary to take this Baptist perspective. The Presbyterian Heidelberg Catechism argues that 'by baptism, as sign of the covenant, [children of believers] must be grafted into the Christian church and distinguished from the children of unbelievers'.[83] In fact, even the Thirty-Nine Articles of Headlam's own Church of England view the sacrament as 'a sign of profession, and mark of difference, whereby Christian men are discerned from others that be not christened, but it is also a sign of Regeneration or New-Birth, whereby, as by an instrument, they that receive Baptism rightly are grafted into the Church'.[84] Here we see that, in the Baptist, Presbyterian and Anglican traditions, baptism, rather than representing universal equality, in fact differentiates between believers – or, the children of believers – and unbelievers.

The same is true of the Lord's Supper: rather than 'enabling all to live the life of brotherhood', the Thirty-Nine Articles – based on 1 Corinthians 11 – restrict the sacrament to Christians, for when non-Christians eat the bread and wine 'in no wise are they partakers of Christ: but rather, to their condemnation, do eat and drink the sign or Sacrament of so great a thing'.[85] Headlam's universal application of the sacraments is therefore denied by one of the foundational documents of his own church. On this basis, Lansbury is also wrong in his view that 'the Communion service to me is not only the sacrifice again of Christ but a reminder of all the good men and women who have made their sacrifices in order to make the world better', for neither the Thirty-Nine Articles nor the Bible suggests that communion should signify the death of any person except Christ.[86] Much of the theological argument underpinning Christian Socialism is therefore questionable at best.

The Christian Socialist method of bringing about socialism – even if we accept that it is revolutionary change by democratic means – is rejected by revolutionary forms of socialism. In *The Communist Manifesto* Marx and Engels appear to reject a parliamentary route to socialism in favour of revolution, arguing: '[T]he bourgeoisie has [. . .] conquered for itself, in the modern representative State, exclusive political sway. The executive of the modern State is but a committee for managing the common affairs of the whole bourgeoisie.' In their conclusion they write: 'The Communists disdain to conceal their views and aims. They openly declare that their ends can be attained only be the forcible overthrow of all existing social conditions.'[87] This revolutionary zeal was incorporated into Marxism-Leninism, Lenin writing that 'the fundamental economic interests of the proletariat can be satisfied only by a political revolution that will replace the dictatorship of the bourgeoisie by the dictatorship of the proletariat'.[88] Lenin reinforced this point in a meeting with George Lansbury, explaining:

> You think you can establish the revolution without violence, I think you will not be able to do so. If in England you are able to do this, well and good. No one wants bloodshed merely for bloodshed's sake, but it is necessary that the workers must arm in order to obtain the revolution. The workers must arm to protect the revolution because I do not believe the capitalist class will give in without a fight.[89]

This is also the syndicalist view, one contributor to the *Syndicalist* contending:

> We part company with the Socialists in thinking that the effectiveness of sending men into a moribund Parliament of a moribund State can in any manner of way compare with the effectiveness of organising men into all-powerful industrial unions. [. . .] [T]o the extent that political action does not distract the workers from industrial unionism we have no quarrel with those who thus employ themselves. [. . .] But to those Socialists who look for a social transformation to come about by the election of a Socialist majority to the House of Commons we can but extend our pity.[90]

Radcliffe argues that '[t]he only way Socialists have ever succeeded in getting into Parliament has been by sacrificing their Socialist principles', and that 'Parliament is essentially a capitalist instrument. It is designed, simply and solely, to give expression to, to extend, and to safeguard capitalist interests. It could be made to do nothing else, even were there a strong party of uncompromising Socialist members seated there.'[91] Revolutionary socialists therefore reject the idea that revolution can be achieved by democratic means.

While Marxists and syndicalists sought to keep the upper classes out of their campaigns, the Fabians took the opposite view, rejecting the idea of working-class involvement. This was a result of what has been described as the Fabian 'distrust or depreciation of political democracy'; the Fabian Society was 'all in favour of government for the people but not necessarily *of* or *by* the people'.[92] Shaw, for example, wrote: 'To hand the country over to riff-raff is national suicide, since riff-raff can neither govern nor will let anyone else govern except the highest bidder of bread and circuses.' The Webbs 'were perfectly conscious that socialism as they understood it had only a tenuous relationship to democracy in the usual sense of the word'.[93] This view is contrary to the Christian Socialist method of persuading a democratic electorate to favour socialism, as well as the enshrining of democracy as a principle of the new society. The Christian Socialist view of equality is also at odds with the belief of leading Fabians in eugenics. It was the view of H. G. Wells – supported by the Webbs and Shaw – that society should delete from within itself the 'feeble, ugly, inefficient, born of unrestrained lusts, and increasing and multiplying through sheer incontinence and stupidity'. The Webbs similarly called for 'intelligently purposeful selection' in order to facilitate the birth of 'well-born' children and 'prevent the persistent multiplication of the congenitally feeble-minded'.[94] These opinions are far removed from the Christian Socialist way of thinking, in which human equality is drawn from idea about God as Father and creator.

The Christian Socialist view of socialist society as being the Kingdom of God would be rejected both by other Christians and by other socialists. The Christian would argue that biblical passages which speak of the return of Christ and the establishment of God's Kingdom speak much of separation, judgement and holiness, but not at all of equality, economic collectivism or democracy. For non-Christian socialists, their vision of a socialist future was more often that religion will cease to exist. Marx and Engels rejected utopian socialism in general, writing that the 'duodecimo editions of the New Jerusalem' aimed at by utopians were no more than 'castles in the air'.[95] Marx explained why religion would vanish under communism: 'The religious reflex of the real world can, in any case, only then finally vanish, when the practical relations of every-day life offer to man none but perfectly intelligible and reasonable relations with regard to his fellowmen and to nature.'[96]

A similar view was taken by the syndicalists. Far from equating a socialist society and the Kingdom of God, religion and socialism had such different perspectives that the former must pass away for the latter to be established: 'It is impossible for most people who are acquainted with modern knowledge to accept the views of the universe taken by the established religions. Therefore the old religions must be swept away in order that the new faith which will inspire revolutionary action may arise.'[97] George Bernard Shaw in *Fabian Essays* also suggestion that religion must pass away for socialism to be established:

> It was pleasant to lose the sense of worldly inequality in the contemplation of our equality before God. But utilitarian questioning and scientific answering turned all this tranquil optimism into the blackest pessimism. Nature was shown to us as 'red in tooth and claw': if the guiding hand were indeed benevolent, then it could not be omnipotent; so that our trust in it was broken: if it were omnipotent, it could not be benevolent; so that our love of it turned to fear and hatred.[98]

For Marx and Engels, the idea of 'the kingdom of God' existed only 'in the imagination'; it could not be realized, because it was not real.[99]

Past, present and future

People, to use Tim Farron's phrase, might well be 'surprised and confused' when they find Christians committed to a left-wing form of politics, but that surprise is the result of lack of familiarity with a well-established tradition of left-wing Christianity in British politics. We cannot refer to a 'Religious Left' in the same manner as we refer to a 'Religious Right' in the United States, for that would imply a movement far more cohesive than the reality, but there is no doubt that the participation of practising Christians in political activity outside that of the conservative right should not come as a surprise to anyone. Christian Socialism, which can trace its history back to the 1848 (and, arguably, beyond), came to maturity over a century ago and was one of the strands of left-wing thought incorporated into the nascent Labour movement and the mainstream British left.

The 'Christian' in Christian Socialism was not just a tactic or rhetorical strategy designed to make socialist arguments more appealing to the masses in an age of higher religious observance. Instead, we have seen that a political commitment to socialism – to equality, cooperation and democracy – was based firmly on an understanding of universal brotherhood derived from a belief in the universal Fatherhood of God. The accuracy of this belief might be questioned from the perspective of non-Christian socialism or non-socialist Christianity, but the genuineness of it cannot be disputed.

Neither is Christian Socialism an anachronism, a relic from a bygone age. Our argument here is that the period from the late nineteenth century to the interwar years was a formative one for Christian Socialism, but that surely isn't where the story ends. Outside the scope of this work lies the Common Wealth Party, the Christian influence on Clement Attlee's post-war Labour government (of which Ellen Wilkinson was a part), the formation of the Christian Socialist Movement in 1960, the Christian response to and critique of Thatcherism and neo-liberalism, and the Christian Socialist elements of the Blair and Brown premierships. The Christian Socialist Movement affiliated to the Labour Party in 1988, and today – now known as Christians on the Left – has over 40 members in the House of Commons and 2,000 members overall. This is clearly no aberration but a vibrant political tradition, and further research on Christian Socialism is to be encouraged.

Questions, however, remain as to whether left-wing Christianity can thrive in the future. Can Christian Socialism make its voice heard in a political arena where the main battle is no longer economics but rather identity politics? Does Christian Socialism have an answer to the view that religious voices should be excluded from public discourse, or to the objection that Christianity – even left-wing Christianity – is not progressive enough for the contemporary world? Is Christian Socialism able to persuade Christians in an age of culture war they need not associate themselves with the political right in response to the secularization of the left? These are all questions for which we must await the answers.

Notes

Introduction

1 P. Lowe, 'Jacob Rees-Mogg Thinks His Anti-abortion Stance Doesn't Matter – Here's Why He Is Wrong', *The Conversation*, https://theconversation.com/jacob-rees-mogg-thinks-his-anti-abortion-stance-doesnt-matter-heres-why-he-is-wrong-83594; accessed 3 March 2018.
2 T. Farron, 'What Kind of Liberal Society Do We Want?', https://www.theosthinktank.co.uk/events/2017/11/28/tim-farron-what-kind-of-liberal-society-do-we-want; accessed 3 March 2018.
3 A. Walton, A. Hatcher and N. Spencer, *Is There a 'Religious Right' Emerging in Britain?* (London: Theos, 2013), p. 8.
4 A. Z. Williams, 'Faith Should Not Dictate Political Affiliation', *New Statesman*, http://www.newstatesman.com/blogs/the-staggers/2011/06/god-debate-faith-grayling; accessed 14 December 2015.
5 D. K. Williams, *God's Own Party: The Making of the Christian Right* (Oxford: Oxford University Press, 2010), p. 193.
6 Walton, Hatcher and Spencer, *Religious Right*, p. 89.
7 C. Bryant, *Possible Dreams: A Personal History of the British Christian Socialists* (London: Hodder and Stoughton, 1996), p. 41.
8 Ibid., p. 80.
9 P. Bartley, *Ellen Wilkinson: From Red Suffragist to Government Minister* (London: Pluto Press, 2014), p. xi.
10 M. Freeden, *Ideologies and Political Theory* (Oxford: Oxford University Press, 1996), pp. 426–38.
11 R. Leach, *Political Ideology in Britain* (Basingstoke: Palgrave Macmillan, 2002), p. 1.
12 Freeden, *Ideologies*, p. 48.
13 G. Dale, *God's Politicians: The Christian Contribution to 100 Years of Labour* (London: HarperCollins, 2000), p. 199.
14 Bryant, *Possible Dreams*, p. 287.
15 Ibid., p. 287; A. Wilkinson, *Christian Socialism: Scott Holland to Tony Blair* (London: SCM, 1998), p. 216.
16 P. d'A Jones, *The Christian Socialist Revival 1877-1914: Religion, Class, and Social Conscience in Late-Victorian England* (Princeton, NJ: Princeton University Press, 1968), pp. 29 and 458.

17 J. Callaghan, *Socialism in Britain Since 1884* (Oxford: Wiley-Blackwell, 1990), p. 58.
18 Ibid., pp. 29–30.
19 G. Foote, *The Labour Party's Political Thought: A History* (Basingstoke: Palgrave Macmillan, 1997), p. 36.
20 S. E. Keeble, *Industrial Day-Dreams: Studies in Industrial Ethics and Economics* (London: R. Culley, 1907 [1896]), p. 13.
21 Wilkinson, *Christian Socialism*, p. 101.
22 J. Bruce Glasier, *Keir Hardie: A Memorial* (Manchester: National Labour Press, 1915), pp. 69–70.
23 Wilkinson, *Christian Socialism*, p. 80.
24 Bryant, *Possible Dreams*, p. 97; Ibid.
25 J. Keir Hardie, 'Labour and Christianity: Is the Labour Movement against Christianity?', in *Labour and Religion: By Ten Members of Parliament and Other Bodies* (London: n.p, 1910), p. 49.
26 W. Wellock, *The Way Out, or the Road to the New World* (London: Labour Publishing, 1922), pp. 35–6.

Chapter 1

1 P. Bickley, *Building Jerusalem: Christianity and the Labour Party* (London: Bible Society, 2010), p. 8.
2 Ibid., p. 30.
3 K. Leech, 'Stewart Headlam, 1847-1924, and the Guild of St Matthew', in M. B. Reckitt, ed., *For Christ and the People: Studies of Four Socialist Priests and Prophets of the Church of England* (London: SPCK, 1968), p. 78; Election pamphlet for Lansbury as candidate for Bow and Bromley, 3 November 1935, London School of Economics [LSE] archive, Lansbury/15 361-2.
4 A. Rigby, *Wilfred Wellock: A Life in Peace* (Bridport: Prism, 1988), p. 11.
5 W. Wellock, *Christian Communism: What It Is and Why It Is Necessary* (Manchester: National Labour Press, 1921), p. 5.
6 J. M. Winter and D. M. Joslin, eds, *R.H. Tawney's Commonplace Book* (Cambridge: Cambridge University Press, 2006), p. 12.
7 M. Beech and K. Hickson, *Labour's Thinkers: The Intellectual Roots of Labour from Tawney to Gordon Brown* (London: I.B. Tauris, 2007), pp. 33–4; C. Bryant, *Possible Dreams: A Personal History of the British Christian Socialists* (London: Hodder & Stoughton, 1996), p. 189.
8 Winter and Joslin, *Tawney's Commonplace Book*, p. 67.
9 J. Clifford, *Socialism and the Teaching of Christ: Fabian Tract No. 78* (London: Fabian Society, 1898), p. 7.

10 S. E. Keeble, *Industrial Day-Dreams: Studies in Industrial Ethics and Economics* (London: R. Culley, 1907[1896]), p. 190.
11 Bryant, *Possible Dreams*, p. 207.
12 J. Keir Hardie, 'Labour and Christianity: Is the Labour Movement Against Christianity?', in *Labour and Religion: By Ten Members of Parliament and Other Bodies* (London: n.p., 1910), p. 54.
13 T. Judge, *Margaret Bondfield: First Woman in the Cabinet* (London: Alpha House, 2018), p. 5.
14 P. Catterall, *Labour and the Free Churches, 1918-1939: Radicalism, Righteousness and Religion* (London: Bloomsbury, 2016), p. 114.
15 J. Keir Hardie, *Socialism and Christianity: Keir Hardie Library No. 4* (London: n.p., 1907), p. 4; S. D. Headlam, *The Socialist's Church* (London: G. Allen, 1907), p. 11. Headlam is here referring to the nation of Israel.
16 Matthew 23.8-9.
17 Ephesians 3.14-15.
18 S. D. Headlam, *The Meaning of the Mass: Five Lectures with Other Sermons and Addresses* (London: S.C. Brown, 1905), p. 119.
19 Catterall, *Labour and Free Churches*, pp. 14–15.
20 Interview with Lansbury from the Christian Commonwealth Newspaper, 11 August 1915, LSE archive, Lansbury/7 213; J. T. Leckie, *Socialism in Britain: From the Industrial Revolution to the Present Day* (New York, NY: Taplinger, 1972), p. 106.
21 Keeble, *Industrial Day-Dreams*, pp. 17 and 214.
22 'The future of the poor law, address by Councillor George Lansbury', reprinted from the East London Observer, 23 October and 6 November 1909, LSE archive, Lansbury/30 a3.
23 G. Lansbury, 'Back to the Galilean!', in *The Religion in the Labour Movement* (London: Holborn, 1919), p. 54.
24 J. Hannan, *The Life of John Wheatley* (Nottingham: Spokesman Books, 1988), p. 11.
25 E. Wilkinson, 'Slaves of Machines', *Burnley News*, 28 November 30.
26 S. Mayor, *The Churches and the Labour Movement* (London: Independent, 1967), p. 203.
27 Keeble, *Industrial Day-Dreams*, pp. 151 and 152. Emphasis in original.
28 H. Scott Holland, ed., *Our Neighbours: A Handbook for the C.S.U.* (London: A.R. Mowbray, 1911), p. 9.
29 I. S. Wood, 'John Wheatley and Catholic Socialism', in A. R. Morton, ed., *After Socialism? The Future of Radical Christianity* (Edinburgh: CTPI, 1994), p. 20.
30 R. H. Tawney, *The Radical Tradition: Twelve Essays on Politics, Education and Literature* (New York, NY: Pantheon, 1964), p. 167.
31 Catterall, *Labour and Free Churches*, p. 201.

32 Newspaper article by Lansbury from the Daily Herald, 'The Dayspring in Russia' 18 March 1920, LSE archives, Lansbury/8 104.
33 W. Temple, *Christianity and the Social Order* (London: Penguin, 1976 [1942]), p. 37.
34 S. E. Keeble, *The Ideal of the Material Life and Other Social Addresses* (London: C. H. Kelly, 1908), p. 161.
35 P. d'A Jones, *The Christian Socialist Revival 1811-1914: Religion, Class, and Social Conscience in Late-Victorian England* (Princeton, NJ: Princeton University Press, 1968), p. 88.
36 A. Wilkinson, *Christian Socialism: Scott Holland to Tony Blair* (London: SCM, 1998), p. 62.
37 Keeble, *Industrial Day-Dreams*, p. 229.
38 Ibid., p. 222.
39 Wilkinson, 'Slaves of Machines'.
40 J. Clifford, *Socialism and the Churches: Fabian Tract No. 139* (London: Fabian Society, 1908), p. 11; Clifford, *Socialism and the Teaching of Christ*, p. 7.
41 Hardie, 'Labour and Christianity', p. 49.
42 Catterall, *Labour and Free Churches*, p. 1.
43 Headlam, *Meaning of the Mass*, p. 73.
44 S. D. Headlam, *Priestcraft and Progress: Being Sermons and Lectures* (London: John Hodges, 1878), p. 7; J. R. Orens, *Stewart Headlam's Radical Anglicanism: The Mass, the Masses, and the Music Hall* (Chicago, IL: University of Illinois Press, 2003), p. 24. Leech, 'Headlam', p. 78.
45 I. S. Wood, *John Wheatley* (Manchester: Manchester University Press, 1990), p. 18.
46 J. Wheatley, *How the Miners Are Robbed: The Duke in the Dock (Startling Court Case)* (London: Pluto, 1973 [1907]), p. 17. Wheatley refers here to Luke 6.24 – 'But woe unto you that are rich! for ye have received your consolation'.
47 G. Dale, *God's Politicians: The Christian Contribution to 100 Years of Labour* (London: HarperCollins, 2000), p. 106.
48 Lansbury, 'Galilean', p. 56.
49 J. Schneer, *George Lansbury* (Manchester: Manchester University Press, 1990), p. 1.
50 Hannan, *Wheatley*, p. 31.
51 Jones, *Christian Socialist Revival*, p. 178; Wilkinson, *Christian Socialism*, p. 72; Holland, *Our Neighbours*, pp. 144–5.
52 S. E. Keeble, *Christian Responsibility for the Social Order* (London: Epworth Press, 1922), p. 29.
53 G. Foote, *The Labour Party's Political Thought: A History* (Basingstoke: Palgrave Macmillan, 1997), p. 44.
54 J. Keir Hardie, *Can a Man Be a Christian On a Pound a Week?* (London: ILP, 1901), pp. 3 and 13–14; J. Keir Hardie, *From Serfdom to Socialism* (London: G. Allen, 1907), pp. 36 and 38.
55 Matthew 5.3, 5.

56 Wellock, *Christian Communism*, p. 12.
57 Lansbury, 'Galilean', p. 54.
58 Matthew 6.24.
59 Matthew 6.24. [ESV].
60 'These Things Shall Be', Church Socialist League, LSE archives, Lansbury/8 127.
61 Newspaper cutting about Lansbury speaking at Llanelly, 1919, LSE archives, Lansbury/8 99.
62 Hughes, *Keir Hardie's Speeches*, pp. 68 and 79.
63 Wellock, *Christian Communism*, p. 4
64 Hardie, *Serfdom to Socialism*, p. 39.
65 Luke 18.22; Luke 16.19-21.
66 Headlam, *Meaning of the Mass*, p. 79; Headlam, *Christian Socialism*, p. 4.
67 Hardie, *Can a Man Be a Christian*, p. 3. 'Dives' is the name traditionally given to the rich man, even though he is not named in scripture.
68 S. E. Keeble, *Money and How to Use It* (London: Epworth Press [?], 1921), p. 2.
69 Holland, *Our Neighbours*, p. 156.
70 Lansbury, 'Galilean', p. 56.
71 Judge, *Bondfield*, p. 114.
72 Matthew 25:31-46; Wilkinson, 'Slaves of Machines'.
73 Headlam, *Meaning of the Mass*, p. 83.
74 Headlam, *Christian Socialism*, p. 4.
75 Hardie, *Socialism and Christianity*, p. 4.
76 Luke 10:25-37; Keeble, *Industrial Day-Dreams*, p. 234.
77 Matthew 6:11; Keeble, *Industrial Day-Dreams*, p. 243.
78 Matthew 20.2-16. [ESV].
79 Keeble, *Material Life*, p. 116. Emphasis in original.
80 Holland, *Our Neighbours*, pp. 38–9.
81 Hardie, 'Labour and Christianity', p. 51.
82 James 5.1, 4.
83 Headlam, *Socialist's Church*, p. 59. The phrase 'Lord of sabaoth' here can loosely be translated 'Lord of armies', hence Headlam's reference to 'the God who fights'.
84 Hardie, *Can a Man Be a Christian*, p. 3; J. Hardie, *Serfdom to Socialism*, p. 39.
85 *Guilty and Proud of It: Poplar's Answer* (London: n.p., 1927), p. 1; James 1.27.
86 Luke 1.46-8, 52-3.
87 Headlam, *Socialist's Church*, p. 20.
88 Keeble, *Ideal of the Material Life*, p. 192.
89 2 Thessalonians 3:10.
90 Orens, *Headlam's Radical Anglicanism*, p. 97; B. Holman, *Keir Hardie: Labour's Greatest Hero?* (Oxford: LIon, 2010), p. 135; see also, Hardie, *Socialism and Christianity*, p. 5 and Hardie, *Serfdom to Socialism*, p. 39.
91 Tawney, *Radical Tradition*, p. 115.

92 Keeble, *Ideal of the Material Life*, p. 201; Keeble, *Christianity and Socialism*, p. 17.
93 Keeble, *Industrial Day-Dreams*, p. 228.
94 Ibid., p. 245.
95 Wilkinson, *Christian Socialism*, p. 105.
96 1 Corinthians 12:20-21, 25-26.
97 Wilkinson, *Christian Socialism*, p. 105.
98 Dale, *God's Politicians*, p. 95.
99 Keeble, *Christian Responsibility*, p. 256.
100 Acts of the Apostles 2:44-5.
101 Hardie, *Can a Man Be a Christian*, p. 11.
102 Headlam, *Priestcraft and Progress*, p. 24; Headlam, *Meaning of the Mass*, p. 29.
103 Temple, *Christianity and the Social Order*, p. 47.
104 1 Corinthians 13.13. [ESV].
105 Bryant, *Possible Dreams*, p. 98.
106 2 Corinthians 10.4-5.
107 J. Clifford, *Socialism and the Churches: Fabian Tract No. 139* (London: Fabian Society, 1908), p. 3.
108 Acts of the Apostles 17:26.
109 Open letter to electorate from Lansbury, General Election May 1929, LSE archive, Lansbury 9/39-41.
110 J. Keir Hardie, *The I.L.P. and All About It* (Manchester: National Labour Press, 1908), p. 8.
111 Keeble, *Material Life*, p. 158.
112 Genesis 1.26-7.
113 Wellock, *Christian Communism*, p. 10.
114 A. Wright, *R.H. Tawney* (Manchester: Manchester University Press, 1987), p. 93.
115 Holman, *Hardie*, p. 167.
116 W. Temple, *The Church Looks Forward* (London: Macmillan, 1944), p. 141.
117 Newspaper article in the 'Liverpool Daily Post' on a speech by Lansbury at Carnarvon, 18 September 1911, LSE archive, Lansbury/4 219.
118 Wood, 'John Wheatley and Catholic Socialism', p. 21.
119 Headlam, *Christian Socialism*, p. 15.
120 Wellock, *The Way Out*, p. 41.
121 'Miss Ellen Wilkinson, M.P., at Neasdon Railwayman's Service', *Willsden Chronicle*, 1 March 31.
122 Headlam, *Meaning of the Mass*, p. 16.
123 Exodus 5.17-19. [ESV].
124 Keeble, *Industrial Day-Dreams*, p. 229.
125 S. E. Keeble, 'Introduction', in S. E. Keeble, ed., *The Social Teaching of the Bible* (London: R. Culley, 1909), p. 19.
126 Headlam, *Socialist's Church*, p. 59.

127 Hardie, *Serfdom to Socialism*, p. 32.
128 Temple, *Christianity and the Social Order*, p. 48.
129 Leviticus 25:8 [ESV]; Wilkinson, *Christian Socialism*, p. 118.
130 Lansbury, *Your Part in Poverty*, p. 31. Exodus 20.8.
131 'The future of the poor law, address by Councillor George Lansbury', reprinted from the East London Observer, 23 October and 6 November 1909, LSE archive, Lansbury/30 a3.
132 Hughes, *Hardie's Speeches and Writings*, p. 92.
133 M. Bondfield, *Socialism for Shop Assistants: Pass on Pamphlets No. 10* (London: Clarion Press, 1909), p. 11.
134 Exodus 20.15; S. D. Headlam, *Christian Socialism – A Lecture: Fabian Tract No. 42* (London: Fabian Society, 1899), p. 15.
135 Exodus 20.4-5; R. H. Tawney, 'The Choice Before the Labour Party', *Political Quarterly*, 3, no. 3 (1932), p. 32.
136 J. Hardie, *Socialism and Christianity*, p. 4; F. Johnson, *Keir Hardie's Socialism* (London: ILP, 1922), p. 12.
137 Keeble, *Material Life*, p. 16.
138 Clifford, *Socialism and the Teaching of Christ*, p. 2.
139 Keeble, *Industrial Day-Dreams*, p. 92.
140 1 Timothy 6:8. [ESV].
141 Headlam, *Christian Socialism*, p. 5.
142 Keeble, *Industrial Day-Dreams*, p. 244.
143 Keeble, *Material Life*, pp. 94–5.
144 Luke 3:14.
145 Keeble, *Material Life*, p. 96.
146 Matthew 5:3; Luke 6:20; Mark 14:7.
147 Headlam, *Christian Socialism*, p. 5.
148 Ibid.
149 Holland, 'Our Neighbours' (1911), cited in A. Bradstock and C. Rowland, eds, *Radical Christian Writings: A Reader* (Oxford: Wiley-Blackwell, 2002), p. 194.
150 Ibid., p. 195.
151 S. E. Keeble, *Is There a Heavenly Father?* (London: C.H. Kelly, 1904), p. 17.
152 Parliamentary Election, 1935, Lansbury/30 b 40-42, LSE archive.
153 Newspaper cutting from the Gravesend Reporter, about Lansbury delivering a speech to the Swanscombe Brotherhood, 21 March 1931, Lansbury/10 52.
154 Wilkinson, *Christian Socialism*, p. 60.
155 Keeble, *Christianity and Socialism*, p. 14. Keeble is not here referring to the second of the Ten Commandments, but the second of the two commandments given by Christ Himself: Mt. 22:9 – 'Thou shalt love thy neighbour as thyself'.
156 Letter from Lansbury to Rev John Charles Carlisle, 22 January 1931, Lansbury/10 2-6, LSE archive.

Chapter 2

1. P. d'A Jones, *The Christian Socialist Revival 1877-1914: Religion, Class, and Social Conscience in Late-Victorian England* (Princeton, NJ: Princeton University Press, 1968), pp. 86–7.
2. C. E. Curran, *Catholic Social Teaching 1891-Present: A Historical, Theological and Ethical Analysis* (Washington, DC: Georgetown University Press, 2002), p. 137.
3. J. R. Orens, *Stewart Headlam's Radical Anglicanism: The Mass, the Masses, and the Music Hall* (Chicago, IL: University of Illinois Press, 2003), p. 61.
4. S. Mayor, *The Churches and the Labour Movement* (London: Independent, 1967), p. 355.
5. S. D. Headlam, *The Socialist's Church* (London: G. Allen, 1907), p. 29; I. S. Wood, *John Wheatley* (Manchester: Manchester University Press, 1990), p. 18.
6. Curran, *Catholic Social Teaching*, p. 101.
7. S. D. Headlam, *Priestcraft and Progress: Being Sermons and Lectures* (London: John Hodges, 1878). Headlam is here referring to the Eucharist as 'the worship of Jesus Christ'.
8. Headlam, *Socialist's Church*, p. 33.
9. S. D. Headlam, *Christian Socialism – A Lecture: Fabian Tract No. 42* (London: Fabian Society, 1899), p. 6.
10. K. Leech, 'Stewart Headlam, 1847-1924, and the Guild of St Matthew', in M. B. Reckitt, ed., *For Christ and the People: Studies of Four Socialist Priests and Prophets of the Church of England* (London: SPCK, 1968), p. 73.
11. G. Taylor, *Socialism and Christianity: The Politics of the Church Socialist League* (Sheffield: IHS, 2000), pp. 77–8.
12. L. Goldman, *The Life of R.H. Tawney: Socialism and History* (Oxford: Bloomsbury, 2013), p. 231. Goldman suggests that Tawney may not have been a theological Anglo-Catholic despite his views about Protestantism and individualism.
13. Wood, *Wheatley*, p. 18.
14. Ibid., p. 20.
15. Mayor, *Churches and Labour Movement*, p. 355.
16. S. E. Keeble, *Industrial Day-Dreams: Studies in Industrial Ethics and Economics* (London: R. Culley, 1907 [1896]), p. 220.
17. S. E. Keeble, *Christian Responsibility for the Social Order* (London: Epworth Press, 1922), p. 21.
18. W. Wellock, *The Way Out, or the Road to the Road to the New World* (London: Labour Publishing, 1922), p. 31.
19. J. Keir Hardie, *From Serfdom to Socialism* (London: G. Allen, 1907), pp. 40–1.

20 Keeble, *Christian Responsibility*, p. 178.
21 Ibid., p. 67.
22 J. Clifford, *The New City of God: The Primitive Christian Faith as a Social Gospel* (London: Alexander & Shepherd, 1888), p. 13. The 'bishop' in question is the Pope, the Bishop of Rome.
23 Wood, *Wheatley*, p. 27.
24 Ibid., p. 26.
25 Hardie, *Serfdom to Socialism*, pp. 40 and 42.
26 Goldman, *Tawney*, p. 183.
27 Keeble, *Christian Responsibility*, pp. 36 and 51.
28 W. Temple, *Christianity and the Social Order* (London: Penguin, 1976 [1942]), p. 47.
29 Hardie, *Socialism and Christianity*, p. 5.
30 Keeble, *Christian Responsibility*, pp. 37–8.
31 Ibid., pp. 39 and 41.
32 S. E. Keeble, *The Ideal of the Material Life and Other Social Addresses* (London: C.H. Kelly, 1908), p. 227.
33 Temple, *Christianity and the Social Order*, p. 50.
34 Keeble, *Christian Responsibility*, pp. 58–9, 68, 71, 72, 73, 76 and 77.
35 Orens, *Headlam's Radical Anglicanism*, p. 1.
36 Headlam, *Priestcraft and Progress*, p. 108.
37 Ibid., pp. 109–10.
38 Leech, 'Headlam', p. 73. Emphasis in original.
39 'What I should like to read about myself' by the Rt. Hon. George Lansbury, extracted from The Listener, 22 July 1936, London School of Economics [LSE] archive, Lansbury/30 a 10. The article was written in the third person.
40 Tawney, *Acquisitive Society*, p. 12. Here Tawney is quoting from the Book of Common Prayer paraphrase of Psalm 68: 'He is a Father of the fatherless, and defendeth the cause of the widows; even God in his holy habitation. He is the God that maketh men to be of one mind in an house, and bringeth prisoners out of captivity'.
41 Wood, *Wheatley*, p. 160.
42 D. Cloutier, 'Modern Politics and Catholic Social Teaching', in D. M. McCarthy, *The Heart of Catholic Social Teaching: Its Origins and Contemporary Significance* (Grand Rapids, MI: Brasos, 2009), p. 106.
43 Curran, *Catholic Social Teaching*, p. 147.
44 Ibid., p. 174.
45 Ibid., pp. 188 and 199.
46 Wood, *Wheatley*, p. 20.
47 Curran, *Catholic Social Teaching*, pp. 138, 150 and 199.
48 Ibid., p. 200.

49 Ibid.
50 P. Bickley, *Building Jerusalem: Christianity and the Labour Party* (London: Bible Society, 2010), pp. 47 and 48.
51 Keeble, *Christian Responsibility*, p. 177.
52 Wood, *Wheatley*, p. 18.
53 Ibid., p. 23.
54 Cloutier, 'Politics and Catholic Social Teaching', p. 135.
55 Wood, *Wheatley*, p. 26.
56 Ibid., p. 27.
57 Ibid., p. 24.
58 Ibid., p. 185.
59 Jones, *Christian Socialist Revival*, p. 28.
60 Headlam, *Socialist's Church*, p. 5.
61 Leech, 'Stewart Headlam', p. 71.
62 Jones, *Christian Socialist Revival*, p. 159.
63 S. D. Headlam, *The Meaning of the Mass: Five Lectures with Other Sermons and Addresses* (London: S.C. Brown, 1905), p. 16.
64 H. Scott Holland, ed., *Our Neighbours: A Handbook for the C.S.U.* (London: A.R. Mowbray, 1911), p. 60.
65 W. Temple, *The Church Looks Forward* (London: Macmillan, 1944), p. 113.
66 Jones, *Christian Socialist Revival*, p. 178; Holland, *Our Neighbours*, p. 60.
67 Mayor, *Churches and Labour Movement*, p. 215.
68 Jones, *Christian Socialist Revival*, p. 177.
69 Headlam, *Socialist's Church*, p. 5. Emphasis added.
70 Holland, *Our Neighbours*, p. 62.
71 Interview with Lansbury from the Christian Commonwealth Newspaper, 11 August 1915, LSE archive, Lansbury/7 213.
72 Headlam, *Meaning of the Mass*, pp. 27–8.
73 The Church of Rome – and in turn Headlam's Anglo-Catholicism – holds that there are seven sacraments, while most Protestant churches consider baptism and communion to be the only two sacraments.
74 Headlam, *Socialist's Church*, p. 7.
75 J. Keir Hardie, *Socialism and Christianity*, Keir Hardie Library No. 4 (London: n.p., 1907), p. 5.
76 J. Clifford, *The State the Church and the Congregation* (London: James Clarke & Co., 1908), p. 9.
77 G. Lansbury, *Your Part in Poverty* (London: Herald, 1917), p. 95.
78 Ibid., p. 3.
79 Headlam, *Christian Socialism*, p. 9.
80 Headlam, *Meaning of the Mass*, p. 56.

81 J. M. Winter and D. M. Joslin, eds, *R.H. Tawney's Commonplace Book* (Cambridge: Cambridge University Press, 2006), p. 71.
82 K. Keir Hardie, *Can a Man Be a Christian on a Pound a Week?* (London: ILP, 1901), pp. 1, 5 and 9.
83 E. Hughes, *Keir Hardie's Speeches and Writings (From 1888 to 1915)* (Glasgow: Forward, 1928), p. 92.
84 J. Keir Hardie, 'Labour and Christianity: Is the Labour Movement Against Christianity', *Labour and Religion: By Ten Labour Members of Parliament and Other Bodies* (London: n.p. 1910), p. 48.
85 Hughes, *Keir Hardie's Speeches*, p. 73.
86 J. Marchant, *Dr. John Clifford, C.H.: Life, Letters and Reminiscences* (London: Cassell, 1924), p. 130.
87 Clifford, *State, Church and Congregation*, p. 10.
88 Headlam, *Priestcraft and Progress*, p. 24.
89 Holland, *Our Neighbours*, p. 57.
90 G. Foote, *The Labour Party's Political Thought: A History* (Basingstoke: Palgrave Macmillan, 1997), p. 74; A. Wright, *R.H. Tawney* (Manchester: Manchester University Press, 1987), p. 99.
91 Draft of Lansbury's broadcast to the United States during his visit, 21 April 1936, LSE archive, Lansbury/16 72-81.
92 Wood, *Wheatley*, p. 29.
93 J. Wheatley, *How the Miners Are Robbed: The Duke in the Dock (Startling Court Case)* (London: Pluto, 1973 [1907]), pp. 14 and 17–18.
94 Wellock, *Christian Communism*, p. 6.
95 Tawney, *Acquisitive Society*, p. 180.
96 '"Twisted Souls". Miss Ellen Wilkinson at Burnley Church', *Northern Daily Echo*, 24 November 30.
97 Keeble, *Industrial Day-Dreams*, p. 91.
98 Lansbury/8 99; Tawney, *Acquisitive Society*, p. 184.
99 Wright, *Tawney*, p. 92.
100 Headlam, *Socialist's Church*, pp. 4–5.
101 Hardie, 'Labour and Christianity', p. 52; Hughes, *Keir Hardie's Speeches*, p. 101.
102 Hughes, *Keir Hardie's Speeches*, p. 37.
103 Ibid., p. 54.
104 B. Holman, *Keir Hardie: Labour's Greatest Hero?* (Oxford: Lion, 2010), p. 200.
105 Ibid., p. 85.
106 Tawney, *Acquisitive Society*, p. 189.
107 A. M. Suggate, 'William Temple', in P. Scott and W. T. Cavanagh, eds, *The Blackwell Companion to Political Theology* (Oxford: Wiley-Blackwell, 2004), p. 169.
108 Clifford, *Socialism and the Churches*, p. 14.

109 Clifford, *New City of God*, p. 11.
110 Wellock, *The Way Out*, p. 42; Keeble, *Industrial Day-Dreams*, p. 19.
111 Headlam, *Priestcraft and Progress*, p. vi. Emphasis in original.

Chapter 3

1. S. E. Keeble, *Industrial Day-Dreams: Studies in Industrial Ethics and Economics* (London: R. Culley, 1907 [1896]), pp. 174–5.
2. R. H. Tawney, *Equality* (London: George Allen & Unwin, 1938 [1931]), pp. 1 and 24.
3. G. Lansbury, *My Quest for Peace* (London: M. Joseph, 1938), p. 13.
4. M. Grimley, *Citizenship, Community, and the Church of England: Liberal Anglican Theories of the State Between the Wars* (Oxford: Oxford University Press, 2004), p. 54.
5. G. Dale, *God's Politicians: The Christian Contribution to 100 Years of Labour* (London: HarperCollins, 2000), p. 72.
6. C. Bryant, *Possible Dreams: A Personal History of the British Christian Socialists* (London: Hodder & Stoughton, 1996), p. 76; B. D. Vernon, *Ellen Wilkinson, 1891-1947* (London: Croom Helm, 1982), p. 9.
7. S. Mayor, *The Churches and the Labour Movement* (London: Independent, 1967), p. 227.
8. Ibid., p. 372.
9. S. D. Headlam, *Maurice and Kingsley: Theologians and Socialists* (London: George Standring, 1909), p. 5.
10. Ibid., p. 10.
11. S. D. Headlam, *Priestcraft and Progress: Being Sermons and Lectures* (London: John Hodges, 1878), p. vi.
12. K. Leech, 'Stewart Headlam, 1847-1924, and the Guild of St Matthew', in M. B. Reckitt, ed., *For Christ and the People: Studies of Four Socialist Priests and Prophets of the Church of England* (London: SPCK, 1968), p. 61.
13. T. MacQuiban, 'Soup and Salvation: Social Service as an Emerging Motif for the British Methodist Response to Poverty in the Late 19th Century', *Methodist History*, 39, no. 1 (October 2000), p. 33.
14. S. E. Keeble, *Christian Responsibility for the Social Order* (London: Epworth Press, 1922), p. 136.
15. M. S. Edwards, *S.E. Keeble: The Rejected Prophet* (Chester: Wesley Historical Society, 1977), p. 10.
16. G. Lansbury, *Your Part in Poverty* (London: Herald, 1917), p. 102; J. Keir Hardie, *From Serfdom to Socialism* (London: G. Allen, 1907), p. 28.
17. S. Spencer, 'William Temple and the "Temple Tradition"', in S. Spencer, ed., *Theology Reforming Society* (London: SCM Press, 2017), pp. 86–7; P. Avis, 'Anglican Social

Thought Encounters Modernity: Brooke Foss Westcott, Henry Scott Holland and Charles Gore', in S. Spencer, ed., *Theology Reforming Society* (London: SCM Press, 2017), p. 69.

18 P. d'A Jones, *The Christian Socialist Revival 1877-1914: Religion, Class, and Social Conscience in Late-Victorian England* (Princeton, NJ: Princeton University Press, 1968), p. 85.

19 E. Norman, 'Stewart Headlam and the Victorian Christian Socialists', *History Today*, 37, no. 4 (1987), p. 29.

20 J. R. Orens, *Stewart Headlam's Radical Anglicanism: The Mass, the Masses, and the Music Hall* (Chicago, IL: University of Illinois Press, 2003), pp. 12–13.

21 J. Morris, 'F.D. Maurice and the Myth of Christian Socialist Origins', in S. Spencer, ed., *Theology Reforming Society* (London: SCM Press, 2017), p. 7; Bryant, *Possible Dreams*, p. 41.

22 A. Wilkinson, *Christian Socialism: Scott Holland to Tony Blair* (London: SCM, 1998), p. 22.

23 Bryant, *Possible Dreams*, p. 60.

24 Mayor, *Churches and Labour Movement*, p. 265.

25 G. Taylor, *Socialism and Christianity: The Politics of the Church Socialist League* (Sheffield: IHS, 2000), p. 13.

26 R. H. Tawney, *The Radical Tradition: Twelve Essays on Politics, Education and Literature* (New York, NY: Parthenon, 1964), pp. 42.

27 Ibid., p. 44.

28 Wilkinson, *Christian Socialism*, p. 103.

29 S. E. Keeble, *The Ideal of the Material Life and Other Social Addresses* (London: C.H. Kelly, 1908), pp. 40–1.

30 Ibid., pp. 110, 115 and 233.

31 S. E. Keeble, *Christian Responsibility*, pp. 151–2; Keeble, *Industrial Day-Dreams*, p. 230; S. E. Keeble, *Christianity and Socialism: Essays for the Times* (London: R. Culley [?], 1906), p. 11.

32 Keeble, *Ideal of Material Life*, p. 54.

33 E. Lansbury, *George Lansbury: My Father* (London: S. Low, Marston & Co., 1934), p. 24.

34 Lansbury, *Poverty*, p. 14.

35 Wilkinson, *Christian Socialism*, p. 27.

36 Ibid., p. 42.

37 Jones, *Christian Socialist Revival*, p. 85.

38 Wilkinson, *Christian Socialism*, pp. 42–3.

39 M. Carter, *T.H. Green and the Development of Ethical Socialism* (Exeter: Imprint, 2003), p. 183.

40 A. Wright, *R.H. Tawney* (Manchester: Manchester University Press, 1987), p. 2.

41 Carter, *Green*, pp. 165 and 176.

42 Ibid., pp. 32, 34 and 35.

43 R. H. Tawney, 'English Politics Today: We Mean Freedom', *The Review of Politics*, 8, no. 2 (1946), pp. 224–5.
44 Ibid., p. 36.
45 Wilkinson, *Christian Socialism*, p. 67.
46 Ibid., p. 43.
47 Carter, *Green*, p. 92.
48 Ibid., p. 122.
49 Keeble, *Christian Responsibility*, p. 30; Bryant, *Possible Dreams*, p. 178.
50 Keeble, *Christianity and Socialism*, p. 36.
51 S. E. Keeble, *COPEC: An Account of the Christian Conference on Politics, Economics, and Citizenship* (London: Epworth Press, 1924), p. 9.
52 Keeble, *Christian Responsibility*, pp. 182 and 185.
53 S. E. Keeble, *The Ethics of Public Ownership* (London: Epworth Press, 1920), p. 16.
54 Hardie, *Serfdom to Socialism*, p. 11; J. Wheatley, *How the Miners Are Robbed: The Duke in the Dock (Startling Court Case)*, (London: Pluto, 1973 [1907]), p. 15.
55 Wilkinson, *Christian Socialism*, pp. 101 and 122–4.
56 Carter, *Green*, p. 179.
57 L. Goldman, *The Life of R.H. Tawney: Socialism and History* (Oxford: Bloomsbury, 2013), pp. 228–9.
58 Carter, *Green*, p. 125.
59 M. Lavalette, *George Lansbury and the Rebel Councillors of Poplar* (London: Bookmarks, 2006), p. 47; N. Branson, *Poplarism, 1919-1925: George Lansbury and the Councillors' Revolt* (London: Lawrence & Wishart, 1979).
60 W. Wellock, *The Way Out, or the Road to the New World* (London: Labour Publishing, 1922), p. 46.
61 Lansbury, *Poverty*, p. 102.
62 Wellock, *The Way Out*, p. 31.
63 J. Marchant, *Dr. John Clifford, C.H.: Life, Letters and Reminiscences* (London: Cassell, 1924), p. 130.
64 T. Judge, *Margaret Bondfield: First Woman in the Cabinet* (London: Alpha House, 2018), p. 44.
65 Jones, *Christian Socialist Revival*, p. 146; P. Bickley, *Building Jerusalem: Christianity and the Labour Party* (London: Bible Society, 2010), p. 23.
66 Jones, *Christian Socialist Revival*, p. 341.
67 Judge, *Bondfield*, pp. 171, 126–7 and 176.
68 Bryant, *Possible Dreams*, p. 179.
69 Goldman, *Tawney*, p. 296.
70 Ibid., pp. 78–9.
71 Mayor, *Churches and Labour Movement*, p. 334.
72 Ibid., p. 197.
73 Orens, *Headlam*, p. 102.

74 Tawney, *Equality*, p. 135.
75 Orens, *Headlam's Radical Anglicanism*, p. 82.
76 Bryant, *Possible Dreams*, p. 232.
77 Keeble, *Industrial Day-Dreams*, pp. 34 and 62.
78 Edwards, *Keeble*, p. 12.
79 Ibid.
80 Goldman, *Tawney*, p. 177.
81 Keeble, *Industrial Day-Dreams*, pp. 164–6.
82 J. Keir Hardie, *Karl Marx: The Man and His Message* (Manchester: National Labour Press, 1910), p. 10.
83 Hardie, *Labour Alliance*, p. 16.
84 Hardie, *Serfdom to Socialism*, pp. 86 and 53.
85 Ibid., p. 89.
86 J. Keir Hardie, *Socialism and Christianity: Keir Hardie Library No. 4* (London: n.p., 1907), p. 3.
87 B. Holman, *Keir Hardie: Labour's Greatest Hero* (Oxford: Lion, 2010), pp. 28, 41 and 132–3.
88 J. Maxton, *Keir Hardie: Prophet and Pioneer* (London: n.p., 1939), p. 14.
89 Keeble, *Industrial Day-Dreams*, p. 70.
90 Hardie, *Labour Alliance*, p. 13.
91 Hardie, *Karl Marx*, pp. 12 and 15.
92 Hardie, *Labour Alliance*, p. 14.
93 Ibid.
94 Keeble, *Industrial Day-Dreams*, p. 164; J. M. Winter and D. M. Joslin, eds, *R.H. Tawney's Commonplace Book* (Cambridge: Cambridge University Press, 2006), p. 69.
95 R. H. Tawney, 'The Choice Before the Labour Party', *Political Quarterly*, 3, no. 3 (1932), p. 26.
96 Wright, *R.H. Tawney*, p. 128.
97 E. Wilkinson and E. Conze, *Why War? A Handbook for Those Who Will Take Part in the Second World War* (London: NCLC, 1934), p. 16.
98 Ibid., p. 54.
99 Ibid., p. 40.
100 P. Bartley, *Ellen Wilkinson: From Red Suffragist to Government Minister* (London: Pluto Press, 2014), pp. 14 and 18.
101 Ibid., p. 26.
102 Ibid., p. 61; 'Miss Ellen Wilkinson', *Patriot*, 4 December 30.
103 J. Schneer, *George Lansbury* (Manchester: Manchester University Press, 1990), pp. 19 and 25.
104 Article by Lansbury entitled 'Socialists and Socialism' from *Daily Herald Newspaper*, 13 January 1913, London School of Economics [LSE] Archives, Lansbury/7 5-7.

105 Newspaper article by Lansbury in 'The Labour Leader' titled 'How I Became a Socialist', 17 May 1912, LSE Archives, Lansbury/5 36.
106 Speech by Lansbury in the House of Commons entitled 'Right to Work', 10 February 1911, LSE Archives, Lansbury/4 172-4.
107 J. Wheatley, *Houses to Let: A Speech in Exposition of Labour's Fifteen Years; Housing Programme* (London: TUC, 1924), p. 7.
108 J. Wheatley, *How the Miners Are Robbed: The Duke in the Dock (Startling Court Case)* (London: Pluto, 1973 [1907]), pp. 11 and 13.
109 S. D. Headlam, *Christian Socialism – A Lecture: Fabian Tract No. 42* (London: Fabian Society, 1899), p. 8.
110 Bryant, *Possible Dreams*, p. 82.
111 H. Scott Holland, *Our Neighbours: A Handbook for the C.S.U.* (London: A.R. Mowbray, 1911), p. 113; W. Temple, *Christianity and the Social Order* (London: Penguin, 1976 [1942]), p. 111.
112 J. Keir Hardie, *Can a Man Be a Christian?*, p. 7.
113 M. Bondfield, *Socialism for Shop Assistants: Pass on Pamphlets No. 10* (London: Clarion Press, 1909), p. 14.
114 Judge, *Bondfield*, pp. 31–2.
115 Dale, *God's Politicians*, p. 100.
116 Bondfield, *Socialism for Shop Assistants*, p. 15; Schneer, *Lansbury*, p. 25.
117 J. Clifford, *Socialism and the Churches – Fabian Tract No. 139* (London: Fabian Society, 1908), p. 3.
118 Ibid., p. 8.
119 See J. Bennett, *God and Progress: Religion and History in British Intellectual Culture, 1845-1914* (Oxford: Oxford University Press, 2019).
120 Lavalette, *George Lansbury*, p. 5.
121 Ibid., p. 14.
122 J. Callaghan, *Socialism in Britain Since 1884* (Oxford: Wiley-Blackwell, 1990), p. 96.
123 G. Lansbury, *What I Saw in Russia* (London: Boni and Liveright, 1920), pp. xii and 28.
124 Ibid., pp. 42 and 107.
125 Bartley, *Wilkinson*, pp. 18–19; 'Miss Ellen Wilkinson: Former Socialist M.P. Visits Lynn', *Lynn Advertiser*, 8/7/32.
126 Bartley, *Wilkinson*, pp. 17–18.
127 Ibid., p. 94; B. D. Vernon, *Ellen Wilkinson, 1891-1947* (London: Croom Helm, 1982), p. 96.
128 Bartley, *Wilkinson*, p. 84.
129 A. Rigby, *Wilfred Wellock: A Life in Peace* (Bridport: Prism, 1988), p. 59.
130 Tawney, *The Radical Tradition*, p. 158.
131 Judge, *Bondfield*, pp. 98 and 103.
132 Jones, *Christian Socialist Revival*, p. 17.

133 H. George, *Thy Kingdom Come* (Glasgow: Scottish Land Restoration League, 1889), p. 12.
134 Jones, *Christian Socialist Revival*, p. 103.
135 Leech, 'Stewart Headlam', p. 189.
136 Bryant, *Possible Dreams*, p. 82; Jones, *Christian Socialist Revival*, p. 114.
137 Headlam, *Christian Socialism*, p. 11.
138 Ibid., pp. 12–13.
139 Ibid., p. 13.
140 George, *Kingdom*, p. 5.
141 Lansbury, *Your Part in Poverty*, p. 102; Hardie, *Serfdom to Socialism*, pp. 117–18.
142 Ibid., p. 118.
143 J. Bruce Glasier, *Keir Hardie: A Memorial* (Manchester: National Labour Press, 1915), p. 13.
144 Holland, *Our Neighbours*, p. 6.
145 George, *Kingdom*, p. 16.
146 R. H. Tawney, *The Acquisitive Society* (London: Bell, 1921), pp. 28 and 14.
147 Bickley, *Building Jerusalem*, p. 43.
148 Temple, *Christianity and the Social Order*, p. 112.
149 Jones, *Christian Socialist Revival*, p. 137. Emphasis in original.
150 G. D. H. Cole, *James Keir Hardie: Fabian Society Biographical Series No. 12* (London: Fabian Society, 1941), p. 13.
151 'To the electors of the Walworth Division of Newington', August 1895, LSE archives, Lansbury/30 b2.
152 Hardie, *Marx*, p. 14.
153 Hardie may only have joined because he had to be a member of a socialist organization to be secretary of the British section of the International (Bickley, *Building Jerusalem*, p. 29).
154 Mayor, *The Churches and the Labour Movement*, p. 190.
155 G. Foote, *The Labour Party's Political Thought* (Basingstoke: Palgrave Macmillan, 1997), p. 30; Clifford, *Socialism and the Churches*, p. 6.
156 Holland, *Our Neighbours*, p. 86.
157 Ibid., pp. 67–8.
158 Jones, *Christian Socialist Revival*, p. 186.
159 Edwards, *Keeble*, p. 30.
160 Keeble, *Industrial Day-Dreams*, p. 74.
161 Goldman, *Tawney*, pp. 170–1.
162 Winter and Joslin, *Tawney's Commonplace Book*, p. 46.
163 Bryant, *Possible Dreams*, p. 146.
164 Mayor, *Churches and Labour Movement*, p. 364.
165 Taylor, *Socialism and Christianity*, pp. 33 and 34.
166 Ibid., p. 31.

167 Bickley, *Building Jerusalem*, p. 44.
168 Tawney, *Acquisitive Society*, p. 99.
169 Ibid., p. 92.
170 Keeble, *Christian Socialism*, p. 224.
171 Hardie, *Serfdom to Socialism*, p. 18.
172 Rigby, *Wellock*, p. 28; W. Wellock, *Christian Communism: What It Is and Why It Is Necessary* (Manchester: National Labour Press, 1921), p. 30.
173 Taylor, *Socialism and Christianity*, pp. 41 and 28.
174 Lansbury, *Poverty*, p. 113.
175 Wright, *Tawney*, p. 69.
176 Ibid., pp. 69–70.
177 Wilkinson, *Christian Socialism*, p. 39.
178 Keeble, *Christian Responsibility*, p. 129.
179 Tawney, *Radical Tradition*, p. 26.
180 M. Beech and K. Hickson, *Labour's Thinkers: The Intellectual Roots of Labour from Tawney to Gordon Brown* (London: I.B. Tauris, 2007), pp. 26 and 32.
181 Tawney, *Radical Tradition*, p. 21.
182 Ibid., p. 18.
183 Goldman, *Tawney*, p. 191.
184 Hughes, *Hardie's Speeches*, p. 47.
185 Ibid., p. 79.
186 Newspaper cutting from the Manchester Daily Despatch 'Mr. George Lansbury, the man who menaced the premier', 26 June 1913, LSE archive, Lansbury/28 72.
187 'The Labour unrest. Its causes, effects and remedies. Wages, wealth, monopoly', parliamentary speeches by George Lansbury and others, 1912, LSE archive, Lansbury/30 a 5.
188 Taylor, *Socialism and Christianity*, p. 3.
189 T. Mann, 'George Lansbury', *Syndicalist* 1, 11, December 1912.
190 Holman, *Hardie*, p. 170.

Chapter 4

1 J. Shepherd, *George Lansbury: At the Heart of Old Labour* (Oxford: Oxford University Press, 2002), p. 15. The poverty and mistreatment Lansbury suffered in Australia persuaded him all the more of the deficiencies and immorality of capitalism.
2 J. Schneer, *George Lansbury* (Manchester: Manchester University Press, 1990), p. 119.
3 Newspaper article in the *Halifax Evening Courier* about a speech by Lansbury at Sowerby Bridge, 26 February 1912, London School of Economics [LSE] archives, Lansbury/5 19.

4   J. Keir Hardie, *My Confession of Faith in the Labour Alliance* (London: ILP, 1909), p. 14.
5   J. Keir Hardie, *From Serfdom to Socialism* (London: G. Allen, 1907), p. 4.
6   E. Hughes, *Keir Hardie's Speeches and Writings from 1888 to 1915* (Glasgow: Forward, 1927), p. 73.
7   J. R. Orens, *Stewart Headlam's Radical Anglicanism: The Mass, the Masses, and the Music Hall* (Chicago, IL: University of Illinois Press, 2003), pp. 21, 105 and 102.
8   K. Leech, 'Stewart Headlam, 1847-1924, and the Guild of St Matthew', in M. B. Reckitt, ed., *For Christ and the People: Studies of Four Socialist Priests and Prophets of the Church of England* (London: SPCK, 1968), p. 84.
9   I. S. Wood, *John Wheatley* (Manchester: Manchester University Press, 1990), p. 155.
10 Wood, *Wheatley*, p. 185; A. Rigby, *Wilfred Wellock: A Life in Peace* (Bridport: Prism, 1988), p. 40.
11 J. Marchant, *Dr. John Clifford, C.H.: Life, Letters and Reminiscences* (London: Cassell, 1924), p. 81.
12 W. Wellock, *The Way Out, or the Road to the New World* (London: Labour Publishing, 1922), pp. 35–6; S. E. Keeble, *Christian Responsibility for the Social Order* (London: Epworth Press, 1922), p. 212.
13 R. H. Tawney, *Democracy or Defeat – By a WEA Soldier* (London: n.p., 1917), p. 9.
14 M. Lavalette, *George Lansbury and the Rebel Councillors of Poplar* (London: Bookmark, 2006), p. 14.
15 B. D. Vernon, *Ellen Wilkinson, 1891-1947* (London: Croom Helm, 1982), p. 58.
16 S. E. Keeble, *Christianity and Socialism: Essays for the Times* (London: R. Culley [?], 1906), p. 8.
17 Keeble, *Christian Responsibility*, p. 204.
18 S. E. Keeble, *The Ideal of the Material Life and Other Social Addresses* (London: C.H. Kelly, 1908), p. 101.
19 Rigby, *Wellock*, p. 67.
20 Antimilitarism speech by Lansbury, *The Arbitrator*, May 1892, LSE archives, Lansbury/1 150.
21 Schneer, *Lansbury*, p. 146.
22 B. Holman, *Keir Hardie: Labour's Greatest Hero?* (Oxford: Lion, 2010), p. 96.
23 Hardie, *Serfdom to Socialism*, p. 28.
24 Hardie, *Labour Alliance*, p. 11.
25 Hughes, *Hardie's Speeches and Writings*, p. 49.
26 Holman, *Hardie*, p. 170.
27 P. Bartley, *Ellen Wilkinson: From Red Suffragist to Government Minister* (London: Pluto Press, 2014), pp. 85 and 115.
28 'Miss Ellen Wilkinson at Burslem', *Staffordshire Advertiser*, 3-2-34.
29 Vernon, *Wilkinson*, p. 226.
30 Wood, *Wheatley*, p. 70.

31 M. Beech and K. Hickson, *Labour's Thinkers: The Intellectual Roots of Labour from Tawney to Gordon Brown* (London: I.B. Tauris, 2007), p. 32.
32 R. H. Tawney, *Equality* (London: George Allen & Unwin, 1938 [1931]), p. 268; R. H. Tawney, *The Radical Tradition: Twelve Essays on Politics, Education and Literature* (New York, NY: Parthenon, 1964), p. 26.
33 G. Lansbury, *Your Part in Poverty* (London: Herald, 1917), p. 119.
34 Letter from Lansbury to John Armitage, 9 March 1940, LSE archive, Lansbury/17 160-2; Letter from Lansbury to Harold Arthur Hill, 14 June 1929, LSE archive, Lansbury/9 173-4.
35 J. Clifford, *Socialism and the Churches: Fabian Tract No. 139* (London: Fabian Society, 1908), p. 6.
36 G. Lansbury, *What I Saw in Russia* (London: Boni & Liveright, 1920), p. 59.
37 Ibid., p. xii.
38 M. S. Edwards, *S.E. Keeble: The Rejected Prophet* (Chester: Wesley Historical Society, 1977), p. 55.
39 Rigby, *Wellock*, p. 59.
40 Newspaper cutting from the Northamptonshire Evening Telegraph, featuring the policies of Lansbury as outlined by him in a public meeting to the people of Rushden, 21 March 1931, LSE archive, Lansbury/10 56.
41 Wellock, *The Way Out*, pp. 35-6 and 38.
42 Rigby, *Wellock*, pp. 29, 56 and 68-9.
43 S. D. Headlam, *The Meaning of the Mass: Five Lectures with Other Sermons and Addresses* (London: S.C. Brown, 1905), p. 68. Emphasis in original.
44 S. D. Headlam, *The Socialist's Church* (London: G. Allen, 1907), pp. 13 and 25.
45 Newspaper article about a speech by Lansbury on socialism, 18 September 1912, LSE archives, Lansbury/6 140.
46 Lansbury, *Russia*, p. 171.
47 Newspaper article from the Daily Sketch by Lansbury, explaining his background to Socialist thought, 18 June 1931, LSE archive, Lansbury/10 69.
48 Parliamentary Election, 1929, LSE archive, Lansbury/30 b 35-7; G. Lansbury, *My Quest for Peace* (London, 1938), p. 19.
49 Interview with Lansbury from the Christian Commonwealth Newspaper, 11 August 1915, LSE archive Lansbury/7 213.
50 Holman, *Hardie*, p. 57.
51 Edwards, *Keeble*, p. 34.
52 Keeble, *Christian Responsibility*, p. 212.
53 Tawney, *Radical Tradition*, pp. 168 and 169.
54 J. Clifford, *The New City of God: The Primitive Christian Faith as a Social Gospel* (London: Alexander & Shepherd, 1888), p. 9; J. Wheatley, *Socialise the National Income!* (London: ILP, 1927), p. 14.

55 T. Judge, *Margaret Bondfield: First Woman in the Cabinet* (London: Alpha House, 2018), p. 109.
56 M. Bondfield, *Why Labour Fights* (n.p., 1941), p. 2.
57 W. Wellock, *Which Way, Britain?* (Hereford: Hereford Times, 1942), p. 4.
58 Ibid., pp. 45–6.
59 Ibid., p. 46.

Chapter 5

1 R. H. Tawney, *The Radical Tradition: Twelve Essays on Politics, Education and Literature* (New York, NY: Parthenon, 1964), p. 177.
2 R. H. Tawney, *Equality* (London: George Allen & Unwin, 1938 [1931]), pp. 273 and 266.
3 J. Keir Hardie, *The I.L.P. and All About It* (Manchester: National Labour Press, 1908), p. 11.
4 M. Bondfield, F. A. Broad, Harold Clay, E. Harold, A. Creech Jones, H. Kegie, Francis Edmund Lawley; Fred Longden, Wilfred Paling, John Paton, Emanuel Shinwell, J. Allen Skinner, Mark Starr, G. W. Thomson, W. M. Watson, E. F. Wise, Brockway Fenner,, *Trade Unions and Socialism* (London: ILP, 1926), p. 3.
5 J. M. Winter and D. M. Joslin, eds, *R.H. Tawney's Commonplace Book* (Cambridge: Cambridge University Press, 2006), p. 31.
6 R. H. Tawney, *The Acquisitive Society* (London: Bell, 1921), p. 180.
7 Ibid., p. 189.
8 S. E. Keeble, *The Ideal of the Material Life and Other Social Addresses* (London: C.H. Kelly, 1908), pp. 104 and 169.
9 Ibid., pp. 12 and 86.
10 S. E. Keeble, *Towards the New Era: A Draft Scheme of Industrial Reconstruction* (London: C.H. Kelly, 1917), p. 4.
11 A. M. Suggate, 'William Temple', in P. Scott and W. T. Cavangh, eds, *The Blackwell Companion to Political Theology* (Oxford, 2004), p. 160.
12 W. Temple, *Christianity and the Social Order* (London: Penguin, 1976 [1942]), p. 115.
13 J. Clifford, *Socialism and the Churches: Fabian Tract No. 139* (London: Fabian Society, 1908), p. 14.
14 G. Lansbury, *Your Part in Poverty* (London: Herald, 1917), p. 43; G. Lansbury, *What I Saw in Russia* London: Boni & Liveright), p. 52.
15 S. D. Headlam, *Priestcraft and Progress: Being Sermons and Lectures* (London: John Hodges, 1878), p. vi. Emphasis in original.
16 S. D. Headlam, *The Socialist's Church* (London: G. Allen, 1907), p. 12.

17 Headlam, *Socialist's Church*, p. 48; S. D. Headlam, *The Meaning of the Mass: Five Lectures with Other Sermons and Addresses* (London: S.C. Brown, 1905), p. 122.
18 W. Wellock, *The Way Out, or the Road to the New World* (London: Labour Publishing, 1922), pp. 25–6.
19 Tawney, *Acquisitive Society*, p. 189.
20 S. E. Keeble, *Industrial Day-Dreams: Studies in Industrial Ethics and Economics* (London: R. Culley, 1907 [1896]), p. 229.
21 S. E. Keeble, *Christian Responsibility for the Social Order* (London: Epworth Press, 1922), p. 275.
22 A. Wright, *R.H. Tawney* (Manchester: Manchester University Press, 1987), p. 33.
23 S. E. Keeble, *COPEC: An Account of the Christian Conference on Politics, Economics, and Citizenship* (London: Epworth Press, 1924), p. 16.
24 Keeble, *Material Life*, p. 15.
25 Headlam, *Socialist's Church*, p. 23.
26 P. d'A Jones, *The Christian Socialist Revival 1877-1914: Religion, Class, and Social Conscience in Late-Victorian England* (Princeton NJ: PUP, 1968), p. 218.
27 J. Schneer, *George Lansbury* (Manchester: MUP, 1990), p. 141.
28 A. Rigby, *Wilfred Wellock: A Life in Peace* (Bridport: Prism, 1988), p. 36.
29 H. Scott Holland, ed., *Our Neighbours: A Handbook for the C.S.U.* (London: A.R. Mowbray, 1911), p. 58.
30 S. D. Headlam, *Christian Socialism – A Lecture: Fabian Tract No. 42* (London: Fabian Society, 1899), p. 9.
31 Headlam, *Meaning of the Mass*, p. 56.
32 J. Clifford, *The State the Church and the Congregation* (London: James Clarke & Co., 1908), p. 9.
33 Ibid., p. 3.
34 W. Temple, *The Church Looks Forward* (London: Macmillan, 1944), p. 117.
35 Suggate, 'Temple', pp. 169–70.
36 Jones, *Christian Socialist Revival*, p. 181.
37 Keeble, *Industrial Day-Dreams*, p. 7.
38 Ibid., p. 22.
39 Keeble, *Christian Responsibility*, pp. 279 and 271.
40 G. Lansbury, 'Power that Re-Makes Men', in *Labour and Religion: By Ten Labour Members of Parliament and Other Bodies* (London: n.p., 1910), p. 74.
41 Ibid., p. 269.
42 J. Maxton, *Keir Hardie: Prophet and Pioneer* (London: n.p., 1933), p. 14.
43 J. Keir Hardie, 'Labour and Christianity: Is the Labour Movement Against Christianity?', in *Labour and Religion: By Ten Labour Members of Parliament and Other Bodies* (London: n.p., 1910), p. 52; E. Hughes, *Keir Hardie's Speeches and Writings from 1888 to 1915* (Glasgow: Forward, 1927), p. 101.
44 Hughes, *Keir Hardie's Speeches*, p. 54.

45 J. Keir Hardie, *My Confession of Faith in the Labour Alliance* (London: ILP, 1909), p. 11.
46 Schneer, *Lansbury*, pp. 31-3.
47 Lansbury, 'Power that Re-makes Men', p. 70.
48 Luke 10:25-37; Keeble, *Industrial Day-Dreams*, p. 234.
49 T. Judge, *Margaret Bondfield: First Woman in the Cabinet* (London: Alpha House, 2018), p. 30.
50 A. Wilkinson, *Christian Socialism: Scott Holland to Tony Blair* (London: SCM, 1998), p. 212.
51 B. D. Vernon, *Ellen Wilkinson, 1891-1947* (London: Croom Helm, 1982), p. 19; G. Dale, *God's Politicians: The Christian Contribution to 100 Years of Labour* (London: HarperCollins), p. 124.
52 G. Armstrong and T. Gray, 'Three Fallacies in the Essentialist Interpretation of the Political Thought of R.H. Tawney', *Journal of Political Ideologies*, 15, 2 (2010), p. 165.
53 Ibid., p. 171.
54 Wright, *Tawney*, pp. 32-3.
55 Ibid., p. 136.
56 Armstrong and Gray, 'Three Fallacies', p. 169.
57 M. Beech and K. Hickson, *Labour's Thinkers: The Intellectual Roots of Labour from Tawney to Gordon Brown* (London: I.B. Tauris, 2007), p. 28.
58 Jones, *Christian Socialist Revival*, p. 334.
59 Ibid., p. 181.
60 Holland, *Our Neighbours*, p. 69.
61 S. E. Keeble, *The Ethics of Public Ownership* (London: Epworth Press, 1920), p. 9.
62 Ibid., p. 15.
63 Headlam, *Christian Socialism*, p. 8.
64 Clifford, *Socialism and the Churches*, p. 9.
65 P. Bartley, *Ellen Wilkinson: From Red Suffragist to Government Minister* (London: Pluto Press, 2014), p. 138.
66 G. Foote, *The Labour Party's Political Thought: A History* (Basingstoke: Palgrave Macmillan, 1997), p. 44.
67 Hughes, *Hardie's Speeches and Writings*, pp. 76 and 69.
68 J. Keir Hardie, *Karl Marx: The Man and His Message* (Manchester: National Labour Press, 1910), p. 11.
69 Lansbury, 'Power that Re-Makes Men', p. 74.
70 S. Mayor, *The Churches and the Labour Movement* (London: Independent, 1967), p. 223.
71 R. H. Tawney, 'The Choice Before the Labour Party', *Political Quarterly*, 3, no. 3 (1932), p. 28.
72 Ibid., pp. 26-7.
73 Ibid., p. 27.

74 Wellock, *The Way Out*, p. 55.
75 Bartley, *Wilkinson*, p. 56.
76 J. Wheatley, *How the Miners are Robbed: The Duke in the Dock (Startling Court Case)*, (London: Pluto, 1973 [1907]), p. 15. Wheatley here suggests that the election of Labour is '[t]he first step'. We may maintain that it is the second, for the persuasion of the electorate is the necessary precursor.
77 I. S. Wood, *John Wheatley* (Manchester: Manchester University Press, 1990), p. 118.
78 Ibid., p. 157.
79 Ibid., p. 181.
80 Vernon, *Wilkinson*, pp. 112 and 138; 'Ellen Wilkinson Sees Britain as Solid for Peace', *New York Morning World*, 18/1/31.
81 Tawney, 'Choice Before Labour', p. 34.
82 Jones, *Christian Socialist Revival*, p. 138.
83 Ibid., pp. 140–1.
84 Headlam, *Socialist's Church*, p. 73.
85 Ibid., p. 54.
86 J. R. Orens, *Stewart Headlam's Radical Anglicanism: The Mass, the Masses, and the Music Hall* (Chicago, IL: University of Illinois Press, 2003), p. 116.
87 Jones, *Christian Socialist Revival*, pp. 217–8.
88 Wilkinson, *Christian Socialism*, p. 51.
89 Ibid., p. 54.
90 M. Carter, *T.H. Green and the Development of Ethical Socialism* (Exeter: Imprint, 2003), p. 125; Wilkinson, *Christian Socialism*, p. 73.
91 Wilkinson, *Christian Socialism*, p. 46.
92 Clifford, *Socialism and the Churches*, p. 6.
93 J. Marchant, *Dr. John Clifford, C.H.: Life, Letters and Reminiscences* (London: Cassell, 1924), p. 147.
94 Ibid.
95 B. Holman, *Keir Hardie: Labour's Greatest Hero?* (Oxford: Lion, 2010), pp. 97 and 118–9.
96 J. Scheer, *George Lansbury* (Manchester: Manchester University Press, 1990), pp. 89–91.
97 Newspaper article about John Burns and the Social Democratic Federation, authored by Lansbury, 25 January 1894, London School of Economics [LSE] archive, Lansbury/1 203.
98 E. Lansbury, *George Lansbury: My Father* (London: S. Low, Marston & Co., 1934), p. 201.
99 Hardie, *Labour Alliance*, p. 7.
100 Hughes, *Hardie's Speeches and Writings*, p. 12.
101 Ibid., p. 7.
102 Ibid., p. 16.

103 Leaflet advertising Lansbury's candidature for Guardian in Bow, 15 December 1894, LSE archives, Lansbury/1 222.
104 Holland, *Our Neighbours*, p. 72.
105 Ibid., p. 81.
106 Tawney, *Acquisitive Society*, pp. 124–5.
107 Wood, *Wheatley*, p. 40.
108 Ibid., pp. 41 and 88.
109 M. Lavallette, *George Lansbury and the Rebel Councillors of Poplar* (London: Bookmark, 2006), p. 12.
110 Wood, *Wheatley*, p. 125.
111 Ibid., p. 126.
112 N. Branson, Poplarism, *1919-25: George Lansbury and the Councillors' Revolt* (London: Lawrence & Wishart, 1979), p. 166.
113 W. Wellock, *Christian Communism: What It Is and Why It Is Necessary* (Manchester: National Labour Press, 1922), p. 33.
114 Schneer, *Lansbury*, p. 40.
115 Article by Lansbury titled 'The Federation of Trade Unions' in 'The Worker', January 1912, LSE archive, Lansbury/5 2-3.
116 Newspaper article authored by Lansbury for how to solve the unemployment problem through state labour colonies, 16 December 1905, Lansbury/2 173.
117 Branson, *Poplarism*, p. 215.
118 Holland, *Our Neighbours*, p. 83.
119 Ibid., p. 86.
120 Ibid., pp. 88–9. A. Swift, *Political Philosophy* (Cambridge: Polity, 2001).
121 J. Keir Hardie, *From Serfdom to Socialism* (London: G. Allen, 1907), pp. 6–7.
122 Wright, *Tawney*, p. 113.
123 Wood, *Wheatley*, p. 166.
124 Wilkinson, *Christian Socialism*, pp. 71–2.
125 Keeble, *Christian Responsibility*, p. 206.
126 Holland, *Our Neighbours*, pp. 88–9.
127 Keeble, *Christian Responsibility*, p. 269.
128 Wellock, *Christian Communism*, p. 15.
129 Hardie, *Marx*, p. 11.
130 Winter and Joslin, *Tawney's Commonplace Book*, p. 52.
131 Ibid.
132 Keeble, *Towards the New Era*, pp. 24, 29–31, 36 and 39.
133 Leaflet advertising Lansbury's Parliamentary Election bid in Bow and Bromley, [August?] 1900, LSE archive, Lansbury/1 334–5.
134 T. L. Jarman, *Socialism in Britain: From the Industrial Revolution to the Present Day* (Ann Arbor, MI: Littlehampton, 1978), pp. 106–7.
135 Wood, *Wheatley*, p. 181.

136 Clifford, *Socialism and the Churches*, p. 4.
137 Keeble, *Industrial Day-Dreams*, p. 134.
138 Wright, *Tawney*, p. 110.
139 J. Callaghan, *Socialism in Britain since 1884* (Oxford: Wiley-Blackwell, 1990), p. 152.
140 F. Johnson, *Keir Hardie's Socialism* (London: ILP, 1922), p. 13.
141 Jarman, *Socialism in Britain*, p. 106.
142 Headlam, *Socialist's Church*, p. 54.
143 M. Bondfield, *Socialism for Shop Assistants: Pass On Pamphlets No. 10* (London: Clarion Press, 1909), p. 14.
144 Wood, *Wheatley*, p. 122.
145 Ibid., p. 139.

Chapter 6

1 P. Bartley, *Ellen Wilkinson: From Red Suffragist to Government Minister* (London: Pluto Press, 2014), p. 85.
2 Interview with Lansbury from the *Christian Commonwealth* Newspaper, 11 August 1915, London School of Economics [LSE] archive, Lansbury/7 213.
3 Bartley, *Wilkinson*, p. 24.
4 G. Lansbury, *My Quest for Peace* (London: M. Joseph, 1938), p. 26.
5 J. Schneer, *George Lansbury* (Manchester: Manchester University Press, 1990), p. 119.
6 Bartley, *Wilkinson*, p. 85.
7 J. Keir Hardie, *My Confession of Faith in the Labour Alliance* (London: ILP, 1909), p. 14.
8 W. Wellock, *The Way Out, or the Road to the New World* (London: Labour Publishing, 1922), pp. 35–6; S. D. Headlam, *The Socialist's Church* (London: G. Allen, 1907), p. 25; Parliamentary Election, 1929, LSE archive, Lansbury/6 140; T. Judge, *Margaret Bondfield: First Woman in the Cabinet* (London: Alpha House, 2018), p. 109; S. E. Keeble, *Christian Responsibility for the Social Order* (London: Epworth Press, 1922), p. 212; J. Wheatley, *Socialise the National Income!* (London: ILP, 1927), p. 15.
9 B. Holman, *Keir Hardie: Labour's Greatest Hero?* (Oxford: Lion, 2010), p. 57.
10 A. Wright, *Socialisms Old and New* (London: Routledge, 1996), p. 57.
11 A case could be made against Holland on this point, that he never aimed at replacing capitalism with socialism, but, again, Holland was not one of those who called for revolution.
12 Ibid., p. 67.
13 H. Tudor and J. M. Tudor, eds, *Marxism and Social Democracy: The Revisionist Debate 1896-1898* (Cambridge: Cambridge University Press, 1988), pp. 34 and 35.
14 Ibid., pp. 19, 21 and 27.

15 Wright, *Socialisms*, p.60. Emphases in original.
16 G. Lansbury, *Your Part in Poverty* (London: Herald, 1917), p. 36.
17 Correspondence between Lansbury and Richard Lee, 16–19 February 1935. Enclosed a copy of the statements made by Lansbury in the House of Commons, 14 September 1931, LSE archive, Lansbury/25 3 o 144-152.
18 J. Wheatley, 'A Deceptive Concoction', in J. Wheatley et al., eds, *Labour Exposes the Pensions Scheme* (London: TUC, 1925), p. 8; J. Hardie, *The I.L.P. and all About It* (Manchester: National Labour Press, 1908), p. 9.
19 Bartley, *Wilkinson*, p. 136.
20 See Chapters 7–9 for details of the society imagined by Christian Socialists.
21 G. Foote, *The Labour Party's Political Thought: A History* (Basingstoke: Palgrave Macmillan, 1997), pp. 79 and 49. Emphasis in original.
22 Holman, *Keir Hardie*, p. 97.
23 L. Goldman, *The Life of R.H. Tawney: Socialism and History* (Oxford: Bloomsbury, 2013), p. 8.
24 P. Bickley, *Building Jerusalem: Christianity and the Labour Party* (London: Bible Society, 2010), p. 29.
25 F. Johnson, *Keir Hardie's Socialism* (London: ILP, 1922), pp. 8 and 14.
26 A. Wright, *R.H. Tawney* (Manchester: Manchester University Press, 1987), p. 145.
27 A. Rigby, *Wilfred Wellock: A Life in Peace* (Bridport: Prism, 1988), p. 35.
28 W. Wellock, *Christian Communism: What It Is and Why It Is Necessary* (Manchester: National Labour Press, 1922), p. 1.
29 Ibid., p. 42.
30 Wellock, *Way Out*, p. 29.
31 Rigby, *Wellock*, pp. 26–7.
32 Wellock, *Christian Communism*, p. 30.
33 Ibid., p. 16.
34 Wellock, *Way Out*, p. 17. See also pp. 14–15.
35 Wellock, *Christian Communism*, p. 32.
36 Newspaper article by Lansbury in 'The Labour Leader' titled 'How I became a Socialist', 17 May 1912, LSE archive, Lansbury/5 36.
37 Wellock, *Christian Communism*, p. 32.
38 Rigby, *Wellock*, p. 50.
39 Ibid., pp. 84–5.
40 Foote, *Labour Party Political Thought*, pp. 79 and 49. Emphasis in original.
41 R. H. Tawney, *The Acquisitive Society* (London: Bell, 1921), p. 188; G. Lansbury, 'Back to the Galilean!', in G. N. Barnes, ed., *The Religion in the Labour Movement* (London: Holborn, 1919), p. 56.
42 G. Lansbury, 'The Power that Re-makes Men', in *Labour and Religion: By Ten Members of Parliament and Other Bodies* (St Albans: WA Hammond, 1910), p. 78.

Chapter 7

1. P. d'A Jones, *The Christian Socialist Revival 1877-1914: Religion, Class, and Social Conscience in Late-Victorian England* (Princeton, NJ: Princeton University Press, 1968), p. 181.
2. W. Temple, *The Place of the Church in Relation to Social Reform* (London: n.p, 1943), pp. 9–10. See also, W. Temple, *The Church Looks Forward* (London: Macmillan, 1944), p. v.
3. S. D. Headlam, *The Meaning of the Mass: Five Lectures with Other Sermons and Addresses* (London: S.C. Brown, 1905), p. 123. Emphasis in original.
4. S. E. Keeble, *Industrial Day-Dreams: Studies in Industrial Ethics and Economics* (London: R. Culley, 1907 [1896]), p. 19.
5. J. Keir Hardie, *From Serfdom to Socialism* (London: G. Allen, 1907), p. 96.
6. Keeble, *Industrial Day-Dreams*, pp. 134 and 136. S. D. Headlam, *The Socialist's Church* (London: G. Allen, 1907), p. 53.
7. Headlam, *Socialist's Church*, p. 53.
8. Ibid., p. 55.
9. By-election address for parliamentary representative of Walworth, February 1894, London School of Economics [LSE] archive, Lansbury/1 204-208; Programme for Guardians' Election, Lansbury as Social-Democratic candidate for Bow and Bromley, [November?] 1894, LSE archive, Lansbury/1 222.
10. Memorandum regarding unemployment by Lansbury, 22 July 1929, London School of Economics [LSE] archive, Lansbury/19 81-94.
11. S. E. Keeble, *The Ideal of the Material Life and other Social Addresses* (London: C.H. Kelly, 1908), pp. 80–1.
12. J. Wheatley, *Houses to Let: A Speech in Exposition of Labour's Fifteen Years' Housing Programme* (London: TUC, 1924), pp. 8 and 11.
13. J. Keir Hardie, *The I.L.P. and All About It* (Manchester: National Labour Press, 1908), p. 6.
14. Hardie, *Serfdom to Socialism*, p. 89.
15. J. T. Leckie, *Socialism in Britain: From the Industrial Revolution to the Present Day* (New York, NY: Taplinger, 1972), pp. 106–7.
16. B. Holman, *Keir Hardie: Labour's Greatest Hero?* (Oxford: Lion, 2010), p. 56.
17. J. Callaghan, *Socialism in Britain since 1884* (Oxford: Wiley-Blackwell, 1990), p. 55.
18. L. Goldman, *The Life of R.H. Tawney: Socialism and History* (Oxford: Bloomsbury, 2013), pp. 122 and 282.
19. M. Bondfield, et al., *Trade Unions and Socialism* (London: ILP, 1926), pp. 4 and 10.
20. Ibid., p. 12.
21. I. S. Wood, *John Wheatley* (Manchester: Manchester University Press, 1990), p. 181.
22. J. Wheatley, *Socialise the National Income!* (London: ILP, 1927), p. 9.

23 E. Norman, 'Stewart Headlam and the Victorian Christian Socialists', *History Today*, 37, no. 4 (1987), p. 31.
24 J. R. Orens, *Stewart Headlam's Radical Anglicanism: The Mass, the Masses, and the Music Hall* (Chicago, IL: University of Illinois Press, 2003), p. 57.
25 Jones, *Christian Socialist Revival*, p. 114.
26 S. Mayor, *The Churches and Labour Movement* (London: Independent, 1967), p. 227.
27 Keeble, *The Ideal of the Material Life*, p. 70.
28 J. Clifford, *Socialism and the Churches: Fabian Tract No.139* (London: Fabian Society, 1908), p. 3.
29 J. Clifford, *Socialism and the Teaching of Christ: Fabian Tract No.78* (London: Fabian Society, 1897), p. 9.
30 Mayor, *The Churches and the Labour Movement*, p. 203.
31 E. Hughes, *Keir Hardie's Speeches and Writings – From 1888 to 1915* (Glasgow: Forward, 1927), p. 70.
32 Jones, *Christian Socialist Revival*, p. 17.
33 Ibid., p. 116.
34 K. Leech, 'Stewart Headlam, 1847-1924, and the Guild of St Matthew', in M. B. Reckitt, ed., *For Christ and the People: Studies of Four Socialist Priests and Prophets of the Church of England* (London: SPCK, 1968), p. 80.
35 G. Lansbury, *Your Part in Poverty* (London: Herald, 1917), p. 117.
36 J. M. Winter and D. M. Joslin, eds, *R.H. Tawney's Commonplace Book* (Cambridge: Cambridge University Press, 2006), p. 52.
37 Hughes, *Hardie's Speeches and Writings*, p. 76.
38 W. Temple, *Christianity and the Social Order* (London: Penguin, 1976 [1942]), p. 101.
39 J. Wheatley, *How the Miners Are Robbed: The Duke in the Dock (startling court case)* (London: Pluto, [1907]), p. 15.
40 Ibid.
41 'To the electors of the Walworth Division of Newington', August 1895, LSE archive, Lansbury/30 b 2.
42 Bow and Bromley Branch of the Social Democratic Federation 'An address to the men and women of Bow and Bromley', 1892, LSE archive, Lansbury/30 a 1.
43 F. Johnson, *Keir Hardie's Socialism* (London: ILP, 1922), p. 11.
44 Headlam, *Socialist's Church*, p. 57.
45 S. Keeble, *Christianity and Socialism: Essays for the Times* (London: R. Culley [?], 1906), p. 18.
46 Middlesborough Election News, 2-11 January 1906, LSE archive, Lansbury/30 c 1. [The newspaper clipping of a story regarding Lansbury's Middlesbrough election campaign also included sections of a lecture by Clifford.]
47 R. H. Tawney, *The Acquisitive Society* (London: Bell, 1921), p. 14.
48 Temple, *Church Looks Forward*, p. 111.

49 Ibid., p. 128.
50 Temple, *Christianity and the Social Order*, p. 112.
51 Keeble, *Material Life*, p. 224. Emphasis in original.
52 Keeble, *Industrial Day-Dreams*, pp. 90 and 272.
53 S. E. Keeble, *Towards the New Era: A Draft Scheme of Industrial Reconstruction* (London: C.H. Kelly, 1917), p. 14. Emphasis added.
54 Ibid., pp. 35 and 32–3.
55 R. H. Tawney, *Acquisitive Society* (London: Bell, 1921), p. 49.
56 Ibid., p. 82.
57 Ibid., p. 114.
58 R. H. Tawney, *Equality* (London: George Allen & Unwin, 1938 [1931]), p. 242.
59 Tawney, *Acquisitive Society*, p. 129.
60 Ibid., p. 145.
61 Tawney, *Equality*, p. 273 and 234–6.
62 J. Keir Hardie, 'Labour and Christianity: Is the Labour Movement against Christianity', in *Labour and Religion: By Ten Labour Members of Parliament and Other Bodies* (St Albans: WA Hammond, 1910), p. 51.
63 Hardie, *I.L.P.*, p. 7.
64 Ibid.
65 Wood, *Wheatley*, pp. 23 and 26.
66 M. S. Edwards, *S.E. Keeble: The Rejected Prophet* (Chester: Wesley Historical Society, 1977), p. 49.
67 Tawney, *Acquisitive Society*, p. 82.
68 Ibid., p. 83.
69 Ibid., p. 79.
70 Temple, *Christianity and the Social Order*, p. 49.
71 Temple, *Church Looks Forward*, pp. 145–6.
72 Acts 2.44-45.
73 Temple, *Christianity and the Social Order*, pp. 46–7.
74 Ibid., p. 36.
75 Temple, *Church Looks Forward*, pp. 146–7.
76 Headlam, *Socialist's Church*, p. 24.
77 Orens, *Headlam*, p. 21.
78 S. E. Keeble, *Money and How to Use It* (London: Epworth Press [?], 1921), p. 10.
79 Lansbury/30 C 1.
80 J. Clifford, *The New City of God: The Primitive Christian Faith as a Social Gospel* (London: Alexander & Shepherd, 1888), pp. 27–8.
81 G. Dale, *God's Politicians: The Christian Contribution to 100 Years of Labour* (London: HarperCollins, 2000), p. 110.
82 Hardie, *Serfdom to Socialism*, p. 101.
83 Lansbury/30 a 1.

84 Wheatley, *Socialise the National Income!*, p. 11. See also, Wood, *Wheatley*, p. 165.
85 Norman, 'Headlam and Victorian Christian Socialists', p. 31.
86 R. H. Tawney, *The Radical Tradition: Twelve Essays on Politics, Education and Literature* (New York, NY: Parthenon, 1964), p. 68.
87 P. Bickley, *Building Jerusalem: Christianity and the Labour Party* (London: Bible Society, 2010), pp. 8–9.
88 Ibid., p. 44.
89 Ibid., p. 46.
90 J. Clifford, *The State the Church and the Congregation* (London: James Clarke & Co., 1908). Emphasis in original.
91 Clifford, *Socialism and the Teaching of Christ*, p. 11; Clifford, *Socialism and the Churches*, p. 5.
92 Clifford, *Socialism and the Teaching of Christ*, p. 5; Clifford, *New City of God*, p. 26. Emphasis in original.
93 P. Catterall, *Labour and the Free Churches, 1918-1939: Radicalism, Righteousness and Religion* (London: Bloomsbury, 2016), p. 200.
94 M. Grimely, *Citizenship, Community and the Church of England: Liberal Anglican Theories of the State between the Wars* (Oxford: Oxford University Press, 2004), p. 54.
95 Temple, *Christianity and the Social Order*, p. 83 Temple speaks of the state subsidising the cost of particular commodities as their being subsidized by 'the whole community', pp. 101 and 112.
96 Temple, *The Church Looks Forward*, pp. 132–3.
97 Temple, *Church in Relation to Social Reform*, p. 11.
98 S. E. Keeble, *Ethics of Public Ownership* (London: Epworth Press, 1920), p. 14; S. E. Keeble, *Christian Responsibility for the Social Order* (London: Epworth Press, 1922), p. 206.
99 Jones, *Christian Socialist Revival*, p. 195.
100 H. S. Holland, ed., *Our Neighbours: A Handbook for the C.S.U.* (London: A.R. Mowbray, 1911), p. 86.
101 Holland, *Our Neighbours*, pp. 88–9; Jones, *Christian Socialist Revival*, p. 195.
102 Holland, *Our Neighbours*, pp. 91 and 99.
103 A. Wilkinson, *Christian Socialism: Scott Holland to Tony Blair* (London: SCM, 1998), pp. 71–2.
104 Ibid., p. 72.
105 Hughes, *Hardie's Speeches and Writings*, p. 18.
106 J. Keir Hardie, *Killing No Murder!: The Government and the Railway Strike* (Manchester: National Labour Press, 1911), p. 22.
107 Holman, *Hardie*, p. 57.
108 J. Schneer, *George Lansbury* (Manchester: Manchester University Press, 1990), p. 27; Manuscript of Lansbury speech on the problem of unemployment delivered to the Christian Social Union, Oxford, May 1907, Lansbury/2 181-98, LSE archive.

109 G. Taylor, *Socialism and Christianity: The Politics of the Church Socialist League* (Sheffield: IHS, 2000), p. 41.
110 Hughes, *Hardie's Speeches and Writings*, p. 29.
111 Anthony Wright, *R.H. Tawney* (Manchester: Manchester University Press, 1987), p. 113.
112 Tawney, *Radical Tradition*, p. 164.
113 Ibid., pp. 164–5.

Chapter 8

1 R. H. Tawney, *The Radical Tradition: Twelve Essays on Politics, Education and Literature* (New York, NY: Parthenon, 1964), p. 170.
2 A. Wright, *R.H. Tawney* (Manchester: Manchester University Press, 1987), p. 103.
3 J. Shepherd, *George Lansbury: At the Heart of Old Labour* (Oxford: Oxford University Press, 2002), p. 3.
4 G. Dale, *God's Politicians: The Christian Contribution to 100 Years of Labour* (London: HarperCollins, 2000), pp. 112 and 114.
5 S. Mayor, *The Churches and the Labour Movement* (London: Independent, 1967), pp. 188 and 193; P. d'A Jones, *The Christian Socialist Revival 1877-1914: Religion, Class, and Social Conscience in Late-Victorian England* (Princeton, NJ: Princeton University Press, 1968), p. 345.
6 B. D. Vernon, *Ellen Wilkinson: 1891-1947* (London: Croom Helm, 1982), p. 106.
7 G. D. H. Cole, *James Keir Hardie: Fabian Society Biographical Series No.12* (London: Fabian Society, 1941), p. 28.
8 E. Hughes, *Keir Hardie's Speeches and Writings – From 1888 to 1915* (Glasgow: Forward, 1927), p. 35.
9 H. Scott Holland, ed., *Our Neighbours: A Handbook for the C.S.U.* (London: A.R. Mowbray, 1911), p. 104.
10 Ibid., p. 133.
11 A. M. Suggate, 'William Temple', in P. Scott and W. T. Cavanagh, eds, *The Blackwell Companion to Political Theology* (Oxford: Wiley-Blackwell, 2004), p. 173.
12 W. Temple, *The Church Looks Forward* (London: Macmillan, 1944), p. 143.
13 Suggate, 'Temple', p. 174.
14 S. E. Keeble, *Christian Responsibility for the Social Order* (London: Epworth Press, 1922), pp. 211–12 and 206.
15 P. Bickley, *Building Jerusalem: Christianity and the Labour Party* (London: Bible Society, 2010), p. 44.
16 L. Goldman, *The Life of R.H. Tawney: Socialism and History* (Oxford: Bloomsbury, 2013), p. 173.

17 R. H. Tawney, *Equality* (London: George Allen & Unwin, 1938 [1931]), p. xvii.
18 Tawney, *Radical Tradition*, pp. 103 and 110.
19 M. Bondfield, et al., *Trade Unions and Socialism* (London: ILP, 1926), p. 3.
20 G. Lansbury, *Your Part in Poverty* (London: Herald, 1917), p. 15.
21 B. Holman, *Keir Hardie: Labour's Greatest Hero?* (Oxford: Lion, 2010), p. 57.
22 Ibid., p. 132.
23 J. Keir Hardie, *The I.L.P. and All About It* (Manchester: National Labour Press, 1908), p. 8. Hardie is here referencing the Apostle Paul's sermon at the Areopagus in Athens, recorded in Acts 17: 'God that made the world and all things therein [. . .] hath made of one blood all nations of men for to dwell on all the face of the earth.'
24 Wright, *Tawney*, p. 70.
25 Keeble, *Christian Responsibility*, p. 261.
26 T. Judge, *Margaret Bondfield: First Woman in the Cabinet* (London: Alpha House, 2018), p. 207.
27 W. Temple, *Christianity and the Social Order* (London: Penguin, 1976 [1942]), p. 37.
28 J. Keir Hardie, *From Serfdom to Socialism* (London: G. Allen, 1907), p. 10.
29 Tawney, *Equality*, p. 24.
30 Lansbury, *Your Part in Poverty*, p. 19.
31 Tawney, *Equality*, p. 62.
32 Ibid., p. 141.
33 Ibid., p. 100.
34 Keeble, *Christian Responsibility*, p. 243; S. E. Keeble, *Christianity and Socialism: Essays for the Times* (London, R. Culley [?], 1906), p. 25.
35 Wright, *Tawney*, pp. 72–3; Tawney, *Equality*, p. 115.
36 J. Clifford, *The Gospel of World Brotherhood According to Jesus* (London: Hodder & Stoughton, 1920), p. 140.
37 Hardie, *I.L.P.*, p. 13.
38 S. D. Headlam, *The Socialist's Church* (London: G. Allen, 1907), pp. 80–1.
39 Hardie, *Serfdom to Socialism*, p. 63.
40 Lansbury, *Your Part in Poverty*, pp. 71–2.
41 J. Bruce Glasier, *Keir Hardie: A Memorial* (London: National Labour Press, 1915), p. 38; Dale, *God's Politicians*, p. 50.
42 Lansbury, *Your Part in Poverty*, p. 119.
43 Shepherd, *Lansbury*, pp. 115 and 131–2.
44 Holman, *Hardie*, p. 164.
45 Vernon, *Wilkinson*, p. 40; Judge, *Bondfield*, p. 47.
46 Judge, *Bondfield*, p. 1.
47 Ibid., p. 150.
48 P. Bartley, *Ellen Wilkinson: From Red Suffragist to Government Minister* (London: Pluto Press, 2014), p. 27; Vernon, *Wilkinson*, p. 80.

49 Vernon, *Wilkinson*, p. 91.
50 J. Marchant, *Dr. John Clifford, C.H.: Life, Letters and Reminiscences* (London: Cassell, 1924), p. 200.
51 S. E. Keeble, 'The City, or Service of the Citizens', in S. E. Keeble, ed., *The Citizen of To-Morrow* (London: C.H. Kelly, 1909), pp. 288–9.
52 S. E. Keeble, *The Ideal of the Material Life and Other Social Addresses* (London: C.H. Kelly, 1908), p. 129.
53 Wright, *Tawney*, p. 146.
54 A. Wilkinson, *Christian Socialism: Scott Holland to Tony Blair* (London: SCM, 1998), p. 111.
55 Goldman, *Tawney*, p. 51.
56 Ibid., p. 301.
57 Tawney, *Radical Tradition*, p. 167. Emphasis added.
58 Manuscript of a speech by Lansbury entitled 'The Chief Need of the Labour Movement', 5 May 1911, LSE archive, Lansbury/4 202-205.
59 Antimilitarism speech by Lansbury, The Arbitrator, May 1892, LSE archive Lansbury/1 150.
60 Hardie, *I.L.P.*, p. 13.
61 Holman, *Hardie*, p. 153.
62 Keeble, *Christian Responsibility*, p. 197.
63 Marchant, *Clifford*, p. 99.
64 E. Wilkinson, 'Colour Bar in Hotels', 17/4/31; M. Bondfield, *Why Labour Fights* (n.p., 1941), p. 2.
65 Jones, *Victorian Christian Socialists*, pp. 198–9.
66 J. Callaghan, *Socialism in Britain since 1884* (Oxford: Wiley-Blackwell, 1990), p. 107.
67 Open letter to electorate from Lansbury, General Election May 1929, LSE archive, Lansbury/9 39-41.
68 Callaghan, *Socialism in Britain*, p. 107.
69 G. Foote, *The Labour Party's Political Thought: A History* (Basingstoke: Palgrave Macmillan, 2007), p. 52.
70 Manuscript of a speech by Lansbury entitled 'The Chief Need of the Labour Movement', 5 May 1911, LSE archive, Lansbury/4 202-205.
71 Keeble, *Christian Responsibility*, p. 197.
72 Suggate, 'Temple', pp. 165–79.
73 Memorandum for interview with Hitler by Lansbury, 19 April 1937, LSE archive, Lansbury/16 145-7.
74 Headlam, *Socialist's Church*, pp. 78–9.
75 Ibid., p. 82.
76 Ibid., pp. 72 and 73.
77 P. Catterall, *Labour and the Free Churches, 1918-1939: Radicalism, Righteousness and Religion* (London: Bloomsbury, 2016), p. 196.

78 Foote, *Labour Party's Political Thought*, p. 43.
79 J. Maxton, *Keir Hardie: Prophet and Pioneer* (London: n.p., 1933), p. 14.
80 Hardie, *I.L.P.*, p. 11.
81 J. Keir Hardie, *Karl Marx: The Man and His Message* (London: National Labour Press, 1910), p. 15.
82 Ibid., p. 11.
83 Hardie, *Serfdom to Socialism*, p. 60.
84 Hardie, *I.L.P.*, p. 6.
85 Ibid., p. 14.
86 R. H. Tawney, *The Acquisitive Society* (London: Bell, 1921), p. 94.
87 Ibid., p. 110.
88 Tawney, *Radical Tradition*, p. 110.
89 R. H. Tawney, 'The Choice before the Labour Party', *Political Quarterly*, 3, no. 3 (1932), p. 27.
90 Tawney, *Equality*, p. 177.
91 Temple, *Christianity and the Social Order*, p. 91.
92 A. Rigby, *Wilfred Wellock: A Life in Peace* (Bridport: Prism, 1988), p. 6.
93 W. Wellock, *Christian Communism: What It Is and Why It Is Necessary* (Manchester: National Labour Press, 1922), pp. 36 and 42.
94 W. Wellock, *The Way Out, or the Road to the New World* (London: Labour Publishing, 1922), pp. 39–40; Rigby, *Wellock*, p. 36.
95 S. E. Keeble, *Industrial Day-Dreams: Studies in Industrial Ethics and Economics* (London: L R. Culley, 1907 [1896]), p. 272.
96 Ibid., p. 168.
97 Interview with Lansbury from the Christian Commonwealth Newspaper, 11 August 1915, LSE archive, Lansbury/7 213.
98 Parliamentary Election, 1918, LSE archive, Lansbury/30 B 29-30.
99 Judge, *Bondfield*, pp. 3 and 5.
100 Jones, Christian Socialist Revival, p. 205.
101 C. Bryant, *Possible Dreams: A Personal History of the British Christian Socialists* (London: Hodder & Stoughton, 1996), p. 96.
102 Wilkinson, *Christian Socialism*, p. 51.
103 Ibid., p. 54.
104 Ibid., p. 46.
105 Jones, *Christian Socialist Revival*, p. 216.
106 Holland, *Our Neighbours*, p. 115.
107 Wilkinson, *Christian Socialism*, p. 47.
108 Ibid., pp. 52–3.
109 M. S. Edwards, *S.E. Keeble: The Rejected Prophet* (Chester: Wesley Historical Society, 1977), p. 32.
110 I. S. Wood, *John Wheatley* (Manchester: Manchester University Press, 1990), pp. 146–7.

111 Vernon, *Wilkinson*, p. 92.
112 Temple, *Church Looks Forward*, pp. 66 and 71.
113 Ibid., p. 76.
114 S. E. Keeble, 'COPEC': *An Account of the Christian Conference on Politics, Economics, and Citizenship* (London: Epworth Press, 1924), p. 12.
115 Keeble, *Industrial Day-Dreams*, p. 90.
116 Ibid., pp. 146 and 147.
117 Keeble, *Christianity and Socialism*, p. 9.
118 J. R. Orens, *Stewart Headlam's Radical Anglicanism: The Mass, the Masses and the Music Hall* (Chicago, IL: University of Illinois Press, 2003), pp. 133–4.
119 G. Lansbury, *What I Saw in Russia* (London: Boni and Liveright, 1920), pp. 48–9.
120 Callaghan, *Socialism in Britain*, p. 50.
121 Jones, *Christian Socialist Revival*, p. 146.
122 Bryant, *Possible Dreams*, p. 92.
123 Orens, *Headlam*, p. 122.
124 Hughes, *Hardie's Speeches and Writings*, p. 66.
125 Ibid., p. 67.
126 Ibid., p. 68.
127 Wood, *Wheatley*, pp. 86 and 172.
128 Keeble, *Industrial Day-Dreams*, pp. 308–9 and 310.
129 Ibid., p. 311.
130 Ibid., p. 309.
131 Leaflet advertising Lansbury's Parliamentary Election bid in Bow and Bromley, [August?] 1900, LSE archives, Lansbury/1 334-335.
132 Catterall, *Labour and the Free Churches*, p. 160.
133 Shepherd, *Lansbury*, p. 345.
134 Tawney, *Radical Tradition*, p. 168.
135 Marchant, *Clifford*, p. 55.
136 S. D. Headlam, *The Meaning of the Mass: Five Lectures with other Sermons and Addresses* (London: S.C. Brown, 1905), pp. 21–2 and 64.
137 Ibid., p. 38.
138 Keeble, *Industrial Day-Dreams*, p. 293.
139 Ibid., p. 90.
140 Keeble, *Material Life*, pp. 179 and 207–9. Emphasis in original.
141 Speech by Lansbury in the House of Commons entitled 'Right to Work', 10 February 1911, LSE archive, Lansbury/4 172-174.
142 Newspaper interview in the 'Morning Post' with Lansbury, 8 November 1905, LSE archive, Lansbury/2 138.
143 Holman, *Hardie*, p. 123.
144 'The position of the Poor Law in the problem of poverty', paper read at a conference, c1905 (slip proof), LSE archive, Lansbury 29/1.

145 Newspaper cutting from the Manchester Daily Despatch 'Mr. George Lansbury, the man who menaced the premier', 26 June 1913, LSE archive, Lansbury/28 72.
146 Lansbury 29/1.
147 F. Field, 'A Blue Labour Vision of the Common Good', in I. Geary and A. Pabst, eds, *Blue Labour: Forging a New Politics* (London: I.B. Tauris, 2015), p. 60.
148 I. Geary and A. Pabst, eds, *Blue Labour: Forging a New Politics* (London: I.B. Tauris, 2015), back cover.
149 Mayor, *Churches and Labour Movement*, pp. 341 and 373.
150 Ibid., p. 373.

Chapter 9

1 P. d'A Jones, *Christian Socialist Revival* (Princeton, NJ: Princeton University Press, 1868), p. 9.
2 G. Dale, *God's Politicians: The Christian Contribution to 100 Years of Labour* (London: HarperCollins, 2000), pp. 36, 75 and 109.
3 Jones, *Christian Socialist Revival*, p. 202.
4 Ibid., p. 344.
5 Ibid., pp. 344–5.
6 J. Clifford, *The State the Church and the Congregation* (London: James Clarke & Co., 1908), pp. 13–4.
7 J. Clifford, *The New City of God: The Primitive Christian Faith as a Social Gospel* (London: Alexander & Shepherd, 1888), p. 35.
8 S. E. Keeble, *Industrial Day-Dreams: Studies in Industrial Ethics and Economics* (London: R. Culley, 1907 [1896]), pp. 272.
9 S. E. Keeble, *The Ideal of the Material Life and other Social Addresses* (London: C.H. Kelly, 1908), p. 167.
10 M. S. Edwards, *S.E. Keeble: The Rejected Prophet* (Chester: Wesley Historical Society, 1977), pp. 26 and 27.
11 Ibid., p. 40.
12 P. Bartley, *Ellen Wilkinson: From Red Suffragist to Government Minister* (London: Pluto Press, 2014), p. 19; 'Woman M.P. Makes Plea Against Arms', *Evening Ledger*, 24/1/31; 'Woman Laborite Calls on World to Disarm Now', *Christian Science Monitor*, 4/4/31.
13 I. S. Wood, *John Wheatley* (Manchester: Manchester University Press, 1990), p. 53.
14 E. Hughes, *Keir Hardie's Speeches and Writings From 1888 to 1915* (Glasgow: Forward, 1927), p. 101.
15 B. Holman, *Keir Hardie: Labour's Greatest Hero?* (Oxford: Lion, 2010), p. 114.
16 J. Maxton, *Keir Hardie: Prophet and Pioneer* (London: n.p., 1933), p. 12.
17 J. Shepherd, *George Lansbury: At the Heart of Old Labour* (Oxford: OUP, 2002), p. 342.

18 E. Lansbury, *George Lansbury: My Father* (London: S. Low, Marston & Co., 1934), p. 175.
19 Shepherd, *Lansbury*, p. 325.
20 Ibid., p. 330.
21 Memorandum for interview with Hitler by Lansbury, 19 April 1937, LSE archive, Lansbury/16 145-47.
22 Telegram from Lansbury to Hitler, 15 April 1939, LSE archive, Lansbury/17 88.
23 Ibid., p. 345.
24 Bartley, *Wilkinson*, pp. 80–1 and 84.
25 'Miss Ellen Wilkinson, M.P.: "Impossible to Leave Our Own Country Defenceless"', *Walsall Observer*, 25-8-37.
26 E. Wilkinson, 'We Must Organise to the Full', *Bristol Evening Post*, 4-3-40.
27 Jones, *Christian Socialist Revival*, p. 216.
28 J. R. Orens, *Stewart Headlam's Radical Anglicanism: The Mass, the Masses, and the Music Hall* (Chicago, IL: University of Illinois Press, 2003), p. 152.
29 Ibid.
30 A. Wilkinson, *Christian Socialism: Scott Holland to Tony Blair* (London: SCM, 1998), p. 39.
31 J. Marchant, *Dr. Clifford, C.H.: Life, Letters and Reminiscences* (London: Cassell, 1924), p. 99.
32 Ibid., p. 153.
33 Ibid., p. 154.
34 G. Foote, *The Labour Party's Political Thought: A History* (Basingstoke: Palgrave Macmillan, 2007), p. 66.
35 Dale, *God's Politicians*, p. 101; M. Bondfield, *Why Labour Fights* (n.p., 1941), p. 3.
36 C. Bryant, *Possible Dreams: A Personal History of the British Christian Socialists* (London: Hodder & Stoughton, 1996); L. Goldman, *The Life of R.H. Tawney: Socialism and History* (Oxford: Bloomsbury, 2013), p. 85.
37 Goldman, *Tawney*, p. 129.
38 Wilkinson, *Christian Socialism*, pp. 98 and 103.
39 Goldman, *Tawney*, pp. 250, 282 and 278.
40 A. M. Suggate, 'William Temple', in P. Scott, and W. T. Cavanagh, eds, *The Blackwell Companion to Political Theology* (Oxford: Wiley-Blackwell, 2004), p. 175.
41 W. Temple, *Church Looks Forward* (London: Macmillan, 1944), p. 3.
42 Ibid., p. 39.
43 S. E. Lammers, 'William Temple and the Bombing of Germany: An Exploration in the Just War Tradition', *Journal of Religious Ethics*, 19, no. 1 (1991), pp. 71–92.
44 K. Leech, 'Stewart Headlam, 1847-1924, and the Guild of St Matthew', in M. B. Reckitt, ed., *For Christ and the People: Studies of Four Socialist Priests and Prophets of the Church of England* (London: SPCK, 1968), p. 68.

45 J. Keir Hardie, *Can A Man Be A Christian on a Pound a Week?* (London: ILP, 1901), p. 8; J. Keir Hardie, *From Serfdom to Socialism* (London: G. Allen, 1907), p. 104.
46 G. Lansbury, 'Back to the Galilean', in G. N. Barnes, ed, *Religion in the Labour Movement* (London: Holborn, 1919), p. 54.
47 The Bow and Bromley Worker, 1 January 1910–December 1914, LSE archive, Lansbury/30 c 2.
48 A. Rigby, *Wilfred Wellock: A Life in Peace* (Bridport: Prism, 1988), p. 22; W. Wellock, *Christian Communism: What It Is and Why It Is Necessary* (Manchester: National Labour Press, 1922), p. 25.
49 Hardie, *Can A Man Be A Christian?*, pp. 7–8.
50 J. Clifford, *The Gospel of World Brotherhood According to Jesus* (London: Hodder & Stoughton, 1920), p. 150.
51 Manuscript of a speech by Lansbury entitled 'The Chief Need of the Labour Movement', 5 May 1911, LSE archive, Lansbury/4 202-205.
52 Draft of Lansbury's broadcast to the USA during his visit, 21 April 1936, LSE archive, Lansbury/16 72-81.
53 Keeble, *Industrial Day-Dreams*, p. 206.
54 P. Catterall, *Labour and the Free Churches, 1918-1939: Radicalism, Righteousness and Religion* (London: Bloomsbury, 2016), p. 207.
55 Ibid., p. 208.
56 S. Headlam, *Christian Socialism – A Lecture: Fabian Tract No.42* (London: Fabian Society, 1899), p. 3; S. D. Headlam, *Socialist's Church* (London: G. Allen, 1907), p. 68.
57 Headlam, *The Socialist's Church*, pp. 12–13.
58 J. Keir Hardie, *The I.L.P. and All about It* (Manchester: National Labour Press, 1908), p. 7.
59 Wood, *Wheatley*, pp. 72–3.
60 J. Clifford, *Socialism and the Teaching of Christ: Fabian Tract No. 78* (London: Fabian Society, 1897), p. 8.
61 Speech by Lansbury in the House of Commons entitled 'Right to Work', 10 February 1911, Lansbury/4 172-4.
62 W. Wellock, *The Way Out, or the Road to the New World* (London: Labour Publishing, 1922), p. 21.
63 Wellock, *Christian Communism*, p. 23; Rigby, *Wilfred Wellock*, p. 28.
64 Wellock, *Way Out*, p. 69.
65 M. Bondfield, *Socialism for Shop Assistants: Pass on Pamphlets No.10* (London: Clarion Press, 1909), pp. 2 and 16.
66 J. Callaghan, *Socialism in Britain since 1884* (Oxford: Wiley-Blackwell, 1990), p. 68.
67 Foote, *Labour Party's Political Thought*, p. 39.
68 P. Bickley, *Building Jerusalem: Christianity and the Labour Party* (London: Bible Society, 2010), p. 4.

69 J. Clifford, *Socialism and the Churches – Fabian Tract No.139* (London: Fabian Society, 1908), pp. 8 and 14.
70 Hardie, *Can a Man be a Christian?*, pp. 8 and 18–19.
71 J. Keir Hardie, 'Labour and Christianity: Is the Labour Movement against Christianity?', in *Labour and Religion: By Ten Labour Members of Parliament and Other Bodies* (St Albans: WA Hammond, 1910), p. 51.
72 Headlam, *Christian Socialism*, p. 2; E. Norman, *The Victorian Christian Socialists* (Cambridge: Cambridge University Press, 1987), p. 109.
73 E. Norman, 'Stewart Headlam and the Victorian Christian Socialists', *History Today*, 37, no. 4 (1987), p. 31.
74 H. Scott Holland, ed., *Our Neighbours: A Handbook for the C.S.U.* (London: A.R. Mowbray, 1911), p. 152.
75 S. E. Keeble, *Christian Responsibility for the Social Order* (London: Epworth Press, 1922), p. 236.
76 S. E. Keeble, 'Preface', in S. E. Keeble, ed., *The Citizen of To-Morrow* (London: C.H. Kelly, 1909), p. xi.
77 Keeble, *The Ideal of the Material Life and Other Social Addresses*, p. 159.
78 Letter from Lansbury to Rev John Charles Carlile, 22 January 1931, LSE archive, Lansbury/10 2-6; G. Lansbury, *Your Part in Poverty* (London: Herald, 1917), p. 12.
79 Wellock, *Christian Communism*, pp. 1 and 14.
80 T. Judge, *Margaret Bondfield: First Woman in the Cabinet* (London: Alpha House, 2018), p. 207.
81 M. Beech and K. Hickson, *Labour's Thinkers: The Intellectual Roots of Labour from Tawney to Gordon Brown* (London: I.B. Tauris, 2007), p. 28.
82 A. Wright, *R.H. Tawney* (Manchester: Manchester University Press, 1987), pp. 20 and 111.
83 Goldman, *Tawney*, pp. 296 and 174.
84 J. M. Winter and D. M. Joslin, eds, *R.H. Tawney's Commonplace Book* (Cambridge: Cambridge University Press, 2006), p. 15.
85 W. Temple, *Christianity and the Social Order* (London: Penguin, 1976 [1942]), p. 61.
86 Ibid., p. 167.
87 S. Headlam, *Priestcraft and Progress: Being Sermons and Lectures* (London: John Hodges, 1878), p. 58; S. D. Headlam, *The Meaning of the Mass: Five Lectures with Other Sermons and Addresses* (London: S.C. Brown, 1905), pp. 9 and 61.
88 Edwards, *Keeble*, p. 8.
89 Letter from Lansbury to John Armitage, 9 March 1940, LSE archive, Lansbury/17 160-2.
90 S. E. Keeble, *COPEC: An Account of the Christian Conference on Politics, Economics, and Citizenship* (London: Epworth Press, 1924), p. 9.
91 Suggate, *Temple*, p. 168. Emphasis added.

92　Temple, *Christianity and the Social Order*, p. 69.
93　Temple, *Church Looks Forward*, p. 165.
94　Ibid., p. 2.

Conclusion

1　R. Leach, *Political Ideology in Britain* (Basingstoke: Palgrave Macmillan, 2002), p. 1.
2　M. Freeden, *Ideologies and Political Theory* (Oxford: Oxford University Press, 1996), p. 48.
3　Matthew 23.8-9.
4　Interview with Lansbury from the Christian Commonwealth Newspaper, 11 August 1915, London School of Economics and Political Science [LSE] archive, Lansbury/7 213; J. T. Leckie, *Socialism in Britain: From the Industrial Revolution to the Present Day* (New York, NY: Taplinger, 1972), p. 106.
5　S. E. Keeble, *Industrial Day-Dreams: Studies in Industrial Ethics and Economics* (London: R. Culley, 1907 [1896]), pp. 17 and p. 214.
6　J. Hannan, *The Life of John Wheatley* (Nottingham: Spokesman Books, 1988), p. 11.
7　Keeble, *Industrial Day-Dreams*, p. 151 and 152.
8　S. Mayor, *The Churches and the Labour Movement* (London: Independent, 1967), p. 203.
9　W. Temple, *Christianity and the Social Order* (London: Penguin, 1976 [1942]), p. 37.
10　S. E. Keeble, *Christian Responsibility for the Social Order* (London: Epworth Press, 1922), p. 261.
11　R. H. Tawney, *The Radical Tradition: Twelve Essays on Politics, Education and Literature* (New York, NY: Parthenon, 1964), p. 167.
12　A. Wilkinson, *Christian Socialism: Scott Holland to Tony Blair* (London: SCM, 1998), p. 105.
13　Keeble, *Industrial Day-Dreams*, p. 200.
14　T. Judge, *Margaret Bondfield: First Woman in the Cabinet* (London: Alpha House, 2018), p. 207.
15　S. D. Headlam, *The Socialist's Church* (London: G. Allen, 1907), p. 57; E. Hughes, *Keir Hardie's Speeches and Writings – From 1888 to 1915* (Glasgow: Forward, 1927), p. 70.
16　W. Temple, *The Church Looks Forward* (London: Macmillan, 1944), pp. 141 and 143.
17　Tawney, *Radical Tradition*, p. 170.
18　M. Bondfield, et al., *Trade Unions and Socialism* (London: ILP, 1926), p. 3.
19　J. Keir Hardie, 'Labour and Christianity: Is the Labour Movement against Christianity?', in *Labour and Religion: By Ten Members of Parliament and Other Bodies* (St Albans: WA Hammond, 1910), p. 49.

20 S. D. Headlam, *The Meaning of the Mass: Five Lectures with Other Sermons and Addresses* (London: S.C. Brown, 1905), p. 73.
21 G. Foote, *The Labour Party's Political Thought: A History* (Baskingstoke: Palgrave Macmillan, 1997), p. 44.
22 J. Keir Hardie, *Can a Man Be a Christian On a Pound a Week?* (London: ILP, 1901 [?]), pp. 13–14 and 3.
23 Headlam, *Meaning of the Mass*, p. 79; S. D. Headlam, *Christian Socialism – A Lecture: Fabian Tract No.42* (London: Fabian Society, 1899), p. 4.
24 Headlam, *Meaning of the Mass*, p. 83.
25 Keeble, *Industrial Day-Dreams*, p. 246.
26 S. D. Headlam, *Priestcraft and Progress: Being Sermons and Lectures* (London: John Hodges, 1878), p. 7; J. R. Orens, *Stewart Headlam's Radical Anglicanism: The Mass, the Masses, and the Music Hall* (Chicago, IL: University of Illinois Press, 2003), p. 24. K. Leech, 'Stewart Headlam, 1847-1924, and the Guild of St Matthew', in M. B. Reckitt, ed., *For Christ and the People: Studies of Four Socialist Priests and Prophets of the Church of England* (London: SPCK, 1968), p. 78;
27 J. Schneer, *George Lansbury* (Manchester: Manchester University Press, 1990), p. 1.
28 Orens, *Headlam's Radical Anglicanism*, p. 97; J. Keir Hardie, *Socialism and Christianity: Keir Hardie Library No.4* (London: n.p., 1907), p. 5; J. Keir Hardie, *From Serfdom to Socialism* (London: G. Allen, 1907), p. 39; J. Wheatley, *How the Miners are Robbed: The Duke in the Dock (startling court case)* (London: Pluto, 1973 [1907]), p. 17; Keeble, *Industrial Day-Dreams*, pp. 228 and 245.
29 Headlam, *Socialist's Church*, p. 59; Hardie, *Can a Man be a Christian?*, p. 3; Hardie, *Serfdom to Socialism*, p. 39. The Biblical reference for the above is James 5.1-2a, 5.
30 Acts of the Apostles 2.44-5.
31 Headlam, *Meaning of the Mass*, p. 29.
32 A. Wright, *R.H. Tawney* (Manchester: Manchester University Press, 1987), p. 93.
33 W. Wellock, *Christian Communism: What It Is and Why It Is Necessary* (Manchester: National Labour Press, 1921), p. 10.
34 Newspaper article in the 'Liverpool Daily Post' on a speech made by Lansbury as Carnarvon, 18 September 1911, LSE archive, Lansbury/4 219.
35 I. S. Wood, 'John Wheatley and Catholic Socialism', in A. R. Morton, ed., *After Socialism? The Future of Radical Christianity* (Edinburgh: CTPI, 1994), p. 21.
36 S. E. Keeble, 'Introduction', in S. E. Keeble, ed., *The Social Teaching of the Bible* (London: R. Culley, 1909), p. 19.
37 Headlam, *Socialist's Church*, p. 59.
38 Hardie, *Serfdom to Socialism*, p. 32.
39 Wilkinson, *Christian Socialism*, p. 118.
40 C. E. Curran, *Catholic Social Teaching 1891-Present: A Historical, Theological and Ethical Analysis* (Washington DC: Georgetown University Press, 2002) p. 174.

41 Ibid., pp. 199 and 188.
42 Headlam, *Socialist's Church*, p. 5.
43 H. Scott Holland, ed., *Our Neighbours: A Handbook for the C.S.U.* (London: A.R. Mowbray, 1911), p. 60.
44 P. d'A Jones, *Christian Socialist Revival 1877-1914: Religion, Class, and Social Conscience in Late-Victorian England* (Princeton, NJ: Princeton University Press), p. 178; Holland, *Our Neighbours*, p. 60.
45 Temple, *Church Looks Forward*, p. 113.
46 Interview with Lansbury from the Christian Commonwealth Newspaper, 11 August 1915, LSE archive, Lansbury/7 213.
47 Mayor, *Churches and the Labour Movement*, p. 215.
48 S. D. Headlam, *Maurice and Kingsley: Theologians and Socialists* (London: George Standring, 1909), p. 5; Headlam, *Priestcraft and Progress*, p. vi.
49 R. H. Tawney, *Equality* (London: George Allen & Unwin, 1938 [1931]), p. 135; J. Keir Hardie, *Karl Marx: The Man and His Message* (Manchester: National Labour Press, 1910), p. 10; E. Wilkinson and E. Conze, *Why War? A Handbook for Those Who Will Take Part in the Second World War* (London: NCLC, 1934); B. D. Vernon, *Ellen Wilkinson, 1891-1947* (London: Croom Helm, 1982), p. 35.
50 Keeble, *Industrial Day-Dreams*, p. 34.
51 W. Wellock, *The Way Out, or the Road to the New World* (London: Labour Publishing, 1922), pp. 35–6.
52 Keeble, *Christian Responsibility*, p. 212.
53 Headlam, *Christian Socialism*, p. 3; Headlam, *Socialist's Church*, p. 68.
54 Headlam, *Socialist's Church*, pp. 12–13.
55 J. Keir Hardie, *The I.L.P. and All About It* (Manchester: National Labour Press, 1908), p. 7.
56 J. Clifford, *Socialism and the Churches – Fabian Tract No.139* (London: Fabian Society, 1908), p. 8.
57 Hardie, 'Labour and Christianity', p. 51.
58 Headlam, *Christian Socialism*, p. 2; E. Norman, *The Victorian Christian Socialists* (Cambridge: Cambridge University Press, 1987), p. 109.
59 Holland, *Our Neighbours*, p. 152.
60 A. Wright, *Socialisms Old and New* (London: Routledge, 1996), p. 21; Freeden, *Ideologies*, p. 431.
61 Hardie, *Karl Marx*, p. 15.
62 H. Tudor and J. M. Tudor, eds, *Marxism and Social Democracy: The Revisionist Debate 1896-1898* (Cambridge: Cambridge University Press, 1988), pp. 35 and 19.
63 G. Lansbury, *Your Part in Poverty* (London: Herald, 1917]) p. 36. Emphasis added.
64 Correspondence between Lansbury and Richard Lee, 16–19 February 1935. Enclosed a copy of the statements made by Lansbury in the House of Commons, 14 September 1931, LSE archive, Lansbury/25 3 o 144-152.

65 P. Bickley, *Building Jerusalem: Christianity and the Labour Party* (London: Bible Society, 2010), p. 8.
66 F. Engels, 'Anti-Duhring', in K. Marx and F. Engels, *On Religion* (New York, NY: Dover, 1964), pp. 147–8.
67 K. Marx, 'Contribution to the Critique of Hegel's Philosophy of Right', in K. Marx and F. Engels, *On Religion* (New York, NY: Dover 1964), pp. 41–2.
68 A. D. Lewis, 'Topical Yarns', *Syndicalist*, 3, 4, July 1914; 'Trite and Tripe', *Syndicalist*, 3, 2, February 1914.
69 J. Radcliffe, 'About Gadflies – and Other Things', *Syndicalist*, 1, 9, October 1912.
70 S. Olivier, 'Moral', in G. Bernard Shaw, ed., *Fabian Essays on Socialism* (New York, NY: Humboldt, 1891), p. 98.
71 Ibid., pp. 126–7; S. Webb, 'Historic', in G. Bernard Shaw, ed., *Fabian Essays on Socialism* (New York NY: Humboldt, 1891), p. 10.
72 Olivier, 'Moral', p. 124.
73 W. Clarke, 'Industrial', in G. Bernard Shaw, ed., *Fabian Essays on Socialism* (New York, NY: Humboldt, 1891), pp. 76–7.
74 G. Bernard Shaw, 'Economic', in G. Bernard Shaw, ed., *Fabian Essays on Socialism* (New York, NY: Humboldt, 1891), pp. 130.
75 John: 8.42 and 44.
76 Hebrews 12.7-9. (ESV)
77 Matthew 6.19.
78 Matthew 13.11.
79 1 Corinthians 12.14, 27 and 28.
80 Some have also advanced the argument that the holding in common of property in Acts does not suggest socialism as it was purely voluntary. This is true, but cannot be used as an argument against a socialist interpretation; there are libertarian, voluntarist and democratic forms of socialism and communism as well as coercive, authoritarian ones.
81 Curran, *Catholic Social Teaching*, pp. 199 and 200.
82 1689 Baptist Confession of Faith, 29:2.
83 Heidelberg Catechism, 74.
84 The Thirty-Nine Articles of Religion, 27.
85 Ibid., 29.
86 Luke 22.19-20.
87 K. Marx and C. Engels, *The Communist Manifesto* (Oxford: Oxford Classics, 1992 [1848]) pp. 5 and 39.
88 C. Read, *Lenin: A Revolutionary Life* (London: Routledge, 2005), p. 14; V. I. Lenin, *What Is to be Done?* (Peking: Foreign Language Press, 1973 [1902]), p. 58.
89 G. Lansbury, *What I Saw in Russia* (London: Boni and Liveright, 1920), pp. 170–1.
90 'What Is Syndicalism?', *Syndicalist*, 1, 3, March–April 1912.

91 J. Radcliffe, 'Syndicalism and Socialism', *Syndicalist*, 1, 5, June 1912.
92 G. Himmelfarb, *Poverty and Compassion: The Moral Imagination of the Late Victorians* (New York, NY: Vintage, 1991), p. 369. Emphasis in original.
93 Ibid., pp. 371–2.
94 Ibid., pp. 367–8.
95 Marx and Engels, *Communist Manifesto*, pp. 36–7.
96 K. Marx, 'Capital', in K. Marx and F. Engels, *On Religion* (New York, NY: Dover, 1964), p. 136.
97 'An International Conspiracy', *Syndicalist*, 3, 2, February 1914.
98 Shaw, 'Economic', p. 159.
99 K. Marx and F. Engels, 'The Holy Family', in K. Marx and F. Engels, *On Religion* (New York, NY: Dover, 1964), p. 60.

Bibliography

Case study sources

Bondfield, M. *Socialism for Shop Assistants: Pass On Pamphlets No. 10* (London: Clarion Press, 1909).

Bondfield, M. *Why Labour Fights* (n.p., 1941).

Bondfield, M., F. A. Broad, Harold Clay, E. Harold, A. Creech Jones, H. Kegie, Francis Edmund Lawley; Fred Longden, Wilfred Paling, John Paton, Emanuel Shinwell, J. Allen Skinner, Mark Starr, G. W. Thomson, W. M. Watson, E. F. Wise, Brockway Fenner. *Trade Unions and Socialism* (London: ILP, 1926).

Clifford, J. *Socialism and the Churches: Fabian Tract No. 139* (London: Fabian Society, 1908).

Clifford, J. *Socialism and the Teaching of Christ: Fabian Tract No. 78* (London: Fabian Society, 1898).

Clifford, J. *The Gospel of World Brotherhood According to Jesus* (London: Hodder & Stoughton, 1920).

Clifford, J. *The New City of God: The Primitive Christian Faith as a Social Gospel* (London: Alexander & Shepherd, 1888).

Clifford, J. *The State the Church and the Congregation* (London: James Clarke & Co., 1908).

[No named author]. *Guilty and Proud of It: Poplar's Answer* (London: n.p., 1927).

Headlam, S. D. *Christian Socialism – A Lecture: Fabian Tract No. 42* (London: Fabian Society, 1899).

Headlam, S. D. *Maurice and Kingsley: Theologians and Socialists* (London: George Standring, 1909).

Headlam, S. D. *Priestcraft and Progress: Being Sermons and Lectures* (London: John Hodges, 1878).

Headlam, S. D. *The Meaning of the Mass: Five Lectures with Other Sermons and Addresses* (London: S.C. Brown, 1905).

Headlam, S. D. *The Socialist's Church* (London: G. Allen, 1907).

Hughes, E. *Keir Hardie's Speeches and Writings from 1888 to 1915* (Glasgow: Forward, 1927).

Keeble, S. E. *Christianity and Socialism: Essays for the Times* (London: R. Culley [?], 1907).

Keeble, S. E. *Christian Responsibility for the Social Order* (London: Epworth Press, 1922).

Keeble, S. E. *COPEC: An Account of the Christian Conference on Politics, Economics, and Citizenship* (London: Epworth Press, 1924).

Keeble, S. E. *Industrial Day-Dreams: Studies in Industrial Ethics and Economics* (London: R. Culley, 1907 [1896]).

Keeble, S. E. 'Introduction', in S. E. Keeble, ed., *The Social Teaching of the Bible* (London: R. Culley, 1909), pp. 5–26.

Keeble, S. E. *Is There a Heavenly Father?* (London: C.H. Kelly, 1904).

Keeble, S. E. *Money and How to Use It* (London: Epworth Press [?], 1921).

Keeble, S. E. 'Preface', in S. E. Keeble , ed., *The Citizen of to-Morrow* (London: C.H. Kelly, 1909), pp. vii–xii.

Keeble, S. E. 'The City, or Service of the Citizens', in S. E. Keeble, ed., *The Citizen of to-Morrow* (London: C.H. Kelly, 1909), pp. 287–305.

Keeble, S. E. *The Ethics of Public Ownership* (London: Epworth Press, 1920).

Keeble, S. E. *The Ideal of the Material Life and Other Social Addresses* (London: C.H. Kelly, 1908).

Keeble, S.E. *Towards the New Era: A Draft Scheme of Industrial Reconstruction* (London: C.H. Kelly, 1917).

Keir Hardie, J. *Can a Man Be a Christian On a Pound a Week?* (London: ILP,. 1901 [?]).

Keir Hardie, J. *From Serfdom to Socialism* (London: G. Allen, 1907).

Keir Hardie, J. *Karl Marx: The Man and His Message* (Manchester: National Labour Press, 1910).

Keir Hardie, J. *Killing No Murder!: The Government and the Railway Strike* (Manchester: National Labour Press, 1911).

Keir Hardie, J. 'Labour and Christianity: Is the Labour Movement Against Christianity?', in *Labour and Religion: By Ten Members of Parliament and Other Bodies* (St Albans: WA Hammond, 1910), pp. 48–54.

Keir Hardie, J. *My Confession of Faith in the Labour Alliance* (London: ILP, 1909).

Keir Hardie, J. *Socialism and Christianity: Keir Hardie Library No. 4* (London: n.p, 1907).

Keir Hardie, J. *The I.L.P. and all About It* (Manchester: National Labour Press, 1908).

Lansbury, G. 'Back to the Galilean!', in G. N. Barnes, ed., *The Religion in the Labour Movement* (London: Holborn, 1919), pp. 49–56.

Lansbury, G. Labour Politician, London School of Economics archive, LANSBURY, 1859–1940.

Lansbury, G. *My Quest for Peace* (London: M. Joseph, 1938).

Lansbury, G. 'The Power that Re-makes Men', *Labour and Religion: By Ten Labour Members of Parliament and Other Bodies* (St Albans: WA Hammond, 1910), pp. 68–78.

Lansbury, G. *What I Saw in Russia* (London: Boni and Liveright, 1920).

Lansbury, G. *Your Part in Poverty* (London: Herald, 1917).

Scott Holland, H., ed. *Our Neighbours: A Handbook for the C.S.U.* (London: A.R. Mowbray, 1911).

Tawney, R. H. *Democracy or Defeat – By a WEA Soldier* (London: n.p., 1917).

Tawney, R. H. 'English Politics Today: We Mean Freedom', *The Review of Politics*, 8, no. 2 (1946), pp. 223-39.

Tawney, R. H. *Equality* (London: George Allen & Unwin, 1938 [1931]).

Tawney, R. H. *The Acquisitive Society* (London: Bell, 1921).

Tawney, R. H. 'The Choice Before the Labour Party', *Political Quarterly*, 3, no. 3 (1932), pp. 21-34.

Tawney, R. H. *The Radical Tradition: Twelve Essays on Politics, Education and Literature* (New York, NY: Pantheon, 1964).

Temple, W. *Christianity and the Social Order* (London: Penguin, 1976 [1942]).

Temple, W. *The Church Looks Forward* (London: Macmillan, 1944).

Temple, W. *The Place of the Church in Relation to Social Reform* (London: n.p., 1943).

Wellock, W. *Christian Communism: What It Is and Why It Is Necessary* (Manchester: National Labour Press, 1921).

Wellock, W. *The Way Out, or the Road to the New World* (London: Labour Publishing, 1922).

Wheatley, J. 'A Deceptive Concoction', in J. Wheatley, J. T. Thomas, Arthur Greenwood, Ellen Wilkinson, Thomas Johnston, F. W. Pethick-Lawrence, R. J. Davies, Hugh Dalton, eds, *Labour Exposes the Pensions Scheme* (London: TUC, 1925), pp. 2-8.

Wheatley, J. *Houses to Let: A Speech in Exposition of Labour's Fifteen Years; Housing Programme* (London: TUC, 1924).

Wheatley, J. *How the Miners Are Robbed: The Duke in the Dock (Startling Court Case)*, (London: Pluto, 1973 [1907]).

Wheatley, J. *Socialise the National Income!* (London: ILP, 1927).

Wilkinson, Ellen. Press Cuttings; Labour History Archives and Study Centre, LP/WI.

Wilkinson, E. and Conze, E. *Why War? A Handbook for Those Who Will Take Part in the Second World War* (London: NCLC, 1934).

Winter, J. M. and Joslin, D. M., eds *R.H. Tawney's Commonplace Book* (Cambridge: Cambridge University Press, 2006).

Other references

[No named author]. 'An International Conspiracy', *Syndicalist*, 3, 2, February 1914.

Armstrong, G. and Gray, T. 'Three Fallacies in the Essentialist Interpretation of the Political Thought of R.H. Tawney', *Journal of Political Ideologies*, 15, no. 2 (2010), pp. 161-74.

Bartley, P. *Ellen Wilkinson: From Red Suffragist to Government Minister* (London: Pluto Press, 2014).

Beech, M. and Hickson, K. *Labour's Thinkers: The Intellectual Roots of Labour from Tawney to Gordon Brown* (London: I.B. Tauris, 2007).

Bennet, J. *God and Progress: Religion & History in British Intellectual Culture, 1845-1914* (Oxford: Oxford University Press, 2019).

Bernard Shaw, G. 'Economic', in G. Bernard Shaw, ed., *Fabian Essays in Socialism* (New York, NY: Humboldt, 1891), pp. 128-64.

Bickley, P. *Building Jerusalem: Christianity and the Labour Party* (London: Bible Society, 2010).

Bradstock, A. and Rowland, C., eds *Radical Christian Writings: A Reader* (Oxford: Blackwell, 2002).

Branson, N. *Poplarism, 1919-1925: George Lansbury and the Councillors' Revolt* (London: Lawrence & Wishart, 1979).

Bruce Glasier, J. *Keir Hardie: A Memorial* (Manchester: National Labour Press, 1915).

Bryant, C. *Possible Dreams: A Personal History of the British Christian Socialists* (London: Hodder & Stoughton, 1996).

Callaghan, J. *Socialism in Britain since 1884* (Oxford: Wiley-Blackwell, 1990).

Carter, M. *T.H. Green and the Development of Ethical Socialism* (Exeter: Imprint, 2003).

Catterall, P. *Labour and the Free Churches, 1918-1939: Radicalism, Righteousness and Religion* (London: Bloomsbury, 2016).

Clarke, W. 'Industrial', in G. Bernard Shaw, ed., *Fabian Essays in Socialism* (New York, NY: Humboldt, 1891), pp. 44–94.

Cloutier, D. 'Modern Politics and Catholic Social Teaching', in D. M. McCarthy, *The Heart of Catholic Social Teaching: Its Origins and Contemporary Significance* (Grand Rapids, MI: Brasos, 2009), pp. 95–112.

Cole, G. D. H. *James Keir Hardie: Fabian Society Biographical Series No. 12* (London: Fabian Society, 1941).

Curran, C. E. *Catholic Social Teaching 1891-Present: A Historical, Theological and Ethical Analysis* (Washington, DC: Georgetown University Press, 2002).

Dale, G. *God's Politicians: The Christian Contribution to 100 Years of Labour* (London: HarperCollins, 2000).

Donovan, J. F. 'Pope Leo XIII and a Century of Catholic Social Teaching', in D. M. McCarthy, *The Heart of Catholic Social Teaching: Its Origins and Contemporary Significance* (Grand Rapids, MI: Brasos Press, 2009), pp. 55–72.

Edwards, M. S. *S.E. Keeble: The Rejected Prophet* (Chester: Wesley Historical Society, 1977).

Engels, F. 'Anti-Duhring', in K. Marx and F. Engels, *On Religion* (New York, NY: Dover, 1964), pp. 145–51.

Farron, T. 'What Kind of Liberal Society Do We Want?', https://www.theosthinktan k.co.uk/events/2017/11/28/tim-farron-what-kind-of-liberal-society-do-we-want; accessed 3 March 2018.

Foote, G. *The Labour Party's Political Thought: A History* (Basingstoke: Palgrave Macmillan, 1997).

Freeden, M. *Ideologies and Political Theory* (Oxford: Oxford University Press, 1996).

Geary, I. and Pabst, A., eds *Blue Labour: Forging a New Politics* (London: I.B. Tauris, 2015).

George, H. *Thy Kingdom Come* (Glasgow: Scottish Land Restoration League, 1889).

Goldman, L. *The Life of R.H. Tawney: Socialism and History* (Oxford: Bloomsbury, 2013).

Grimley, M. *Citizenship, Community, and the Church of England: Liberal Anglican Theories of the State Between the Wars* (Oxford: Oxford University Press, 2004).

Hannan, J. *The Life of John Wheatley* (Nottingham: Spokesman Books, 1988).

Himmelfarb, G. *Poverty and Compassion: The Moral Imagination of the Late Victorians* (New York, NY: Vintage, 1991).

Holman, B. *Keir Hardie: Labour's Greatest Hero?* (Oxford: Lion, 2010).

Jarman, T. L. *Socialism in Britain: From the Industrial Revolution to the Present Day* (Ann Arbor, MI: Littlehampton, 1978).

Johnson, F. *Keir Hardie's Socialism* (London: ILP, 1922).

Jones, P. d'A *The Christian Socialist Revival 1877-1914: Religion, Class, and Social Conscience in Late-Victorian England* (Princeton, NJ: Princeton University Press, 1968).

Judge, T. *Margaret Bondfield: First Woman in the Cabinet* (London: Alpha House, 2018).

Lammers, S. E. 'William Temple and the Bombing of Germany: An Exploration in the Just War Tradition', *Journal of Religious Ethics*, 19, no. 1 (1991), pp. 71–92.

Lansbury, E. *George Lansbury: My Father* (London: S. Low, Marston & Co., 1934).

Lavalette, M. *George Lansbury and the Rebel Councillors of Poplar* (London: Bookmarks, 2006).

Leach, R. *Political Ideology in Britain* (Basingstoke: Palgrave Macmillan, 2002).

Leckie, J. T. *Socialism in Britain: From the Industrial Revolution to the Present Day* (New York, NY: Taplinger, 1972).

Leech, K. 'Stewart Headlam, 1847-1924, and the Guild of St Matthew', in M. B. Reckitt, ed., *For Christ and the People: Studies of Four Socialist Priests and Prophets of the Church of England* (London: SPCK, 1968), pp. 61–88.

Lenin, V. I. *What Is to Be Done?* (Peking: Foreign Languages Press, 1973 [1902]).

Lewis, A. D. 'Topical Yarns', *Syndicalist*, 3, no. 4, July 1914.

Lowe, P. 'Jacob Rees-Mogg Thinks His Anti-abortion Stance Doesn't Matter – Here's Why He Is Wrong', *The Conversation*, https://theconversation.com/jacob-rees-mogg-thinks-his-anti-abortion-stance-doesnt-matter-heres-why-he-is-wrong-83594; accessed 3 March 2018.

MacQuiban, T. 'Soup and Salvation: Social Service as an Emerging Motif for the British Methodist Response to Poverty in the Late 19th Century', *Methodist History*, 39, no. 1 (October 2000), pp. 28–42.

Marchant, J. *Dr. John Clifford, C.H.: Life, Letters and Reminiscences* (London: Cassell, 1924).

Marx, K. 'Capital', in K. Marx and F. Engels, *On Religion* (New York, NY: Dover, 1964), pp. 135–41.

Marx, K. 'Contribution to the Critique of Hegel's Philosophy of Right', in K. Marx and F. Engels, *On Religion* (New York, NY: Dover, 1964), pp. 41–58.

Marx, K. and Engels, F. *The Communist Manifesto* (Oxford: Oxford Classics, 1992 [1848]).

Marx, K. and Engels, F. 'The Holy Family', in K. Marx and F. Engels, *On Religion* (New York, NY: Dover, 1964), pp. 59–68.

Maxton, J. *Keir Hardie: Prophet and Pioneer* (London: n.p, 1933).
Mayor, S. *The Churches and the Labour Movement* (London: Independent, 1967).
Norman, E. 'Stewart Headlam and the Victorian Christian Socialists', *History Today*, 37, no. 4 (1987), pp. 27–32.
Norman, E. *The Victorian Christian Socialists* (Cambridge: Cambridge University Press, 1987).
Olivier, S. 'Moral', in G. Bernard Shaw, ed., *Fabian Essays on Socialism* (New York, NY: Humboldt, 1891), pp. 95–127.
Orens, J. R. *Stewart Headlam's Radical Anglicanism: The Mass, the Masses, and the Music Hall* (Chicago, IL: University of Illinois Press, 2003).
Preston, R. H. 'Locked in a Time Warp: The Latest Christian Socialist Manifesto', *Theology*, 104, no. 817 (2001), pp. 15–17.
Radcliffe, J. 'About Gadflies – and Other Things', *Syndicalist* 1, 9, October 1912.
Radcliffe, J. 'Syndicalism and Socialism', *Syndicalist* 1, 5, June 1912.
Read, C. *Lenin: A Revolutionary Life* (London: Routledge, 2005).
Rigby, A. *Wilfred Wellock: A Life in Peace* (Bridport: Prism, 1988).
Schneer, J. *George Lansbury* (Manchester: Manchester University Press, 1990).
Shepherd, J. *George Lansbury: At the Heart of Old Labour* (Oxford: Oxford University Press, 2002).
Stoicoiu, R. 'Eucharist and Social Justice', in D. M. McCarthy, *The Heart of Catholic Social Teaching: Its Origins and Contemporary Significance* (Grand Rapids, MI: Brasos, 2009), pp. 45–54.
Suggate, A. M. 'William Temple', in P. Scott and W. T. Cavanagh, eds, *The Blackwell Companion to Political Theology* (Oxford: Wiley-Blackwell, 2004), pp. 165–79.
Swift, A. *Political Philosophy* (Cambridge: Polity, 2001).
Taylor, G. *Socialism and Christianity: The Politics of the Church Socialist League* (Sheffield: IHS, 2000).
[No named author]. 'Trite and Tripe', *Syndicalist*, 3, 2, February 1914.
Tudor, H. and Tudor, J. M., eds *Marxism and Social Democracy: The Revisionist Debate 1896-1898* (Cambridge: Cambridge University Press, 1988).
Vernon, B. D. *Ellen Wilkinson, 1891-1947* (London: Croom Helm, 1982).
Walton, A., Hatcher A. and Spencer, N. *Is There a 'Religious Right' Emerging in Britain?* (London: Theos, 2013).
Webb, S. 'Historic', in G. Bernard Shaw, ed., *Fabian Essays on Socialism* (New York, NY: Humboldt, 1891), pp. 1–43.
[No named author]. 'What Is Syndicalism?', *Syndicalist* 1, 3, March–April 1912.
Wilkinson, A. *Christian Socialism: Scott Holland to Tony Blair* (London: SCM, 1998).
Williams, A. Z. 'Faith Should Not Dictate Political Affiliation', *New Statesman*, http://www.newstatesman.com/ blogs/the-staggers/2011/06/god-debate-faith-grayling; accessed 14 December 2015.
Williams, D. K. *God's Own Party: The Making of the Christian Right* (Oxford: Oxford University Press, 2010).

Wood, I. S. *John Wheatley* (Manchester: Manchester University Press, 1990).
Wood, I. S. 'John Wheatley and Catholic Socialism', in A. R. Morton, eds, *After Socialism? The Future of Radical Christianity* (Edinburgh: CTPI, 1994), pp. 18–22.
Wright, A. *R.H. Tawney* (Manchester: Manchester University Press, 1987).
Wright, A. *Socialisms Old and New* (London: Routledge, 1996).

Index

anarchism 28, 73
Anglican 3-4, 17, 31, 34, 39, 42, 45, 52, 55, 88, 177, 180
Anglo-Catholicism 2, 16, 33-4, 42, 49
Augustine of Hippo 33, 38

baptism 5, 33-5, 42-3, 172, 179-80
Baptist 3, 12, 16, 31, 36, 58, 179, 180
Benn, Tony 5
Bible 3, 11-13, 15, 16, 18, 21, 27-8, 31-4, 48, 49, 51-2, 74, 87, 167-8, 171, 180
Boer War 96, 153-6
Bondfield, Margaret 3-4, 12, 19, 28, 58, 64, 66-7, 69, 82, 86, 90, 93, 102, 105, 119, 134, 136-7, 139, 141, 145, 148, 157, 160, 162, 164, 168-9
brotherhood 6-7, 11-16, 21, 23-5, 42-3, 52, 64, 120, 130, 145, 158-60, 166-9, 171-2, 175, 178, 180, 183

Calvinism 35, 65
capitalism 3, 7, 11-14, 16, 18-19, 25, 28, 33, 40, 50, 57, 59, 61-5, 77-8, 81, 84-7, 89, 92, 94-6, 98-9, 102, 106-8, 117-18, 120, 124-5, 128, 130, 142, 145, 147-8, 151, 155, 157, 160, 166-7, 170-1, 173-5, 177, 179
Chartism 52, 72-3
Christian Socialist Movement 2-3, 151, 183
Christian Social Union (CSU) 3, 6, 52, 54-5, 69, 78, 88, 91, 95, 115, 156
Church of England 3, 58, 88, 178-9
Church Socialist League 35, 52, 71
class 4, 17, 18, 20, 22-4, 26-7, 29-30, 40-3, 48, 56, 59, 61, 63-4, 69, 72-3, 78-9, 81, 83, 89-90, 93-7, 105, 108, 111, 121-2, 125-6, 133, 136, 138-46, 148-50, 158, 162, 168, 170-3, 175, 177, 180-1

Clifford, John 3-4, 12, 14, 16, 24, 28, 36, 44-6, 49, 57-8, 64-5, 69, 72, 78, 80, 82, 87-8, 91-2, 96, 101-2, 111, 120-1, 127-9, 134, 138, 140-1, 149, 154, 156, 158-61, 167, 174, 177
collectivism 7, 24, 32, 34, 66, 92, 115, 120-1, 123, 127, 129, 132-3, 153, 182, 199
communion 5, 33-4, 42-3, 160, 172, 174, 180
communism 17-18, 21, 23-4, 33, 36-7, 40, 42-4, 60-2, 65-7, 81, 98, 109-10, 118, 124, 126, 130, 144-5, 162, 164, 170-4, 180, 182
Communist Party of Great Britain 62, 66-7, 104, 173
concepts 2-3, 7, 24, 166-7, 175
Conference on Christian Politics, Economics and Citizenship (COPEC) 57, 147, 164
conservatism 1, 2, 93-4, 133, 145-52, 183
Conservative Party 1, 79, 95-6, 123, 134
co-operation 11-12, 16, 39, 53, 66-7, 108, 111, 136, 159, 169

democracy 7, 25, 42, 56, 70-2, 77, 79-80, 82-3, 93, 96, 101, 104, 106-7, 115, 117, 119, 132, 133-6, 151-5, 166-9, 173-5, 177-8, 180-3

economics 4, 16, 49, 55, 54, 60, 145, 173, 183
election 7, 69, 79, 82, 85, 92, 95-6, 98, 103, 128, 139, 149, 155, 181
Engels, Friedrich 59-62, 173, 176, 180, 182
equality 7, 13, 15, 24, 27-8, 32, 34-5, 38, 40, 42-3, 49, 51, 56, 59. 66, 71-2, 102, 115, 133, 136-45, 151-4, 163, 167-9, 172-5, 178-83

Index

ethical socialism   11, 55, 61, 128, 161, 175–6
evangelical   1, 16, 34

Fabian   11–12, 16, 19–20, 28, 30, 44, 52, 60, 63, 65, 67, 69–70, 73, 78, 88, 91–2, 95, 161, 177, 181–2
faith   1, 12, 15, 24, 45–7, 53, 91, 137, 151, 155, 168, 178–9, 182
false consciousness   64, 176
fascism   130, 156
Fatherhood of God   7, 11, 13–15, 21, 22, 33, 51–2, 137, 158, 162, 167–9, 175, 178, 181, 183
female suffrage   80, 134, 139–40
First World War   18, 78, 130, 153, 155–7
Free Church Socialist League   14, 120, 167

George, Henry   6, 52, 67–9, 74, 120
Gore, Charles   6, 57
Gospel   13, 16, 19, 21, 25, 29–30, 37, 48–9, 53, 55, 90, 124, 151, 154–5, 167, 178
government   2, 4, 40, 44, 58, 66, 73, 79–80, 82, 85, 92, 94–7, 99–103, 106, 111, 120–1, 124, 128, 131, 135, 139, 161, 170, 173, 179, 181, 183
Green, Thomas Hill   52, 55–7, 59
Guild of St Matthew   2, 3, 22, 42–3, 52, 54, 64, 67, 69, 119, 120, 145–6
guild socialism   52, 70–2

Headlam, Stewart   2–5, 11–13, 16–17, 19–22, 24, 26–30, 34–5, 39, 42–7, 49, 51–9, 63–4, 67, 69, 78, 71, 81, 87–8, 91–2, 95, 97, 102, 105, 111–12, 115–22, 126, 128, 134, 138, 142–9, 151, 156, 158–60, 162, 164, 168–74, 177, 179, 180
Hitler, Adolf   142, 155–6
Holy Spirit   16, 49
housing   27, 63, 101–2, 117, 171

idolatry   28, 46, 154
incarnation   17, 78
Independent Labour Party (ILP)   64, 79, 93–6, 107, 110, 119, 139, 157

industry   12, 14, 18, 29, 46, 54, 57, 60, 68, 70–2, 86, 92, 117, 119–25, 128, 131–2, 135–6, 151, 159, 167–70
injustice   14, 29–30, 58, 78, 99, 122, 138, 140, 173
Israel   26, 28, 171, 179

Jesus Christ   5, 13–14, 16, 20, 24, 30, 34, 43, 46, 61, 120, 153–4, 161, 167, 169, 179
Jubilee   27, 171
justice   18, 20, 27, 37, 46, 54–6, 58, 64, 72, 78, 93, 99, 102, 120, 126–8, 130–1, 134, 140, 151, 154, 159

Keeble, Samuel   4–5, 12–17, 19–20, 22–3, 25–31, 35–8, 41, 47, 49, 51–5, 57, 59–62, 70–2, 78–80, 82, 86–92, 100–2, 105, 111, 115–17, 119–25, 130, 135, 137–8, 140–2, 145–50, 154, 159, 162, 164, 167–8, 170–1, 173, 179
Keir Hardie, James   2–4, 6, 11–13, 16, 19–25, 27–9, 36–8, 44–6, 48, 50, 53, 57–8. 60–2, 64, 68–9, 71, 73, 77–9, 82–3, 85, 89, 90, 93, 96–7, 100–2, 105, 107–8, 110–11, 116–21, 124–5, 127, 130–1, 134, 136–9, 141–4, 148–51, 153, 155–60, 162–3, 167, 169–71, 173–5, 178
Kingdom of God   24, 57, 81, 111, 158, 161–4, 174–5, 182
Kingdom of Heaven   7, 18, 30, 35, 44–5, 53, 81–2, 88, 153, 158, 161–4, 174–5, 179
Kingsley, Charles   2, 52–4, 172, 178

Labour Church   5, 69
Labour movement   2, 16, 18, 20, 23, 35, 41, 48, 58, 59, 61–2, 79, 82, 90, 93, 96, 141, 157, 164, 166, 169, 183
Labour Party   2–4, 7, 28, 53, 58, 61–2, 67, 79, 82–3, 85, 91–9, 103, 108, 111, 119, 121, 124, 128, 138–9, 141, 143, 146, 149, 151, 155–6, 173, 183
Lansbury, George   2, 4, 11–13, 15, 17–19, 21, 24–7, 31, 39, 43–4, 46–7, 51, 53, 55, 58–8, 62–6, 68–9, 71–3, 77–83,

89–90, 93, 96–9, 101, 104–5, 107, 110–11, 117, 119–21, 127, 131, 134, 136–9, 141–2, 145, 147, 149–51, 153, 155, 158–60, 162, 164, 167, 170–2, 175, 180
Lenin   65–6, 82, 87, 180
liberalism   40, 50, 53, 55, 74, 148
Liberal Party   93–6, 119, 127, 146
liberty   21, 27, 56–7, 69, 71–2, 99–100, 128–30, 137, 141, 156, 183
Ludlow, John   2, 54, 70

Mammon   18–19, 42, 148, 159, 170, 178–9
marriage   1, 44, 138, 141, 145–8
Marx, Karl   5–6, 52, 59–62, 64–5, 69, 72–3, 118, 150, 159, 173, 175–6, 180, 182
Marxism   11, 16, 41, 59–65, 108, 128, 131, 173, 176, 181
Maurice, Frederick Denison   2, 52–5, 59, 70, 172, 178
Maxton, James   61, 101, 119, 143, 155
Methodism   3–4, 12, 16, 35–6, 57, 59, 70, 72, 82, 91, 143, 146, 154
mines   17, 63, 69, 101, 119, 121–2
municipal   79, 82, 98–101, 116, 120, 122, 131, 138

nationalization   14, 101–2, 120, 122–4, 128, 167
New Testament   11–12, 21–5, 45, 47, 59, 161, 170
Noel, Conrad   6, 151
Nonconformism   3–4, 13, 15–17, 34–5, 90, 148, 154, 177

Old Testament   11–12, 21, 25–8, 42, 170–1, 179

pacifism   4, 79, 105, 115, 153–9, 164
Parliament   7, 42, 44, 46, 63, 73, 78, 83, 86, 89, 92–7, 99–101, 104–7, 112, 119, 134, 139, 149, 151, 173, 180–1
Poplar   4, 21, 58, 98–9, 150
poverty   7, 12, 18–19, 30–1, 41, 55, 58, 63, 77, 94, 120, 125, 137, 143–5, 148, 150–3, 159–60, 163, 165, 173

property   18, 20, 23, 27, 38, 40–1, 54, 68, 77, 86, 101, 105, 117, 120–6, 130, 137, 140, 143, 146, 170–1, 178–9
Protestant   33–6, 44, 49, 51, 177
public ownership   41, 57, 71, 79–80, 83, 92, 101–2, 119, 123, 125, 127, 135–6

revolution   2, 6–7, 17, 22, 26, 35, 40, 43, 47, 51, 59, 61–2, 64–6, 77–85, 87, 94, 99, 103–12, 133, 147, 166, 170, 172–3, 175, 180–2
Roman Catholic Church   3–4, 13, 17, 33–6, 39–42, 44, 50–1, 71, 147, 171, 177, 179
Ruskin, John   52–5, 59, 147
Russian revolution   65–6, 78, 80, 82, 87, 104, 147

Sabbath   27–8, 45
sacraments   5–6, 11, 15–16, 33–4, 42–4, 48–9, 51, 147, 172, 179, 180
Scott Holland, Henry   3–6, 14, 17, 19–20, 24, 30–1, 43, 46, 51, 53, 55–9, 64, 68–70, 78, 88–9, 91–2, 95–6, 98–100, 106, 115–16, 129, 130–1, 134–5, 145–6, 151, 153, 156, 162, 172, 174
Second World War   83, 153, 157, 159
Social Democratic Federation (SDF)   16, 61–2, 64, 90, 96, 117
Soviet Union   65–6, 80, 83, 99, 131
Stalin   66, 80
state   30, 33, 38–41, 44–5, 49, 51, 55, 60, 68–9, 73, 77, 82, 86–7, 93, 97–101, 105, 111, 116–18, 120, 122, 123, 127–34, 138–9, 143, 146, 159, 161, 173
syndicalism   73, 176–7, 181–2

Tawney, Richard Henry   2, 4–5, 11, 14, 22–3, 25, 28, 35, 37–9, 45–9, 51, 53–62, 66, 68–72, 78, 80, 82, 65–87, 91–5, 98, 100–2, 108, 110–11, 119–21, 123–5, 128, 131–3, 135–8, 140–1, 144, 146, 149, 151, 157–8, 163–4, 168–9, 171, 173
temperance   148–9
Temple, William   4, 15, 23–5, 27, 37–8, 43, 49, 51–3, 57–8, 64, 68–9, 86–7,

89, 93, 115–16, 119–20. 122, 125–6, 128–30, 135, 137, 142, 144, 147, 157–8, 163–4, 168–9, 171–3

trade unions   3, 64, 71, 82, 88, 90, 98, 146

utopian   7, 153–8, 161, 163–5, 173, 175, 182

Wellock, Wilfred   4, 7, 11, 14, 18–19, 25–6, 36, 38, 47, 49, 51, 58, 65–6, 71, 78–81, 83, 87–8, 94, 98, 100–6, 108–10, 112, 118, 143–5, 154, 158–60, 162, 171, 173

Wesleyan Methodist Union for Social Service   4, 57, 70, 91, 146

Wheatley, John   4, 13–14, 17, 22, 26, 34–6, 39–42, 47, 49, 51, 53, 57–8, 63, 65, 78, 80, 82, 93–5, 98–102, 104–5, 107, 117, 119, 121, 125, 127, 141, 146, 148, 151, 153, 155, 160, 167, 170–2

Wilkinson, Ellen   2, 4, 14, 16, 19, 26, 47, 51, 62, 66, 69, 78–80, 90, 93–5, 104–5, 107, 134, 139, 141, 147, 154–7, 165, 173, 183

www.ingramcontent.com/pod-product-compliance
Lightning Source LLC
Chambersburg PA
CBHW072144290426
44111CB00012B/1972